Open prisons

International Library of Social Policy

General Editor   Kathleen Jones
Professor of Social Administration
University of York

Arbor Scientiæ
Arbor Vitæ

A catalogue of the books available in the **International Library of Social Policy** and other series of Social Science books published by Routledge & Kegan Paul will be found at the end of this volume

Open prisons

Howard Jones
Professor of Social Administration,
University College, Cardiff

and

Paul Cornes
Head of the Employment Rehabilitation Research
Centre, Employment Service Agency

assisted by

Richard Stockford

Routledge & Kegan Paul
London, Henley and Boston

First published in 1977
by Routledge & Kegan Paul Ltd
39 Store Street,
London WC1E 7DD,
Broadway House,
Newtown Road,
Henley-on-Thames,
Oxon RG9 1EN and
9 Park Street,
Boston, Mass. 02108, USA
Set in 10 on 12pt English
and printed in Great Britain by
The Lavenham Press Ltd
Lavenham, Suffolk

British Library Cataloguing in Publication Data

Jones, Howard, b.1918

Open prisons. — (International library of social
policy).
1. Open prisons — Great Britain
I. Title II. Cornes, Paul III. Series
365'.3 ⋏ʊℸ HV9647   77-30063

ISBN 0 7100 8602 4

Contents

Illustrations

Figures

Tables

Preface

This research was designed and directed throughout by Professor Howard Jones, and the report written jointly by Professor Jones and Mr Paul Cornes. Much of the fieldwork was carried out (under Professor Jones's direction) by Mr Richard Stockford, who, however, left to take up an appointment as Research Officer in the Social Services Department of Norfolk County Council before the data was analysed and the report prepared.

Thanks are due to the Social Science Research Council for financial support, and to the Home Office for providing facilities in the research prisons. We are grateful also to prison staff members of the Prison Officers' Association and the Civil Service Union, and to the Governors and their Assistants, for their co-operation in the research. We hope that they will feel it was all worthwhile.

H.J.
P.C.
R.S.

1   Open prisons: their origin and aims

The open prison, the so-called 'prison without bars', has been a very late development within the prison system—largely a creation of the last forty years. This in spite of nearly two hundred years of penological speculation and reform dating back to Beccaria[1] and John Howard.[2] The reason for this is fairly clear. Historically, prisons have always been places in which criminals could be securely confined[3] and this 'containment' function has continued to predominate in spite of the gradual emergence of other aims for imprisonment, such as deterrence or rehabilitation. Containment here means not only that prisoners must be kept out of circulation, but also that their deviations, even within the prison, must not be on such a scale as to disturb the peace of mind of the man-in-the-street. The open prison thus begins to appear like a contradiction in terms; a denial of the essential nature of the institution of which it purports to be merely a variant.

The preoccupation with 'containment' probably reflects a fairly realistic assessment of the possibility of using penal institutions to 'change' offenders in view of the current rudimentary level of our technology in the correctional field. However, it may spring from a more fundamental cause; the possibility that crime is evidence of a rival system of norms within the society, arising out of class and communal differentiation. If there is no real consensus about social values, correctional work with prisoners looks both less hopeful and less justifiable.[4] If such is the situation, a preventive rather than a corrective penal system seems almost inescapable.[5]

However that may be, the spectre of security does constantly haunt prison administrators. Most of their procedures, even those ostensibly directed towards the more correctional objectives, are ultimately reshaped towards ensuring secure containment. There is no suggestion, where such a displacement of aims takes place, that it is always deliberately and cynically engineered by prison administrators who thus use rehabilitative pretensions as a respectable cover for other things. This does happen, but more important seems to be the structural situation of prisons in society; what the public

1

expect of them, and the pressures which are thus brought to bear upon prison staff and the prison authorities. This is seen in many ways. There are, for instance, the attempts to reassure a local community about security when planning a prison in its area for the first time; experience often alleviates such local anxieties, showing how unnecessary they were, and may even lead to the development of economic and social interdependence between neighbourhood and prison, as in the relationship between Dartmoor Prison and the village of Princetown.

Even more revealing is the way in which any official suspicion of ioopholes in security leads to the sacrifice of all other considerations (deterrence, rehabilitation, etc.) in the interest of a better achievement of the containment objective. The most recent example of this was the report of the Mountbatten Committee in 1966[6] after an apparent increase in escapes. This led to the retrenchment of the hostel scheme, and of groupwork and other ideas intended to improve the rehabilitative efficiency of the prisons. The training of prison officers reflects the same preoccupation. Although they are taught many things these days including aspects of the sociology of crime, some psychology, and rehabilitative techniques such as groupwork, the core of their training and the aspects on which most time is spent remain those which are primarily concerned with security.

Obviously, in such a situation, open prisons with their limited physical means of containment must be under constant pressure. Thus their intake tends to be selected mainly with security in mind; very rarely are high-escape-risk prisoners placed in them, and any such are speedily removed if they show any signs of continuing to be security hazards. This is perfectly consonant with a view of prisons as primarily 'containment' agencies, but by the same token it represents a denial of the rehabilitative role of the open prison. It is sometimes argued that the emphasis on security is not inconsistent with rehabilitative objectives, on the grounds that 'You must be able to keep them if you are going to treat them.' Against this it might be contended that a potential escaper who never has the opportunity to do so, will never be anything else but a potential escaper. The categorisation of a prisoner as a potential escaper is also a subjective and uncertain matter, and seems to be influenced by the nature of the crime; the more serious the crime is considered to be, and therefore, presumably, the greater the danger to the public if containment fails, the lower the level of risk which appears to be acceptable. This, even though somebody very properly described as a danger to the public is not necessarily therefore less amenable for rehabilitation. The issues of containment and rehabilitation are separate, but are often not kept clearly apart in official thinking about open prisons.

These are not, of course, the only arguments which could be deployed against present practice. It may be that this question of the nature of the inmate intake is critical for the rehabilitative success of open prisons. The suitability of the kind of inmates usually selected is clearly relevant, but we are better supplied with opinions than with knowledge about which are the most suitable. So also important may be the reluctance of the authorities (with security in mind) to place a substantial proportion of our prison population in open institutions. The adoption of a parole system in Britain in the Criminal Justice Act of 1967 led to the early discharge of some of the inmates of open prisons. As a result of this and of suspended sentences, also introduced in the 1967 Act, the proportion of prisoners placed in open institutions fell from 1968 onwards (Table 1.1), the population of a number of these prisons falling to a very low level, presumably because of the maintenance of fairly rigid security criteria for transfer to them. With increases in the total number of receptions into prison, the open prisons began to fill up again though, as Table 1.1 shows, they contained a much smaller pro-

Table 1.1   Average daily population of prisons in England and Wales 1965-75

	Open prisons	Closed prisons	Open % of total
1965	3582	20,516	14·9
1966	3798	22,428	14·5
1967	3964	22,208	15·1
1968	3238	20,640	13·6
1969	3392	25,809	11·6
1970	3739	25,421	12·8
1971	3957	26,115	13·2
1972	3742	25,366	12·9
1973	2118	24.563	7·9
1974	3283	24,219	11·9
1975	3230	26,435	10·9

Source: Annual Reports of the Prison Department 1965-75.

portion of the total daily average population in prisons of all kinds than used to be the case. A sudden further dip in this percentage in 1973 led to a government decision actually to close three open prisons, rather than to relax the narrow security criteria in use—a striking proof of the overriding importance attached, even in open prisons, to the aim of containment. In fact only one of these prisons has been closed to date (1975).

It is against this kind of background that the emergence of the open prison has to be seen, if its slow development and chequered history are to be understood. And this may be as true of the situation in the USA and in Scandinavia as in this country if, as is suggested, the problems in question arise out of the structural position and cultural role of the prison in society.

The first open prison was almost certainly Witzwil, established in Switzerland in 1891. However, Witzwil was not a thoroughgoing minimum security establishment; it had closed sections. Nor did other countries follow the lead given by the Swiss. Witzwil was the result of the vision of a particular individual, Otto Kellerhals.[7] Other countries were more cautious, gradually developing the minimum security idea pragmatically. Thus in 1916 the Lorton Reformatory, in the District of Columbia, USA, was built without a containing wall, and other similar institutions followed. However, these were not open prisons in the sense in which we understand the word, consisting as they usually did of secure blocks arranged so as to fully enclose a central quadrangle. Another modification of the maximum security regime, and one which has aroused interest in Britain in recent years,[8] was the experiment by Howard Gill at Norfolk, Massachusetts. The Norfolk Penal Institution was based on the idea of a maximum security perimeter, making possible a high degree of free movement within that perimeter.

Gill's idea opens up the possibility of combining some elements of a corrective regime with the fulfilment of the containment function, but it does not ensure that this happens. On the one hand it releases the regime from the constant head-counts, inspections, discipline, and suspicion, inherent in a thoroughgoing maximum security regime of the orthodox kind (what Barnes and Teeters[9] call the 'lock psychosis'), and also makes it possible to clarify staff roles, otherwise in conflict between custodial and correctional functions, by separating 'guard' from 'therapist'. It has been claimed that the latter may not only be a help to the staff, who are no longer required to carry out what they might regard as incompatible duties, but also may improve inmate attitudes towards correctional staff, if they are less associated in the minds of prisoners with restraining and incarcerating them. On the other hand the very freedom facilitated by the Norfolk experiment opens up opportunities for coercive and exploitative activity by 'barons' and other power figures among the prisoners, and for the freer operation of the corrupting criminal cultures which are said to exist in all prisons, but normally operate, in the orthodox institution, under the disadvantages of constant staff surveillance. As will be seen later, similar anxieties have been voiced in more recent years about open prisons.

The real breakthrough came in the 1930s in Britain, and the 1940s in the USA. In the United Kingdom, Sir Alexander Paterson (a member of the Prison Commission from 1922 to 1947) began to place his liberalising stamp upon our penal system. In his dictum 'A man is sent to prison as a punishment and not for punishment' he tried to set limits to the role of retribution in prisons, and make room for what he called 'training'. And having established the viability of such a correctional aim side by side with more traditional objectives, it was natural that he should consider the suitability of existing prisons for such a 'training' role. He set out to define what he meant by 'training', and to equip prison staffs to perform it. Nevertheless he seems always to have had some doubts about the possibility of achieving anything effective within the framework of the conventional closed prison. Hence his second famous aphorism: 'You cannot train a man for freedom under conditions of captivity', which led to the opening in 1933 of the first British open prison, New Hall Camp, as a satellite of Wakefield Prison. Here there were no walls, and indeed not even a boundary fence—'the men sleeping in wooden huts and the bounds designated if at all, by whitewash marks on the trees.[10] But the aim of containment persisted: Sir Lionel Fox, a former chairman of the Prison Commission, in writing about New Hall Camp, saw as the achievement most worth mentioning that in the first fifteen years of its life only seven prisoners had absconded. Other open institutions followed: Leyhill Prison in Gloucestershire about ten years later, and Aldington, near Maidstone, in 1947. There were in 1975, thirteen open prisons of various kinds in Britain, with, as we have seen, a total population of 3,230.

The Americans also moved forward, beginning at about the same time as Britain, with open farm camps associated with neighbouring closed prisons. Among the most famous American open prisons are the Californian Institution for Men at Chino in Southern California, and Seagoville, an open federal prison in Texas. The first warden of Chino was Kenyon Scudder, an American penal reformer of great distinction, who developed a remarkable training regime at Chino, and also contributed to the common store of ideas on the nature of open prisons and their potentialities.[11]

But what is the purpose of it all? The basic justification remains that put forward by Sir Alexander Paterson, 'You cannot train a man for freedom under conditions of captivity'. The implication of this is that social behaviour is learned by social experience, and that the restricted life of the closed prison teaches the wrong lessons. The effect thus produced on the individual inmate was called 'prisonisation' by D. Clemmer,[12] who carried out, at a maximum security institution in Illinois, the first serious sociological study of prisons. Although an important step forward, it became clear that the concept of 'prisonisation' lacked clarity. In particular, it included at least two quite distinct processes: (*a*) institutionalisation: adaptation to a standardised mass-regime leading to apathy, dependence, and routinised, inflexible responses; (*b*) criminalisation: the acquisition of criminal attitudes, skills and associates, as a result of sustained and socially functional interaction with criminals.

In what ways, if at all, may open prisons make 'institutionalisation' and 'criminalisation' less likely? To the extent, it might be argued, as far as institutionalisation is concerned, that its regime is less stereotyped and controlling, and makes more 'normal' social learning experiences possible for inmates. This will be effected partly through the daily programme of the prison (the regime), and partly through the greater permeability of its boundaries with the surrounding community—with prisoners going out into the community more often for work or recreation, and members of the outside society visiting the institution more freely, as friends, experts of various kinds, tradesmen, visiting teams and so on.

Both of these steps have been advocated by reformers, who have sought, while retaining closed prisons, to introduce modifications in them to reduce institutionalisation. They have proposed (and sometimes been able to bring about) easier visiting arrangements; more liberal rules about letters, home visits and holidays at home; and hostels, which are within the purlieu of the prison but offer many opportunities during the day for going out into free society. Special interest is being shown in the reform of prison work programmes, so as to render them more realistic, by replacing the traditional programmes of either craft-orientated or sometimes trivial (and in either case, unproductive) work, by a prison 'factory' system using modern machinery, working under normal industrial pressures and disciplines, and with payment according to results, on a scale which could introduce incentives similar to those encountered outside.[13] If it were not for the critical question of 'containment', the idea of an open prison could be seen as merely taking this process a stage further.

In more general terms, it is necessary to reduce those characteristics of the prison which made it what Goffman[14] calls a 'total institution'—an institution which confines prisoners and all their activities within a single establishment. This is of course simply one way of describing the objective of containment. To achieve it prisoners are 'shaped' and 'trimmed' for better adjustment to institutional life, and cut off from counter-influences from outside, producing the effect which we call 'institutionalisation'. The 'total' characteristics of the prison and therefore the degree of institutionalisation can be reduced, but this can be taken beyond a certain point only by rejecting the claim that the containment aim must continue to be of overwhelming importance, with the further implication presumably that we go on to establish real open prisons. At least this is the argument which is put forward by the protagonists of this form of institution.

The other component of prisonisation, the process of criminalisation, probably results from the fact that prisoners spend so much of their time interacting with one another, in an inmate subculture which is largely cut off from staff influence. It is well known that staff control in prisons is confined to the more superficial aspects of prisoners' behaviour: that though prisoners conform to institutional demands on the surface, an active inmate social life goes on autonomously behind this façade. It is also generally agreed that there is not much that the staff can do about this. As Gresham Sykes has pointed out,[15] the overwhelming formal power of the staff does not enable them to dispense with the co-operation of the inmates, which they must therefore buy with some informal relaxation on their part. Out of this situation emerges, in prisons everywhere, an implicit understanding (the custodial compromise)[16] that capricious interference by staff in the relationships and daily life of prisoners will not take place so long as they are careful to 'behave themselves'. A tactless prison officer or the actively hostile prisoner, either of whom is likely to disturb this delicate balance, is as unpopular with experienced officers as with experienced prisoners. Both sides, in their own way, have learned 'how to do bird'.

There will probably be little argument about this account of the way in which the divided community of the prison emerges, or about its effect in shutting out the staff from intervention in the prisoners' side of it. There is more debate about how the norms of this inmate society are formed. One would expect a community of criminals, if cut off from social interaction with non-criminals, to reinforce each other's anti-social views; L. T. Wilkins sees this as one very important dysfunction of segregation into penal institutions of any kind.[17] One would expect such an intensification of criminal attitudes to be increased also by a 'splitting' process, which skimmed off the cream, i.e. the more conformist side of the prisoners' behaviour, for expression within the orderly pattern of surface life in the prison— which is the prison to the official or casual visitor. Not only does this leave little law-abiding enthusiasm to be expended in the subterranean inmate world, but it is likely to produce a resentful reaction in the opposite direction. 'Any action produces an equal and opposite reaction' may be true of other aspects of reality besides the world of physical science.

However, the last point raises the question of whether the unco-operative, and indeed inimical attitude of the prisoners to the staff and the institution derives solely from the initial anti-social orientation of prisoners, or may not be at least in part a response to, and a compensation for the 'pains of imprisonment'.[18] Such research as has been carried out on this question (by Cline and Wheeler) does not support the latter view—though the authors emphasise the imperfections of their study.[19] It would seem not unreasonable to suppose that criminals, when they become prisoners, would use the inmate culture in such an anti-authority way—and incidentally provide themselves with an escape from some of the institutionalising influences emanating from large-scale organisational life. Nevertheless, if the inmate culture is partly compensatory in this latter sense, this would be a matter of the greatest importance for the present study, for one of the results of establishing an open prison may be to ameliorate some of these 'pains' by the more normal, relaxed and open life available in it. Unfortunately researchers are usually identified with the staff, and excluded with them from this inmate world. We were no exception, and had to rely on such few and indirect cues as could be derived from observation 'from outside' as it were, or from responses to a formal research instrument, like the CIES (see below).

Whatever the reason, the outcome is clear: the existence of an inmate culture largely criminal in orientation, which is insulated from the corrective or disciplinary activities of the staff, and thus maximises opportunities for acquiring criminal contacts and skills, and learning criminal attitudes. Most commentators see the weakening of this inmate culture as a *sine qua non* for improving the correctional effectiveness of prisons.

There are a number of ways in which the closed prison may be seen as exacerbating these problems. First of all, the custodial compromise, described above, itself arises out of the need to maintain security—the containment function of the closed prison. Given a freer climate, it is argued, the inmate culture, and therefore the custodial compromise, will lose much of its force. Also, as we have seen, some believe that the frustrations implicit in a closed institution lead to resentment on the part of the prisoners, strengthening the negative aspects of their response to the ministrations of the staff even when the latter are intended to be helpful. Meanwhile the staff are themselves also put into depriving roles, which they tend to justify to themselves by imputing a variety of undesirable traits to the prisoners, who can thus be seen as deserving what is happening to them. Interaction theorists argue that these kinds of attitude produce a like response in the other person, in this case in the prisoners with whom the officers are interacting, causing tensions of this kind to mount.[20] The open prison might perhaps enable this cumulative process to be reversed. Add to this the reduction in tension which must result from freer movement over a more extensive terrain, and one can understand why many feel it easier to develop a progressive correctional regime in an open prison. This also may be cumulative: once prisons are seen as places in which a constructive job of rehabilitation can be attempted, people capable of and wanting to do such a job may become interested in working in prisons.

A variety of other justifications have been presented. Kenyon Scudder, the great Warden of Chino, wrote:

The open fields, the absence of gun guards, no regimentation, men allowed to go to meals and to work unescorted, challenge each individual to begin again to stand on his own feet. Here he is constantly faced with the ease of escape. The fact that he rejects this possibility . . . indicates he has taken a great moral step, a great social step. By accepting this responsibility, he has admitted to himself that he wishes to be a social rather than an asocial individual.[21]

Scudder was realistic enough to recognise that this was sometimes an objective to be aimed at by new inmates, rather than one which they could realise at a stroke, so he provided cells at Chino in which a man could opt to be locked up if he felt that he could not trust himself not to abscond. Many may see only the containment implications of such an innovation, but Scudder is pointing to some possible progress in choice on the part of a prisoner, beyond that of simply concurring in his incarceration under circumstances where he could not escape anyway. The acceptance of one's sentence under the conditions of the open prison is an approach also to an acceptance of the social consensus by which that sentence is supposed to be legitimated.

Scudder, like Sir Lionel Fox a former chairman of the Prison Commission in this country,[22] clearly sees it also as an approach towards an even broader acceptance by the prisoner of responsibility for his own behaviour, in place of relying on the constraints provided by the institution. For besides the opportunity it gives of choosing not to escape, the freer regime of the open prison provides many other occasions for accepting responsibility for one's behaviour. These would certainly seem to be a major prophylactic against the institutionalising effect of the prison, reducing the dependent tendencies generated by a more controlling and supportive regime. However, the same reluctance to accept responsibility for one's behaviour, reinforced by lack of practice and a variety of rationalisations about 'powerlessness', 'them', and 'it's not my fault' is also a powerful criminogenic factor.[23] As a result of institutionalisation it leads to the apathy and dependence of the old lag. As a criminalising factor it provides the matured criminal with excuses which enable him to evade responsibility for his own behaviour: allows him to protect an illusory self-image by blaming what he does (or does not do), and what happens to him in the prison, on those who control so much of his life there.

Behind all these pragmatic arguments for open institutions has often lain a more general if less clearly formulated 'feeling' based on a humane repugnance at the idea of putting human beings under lock and key. It is difficult to escape a sense that, as in so many other fields of social policy, people have sometimes started with a moral or emotional response like this, and have then searched for justifications of a practical kind. This does not of course invalidate the arguments put forward for open prisons in such circumstances. Nor does it follow that effectiveness is the only criterion. One could conceive of ways of dealing with criminals which would be more effective, in terms of reducing recidivism, but which we might find morally intolerable as ways of treating our fellow human beings. It may be that the moral quality of our social life is indicated as much by the way we treat our criminals, as by the incidence of crime itself.

These then are the kinds of arguments which have been put forward in support of the open prison. What we lack is any firm evidence that any of these purposes are in fact realised. While the differences in security measures are apparent enough, serious research on open prisons is virtually non-existent, and the little that has been carried out appears to be indecisive. Hermon's small study of the Maassiahu Camp in Israel predictably commences with the usual genuflexion in the direction of containment, by pointing out how few prisoners in this open establishment attempt to escape or become involved in disciplinary proceedings (there are, alas, in open prison experience, plenty of contrary examples). Reconvictions within 12-18 months of discharge were 43 per cent for those previously imprisoned, but only 7 per cent for those without previous sentences. No comparisons with closed institutions were given, so it is really quite impossible to evaluate these results.[24]

Studies in Holland and Finland, though better designed, give no clearer indication of any relative advantages possessed by open or closed prisons. Both researches centred on a comparison of the conviction rates of the two types of establishment, taking into account differing risk categories—i.e. allowing for differences in the 'quality' of their intake, as measured statistically on the basis of past experience with similar kinds of case. The conclusion of the Dutch study is that 'treatment in an open institution hardly matters as regards later recidivism'. Any differences between the different kinds of institution are attributed to the quality of the intake.[25] The Finnish research by Uusitalo compared 298 male prisoners from a closed prison with 308 from three open 'labour colonies'. The two groups were found to be practically identical in a wide range of prior social and personal variables, including those relating to type of crime and criminal career. This is rather surprising, suggesting a more or less random allocation between the two types of institutions. But it did mean that a direct comparison of their rates of recidivism ought not to be invalidated by those differences in the quality of intake referred to in the Dutch study. However, it was possible that groups of different quality might be differentially helped by the two kinds of regime, so each risk category was also compared separately for each type of institution. The test applied was recidivism during the ten years following release; and differences in these results between the two types of institution were found to be non-existent. When 'risk categories' were compared individually, no consistent differences in recidivism were found, nor do such differences as exist change systematically from high to low risk groups.[26]

In spite of these negative results, this research is of great interest from the methodological point of view. And if there really is no difference in rehabilitative efficiency between open and closed prisons, as this work and that of Jonkers and his collaborators in the Netherlands may indicate, there would seem to be justification for adopting the less costly and less socially depriving solution of the open prison on these latter grounds alone. The fact is, however, that one probably cannot make such an assumption. Our research, for instance (as will be seen) shows that the categories of open and closed prisons are not really homogeneous: that what we should really be talking about is 'regimes', conditioned as these are by other factors besides 'openness' and 'closedness'.

Not a single serious study of relative effectiveness has been carried out in British open prisons. The research work of the Prison Department has been limited to a number of 'experiments', like that undertaken in Ashwell Prison in 1962 in which the researchers examined the extent to which open prisons are escape-proof for certain categories of offender. The preoccupation with absconding has both precluded other research, and prevented a fuller exploration of the rehabilitative potential of the open institution for large sections of the offender population—most notably those who are convicted, even though for the first time, of sexual offences or offences of violence against the person.

The case for open prisons therefore remains entirely *a priori*. It is probably partly for this reason that (as the figures given above show), they continue as a small-scale fringe activity within the prison system of this as of all countries. They are alien bodies within a containment-oriented system. Because they cannot justify themselves on containment grounds, they need to be all the more firmly in possession of other justifications if they are to make headway. And this means that they have to define their aims more clearly, and be able to show that they do achieve something worthwhile. These are not distinct operations. Initial hopes for open prisons may be dashed in the light of research, but the purposes which they are actually found to be realising may prove just as acceptable as those originally credited to them.

Arguments are not lacking on the other side. The 'containment' argument that open prisons mean greater risk to the public goes without saying, though it might be asserted against it that the best protection for the public is an effectively rehabilitative prison system. There is also the oft-quoted objection that open prisons are too 'soft', failing as deterrents by comparison with the orthodox closed prison. There is no support for this in the Finnish study mentioned above. Another commonly expressed fear is that freer interaction between criminals could only result in their corrupting each other. Those who believe this would obviously view with misgiving the increase in freedom of movement permitted to inmates of the open prison. The difference between this standpoint and that of others who take up a more optimistic position seems to be in the low value attributed here to the work of the staff. Certainly the prison staff appear to be largely excluded from effective intervention by the divided community in the closed prison, leaving the field free to 'barons' and the rest. The most that could be said about the open prison from this point of view is that it could possibly provide more opportunities for fruitful rehabilitative work by the staff; they still have to display a willingness and the ability to make use of it. The kind of people recruited for the work, and the quality of their training, would be absolutely decisive, and something will be said about this later in this report.

Related to the contamination objection is that of middle-class prisoners that they are not protected in the open prison from social contacts which they find disagreeable, particularly where cells for sleeping are replaced by dormitories.[27] Indeed, quite apart from any specific invasions of which they may complain, the general lack of the quality of privacy in open prisons may itself be destructive of certain reticences important in some people's lives, and also damaging to their self-image. Anthropological studies of class differences in life-style[28] suggest that such elements of privacy are of greater importance to members of middle-class groups than to the lower working class who are believed to provide most of our convicted offenders. One might have less sympathy with the related complaint of the 'old lag' that he misses the seclusion and freedom from interference which he found in his cell. In many cases this may be because he has become institutionalised by cell life in a closed prison, and resists the awakening of his social abilities which a more active social life might tend to bring about.

In other words, open prisons do have a case to answer. And it is the function of research to try to determine where the truth lies. The present research undertakes a comparison of three open and three closed prisons with the idea of trying to settle some of these questions. No attempt has been made here to follow Jonkers and Uusitalo by embarking on a study of recidivism. Attention has been directed instead towards the institutions themselves. What are they like? How are they organised? How do staff and inmates perceive and respond to them? And do different forms of organisation tend to lead to different perceptions and responses from those who live and work in them? Though lacking the apparently compelling logic of the recidivism study, this approach may do less violence to the true nature of the experience of imprisonment and of how people are affected by it, simply because it is not content with over-simplified conventional categories like reconviction; or those which are involved in straight comparisons between open and closed prisons with their over-facile assumption that all open or all closed prisons are alike. Or perhaps a number of such different approaches are required if we are to make any real progress in understanding such complex social institutions.

The aim of the project then was to compare three open and three closed prisons, paired for research purposes according to whether the men received into them were principally in long-, medium- or short-term sentence categories. The closed prisons selected were all officially designated as training prisons, and therefore were not typical of closed establishments as such (there are also local prisons, whose functions are principally those of servicing the courts, holding short-term and civil prisoners and the reallocation of inmates to other establishments). However, they were selected because both they and open prisons ostensibly had a similar 'training' aim, making a more valid comparison than between, say, open prisons and closed locals. Both open and closed training prisons receive men from local prisons, tend to hold them for the duration of their sentences, and offer a training programme, based on a full day of industrial employment—employment of a kind that is not usually specified for, or easy to operate within, closed local prison conditions.

Research instruments

Usually where prisons have been compared it has been on the assumption of the objective existence of regimes to which inmates and staff may then be seen as responding. Berk,[29] for instance, compared three American medium-security closed prisons which differed in the emphasis placed on treatment as a formal goal of the organisation. The degree of treatment orientation was measured by the number of staff employed for that purpose and this index was found to be related to other variables such as staff/inmate interaction, the extent to which counselling facilities were available, and positive attitudes towards the notion of treatment by both staff and inmates. While it would be incorrect to dismiss such objective approaches to the measurement of organisational climate as irrelevant, recent evidence from studies using tests designed to ascertain the perceived qualities of an organisational climate suggests that they need to be supplemented by other approaches. It is arguable that how people respond to a social situation will depend more on how they see it than on how it actually is. These studies have indicated that there is not necessarily a close correspondence between the perceived qualities of a regime and objective indicators of the same regime, and that it is essential that attention should be paid to both aspects. This was the view of the US National Council of Crime and Delinquency in their planning of an international collaborative study 'Assessment of the Prison Community' when, at an early stage, it was decided 'that both objective and inferential measures of the environment must be taken into account in order to obtain an adequately differentiated description of the environments of correctional facilities'.[30]

We have, in consequence, used methods designed to elicit both objective and perceptual assessments of the organisational characteristics of the prisons. For the latter purpose we have largely used the instrument adopted by the National Council of Crime and Delinquency, the Moos 'Correctional Institutions Environment Scale' (CIES). It was thought that this instrument would provide a useful basis for a systematic comparison of perceived differences (e.g. open/closed differences) in the social climates of the prisons in our study. Further information about this research tool will be given in chapter 4.

The more objective data, on the other hand, were collected with the aid of a number of approaches and instruments, as follows.

Demographic information concerning inmates was obtained by means of a population census, taken in two stages. First, basic information about each inmate was extracted from the nominal index record cards. These cards maintained by the prisons constitute an up-to-date record of all inmates in the prison at any time. Further material, for instance concerning previous convictions and time spent in the initial allocation prison, was obtained by examining the inmates' full records. These records also provided data for each of the prisoners on age, sentence-length, present and previous offences, age at first conviction, security category, marital status, occupation, race and religion. Demographic information about members of staff was obtained by asking the management at each prison to provide updated lists of men in post with details of rank, and separate lists containing anonymous details of age and length of service. The demographic information was used to compile total population statistics, and in some cases provided the details necessary in order to test the representativeness of samples.

A prison officer's diary was developed and administered to all members of the uniformed staff in each prison. The diary contained blank timetables which officers were expected to complete each day during a specified three-day period. The timetables were divided into half-hour periods and officers were required to record their activity for each half hour of their working day. Response categories were pre-coded and included duties such as security, supervision, rehabilitation and staff training. The aim of the diary was to produce a picture both of the length of the working day and of the way in which time was apportioned to various duties. It was expected that the information produced by the diary would test the claims that have been made that open regimes offer opportunities for staff to be used in a different and more constructive way. The diary is described further in chapter 6.

A prison officer's questionnaire. This instrument was designed to elicit a range of details about the career, attitudes and social situation of uniformed prison staff. Questions were asked about training postings, attitudes towards aspects of the penal system and towards training for the prison service, as well as about duties performed, previous occupations, career alternatives, current domestic circumstances and social life. (For the questionnaire see appendix 2.)

A data collection sheet was compiled for each prison. The aim of this instrument was to provide details of the history, structure and functioning of each establishment. Information for the data collection sheet was accumulated in a variety of ways including library research, the examination of administrative records, and casual conversations with members of staff. The principal source of information, however, was a series of interviews conducted with strategically located members of staff in each prison. Such persons always included the Governor and Chief Officer, the Chaplain, the Administration Officer, the Industrial Manager, the Senior Foreman of Works, a representative of the Welfare Department, all shop supervisors and other members of staff responsible for such duties as security, hospitals, inmate labour allocation, kitchens, stores, reception and discharge, parole and induction schemes.

A sociometric measure was developed in order to make possible a comparison of patterns of personal interaction and subgrouping. An attempt was made to apply this device in one prison. Its application caused immediate concern among the rather sophisticated inmate population, and all other aspects of research with inmates (e.g. that based on the CIES) were placed in jeopardy. A decision was made to withdraw this instrument from use but it was hoped that the CIES scales and objective indices measuring involvement and the degree and pattern of staff/inmate interaction would provide part of the information that this instrument was intended to obtain.

In addition to these more formal means of data collection (and of equal importance), members of the research staff lived and worked intensively in each prison for periods of up to two months. During these periods, and on later visits to each prison, therefore, they had many opportunities to observe proceedings and to meet and converse with staff and inmates in more informal ways. The information about everyday affairs and problems of each prison which this experience provided was viewed as an important and in no way secondary data source. Observational accounts based upon these experiences were, therefore, prepared for each prison included in the study, thus providing a rich and complementary source of information which could be called upon to fill out and inform the picture created by the more empirically based approaches.

Sampling

Research instruments were administered to all uniformed staff in the research, and to a variable ratio sample of inmates, giving a sample of 100 in each prison (see p. 97). While the responses from inmates were large enough to provide representative samples in each case, the results from two staff samples (those from the long-term and short-term closed prisons) were not. Consequently, results from these two closed prisons have been excluded from the statistical analysis. This does mean, however, that the results from staff and inmates, particularly in relation to the problems of the assessment and comparison of prison regimes, are not entirely parallel. In other words, because of the exclusion of the results from these two staff samples, the fifteen possible comparisons between six prisons for the inmate data are reduced to only six from four prisons in the case of staff. However, raw scores and results from the two prisons from which unrepresentative data were obtained have occasionally been tabulated purely for comparison. Actual sampling statistics are provided in each chapter where relevant.

Course of the project

Once the research instruments had been designed and piloted both they and the aims of the research were put before the governors of the prisons we intended to visit at a meeting arranged in Manchester by the regional director of the Northern Region of the Prison Department. Similar discussions with the directors of the Midlands and South Western Regions had already taken place. An open prison in each of the latter regions had been selected for the study and the Manchester meeting was attended by the Governor of one and the deputy governor of the other. It was hoped that the meeting would inform the governors of our intentions, allow them to discuss the proposed research informally with us and thus place them in a position to pass on to their institutions an accurate picture of our aims.

After the meeting at Manchester, the Prison Officers' Association and the Civil Service Union were approached in order to answer any questions they might have and to ask them to support the research so that co-operation from their members in each establishment might be secured. Both organisations willingly offered their co-operation, expressed active interest in the project and offered to write urging support for us from the branches of their organisations affected.

The next step was for two members of the research team to visit each prison to speak to staff and, wherever possible, to hold a general staff meeting at which the research proposals could be outlined and any questions answered. These visits were also used in order to negotiate final details of the research—for instance its proposed duration and date, and accommodation and facilities for the research staff within the prison.

Finally six prisons were visited in order to carry out fieldwork as follows: long-term open: June-July 1970; short-term open: August-September 1970; short-term closed: September-October 1970; medium-term open: October-November 1970; medium-term closed: November-December 1970; long-term closed: January-February 1971.

There was no special reason for visiting the prisons in the above order except that there had been a recent change of Governor at the long-term closed prison and it was suggested to us that this prison be visited as late as possible in the research. Apart from this, it seemed most sensible to visit the open prisons where possible during the summer and the closed prisons in the autumn and winter. The long-term open camp was visited first because of its relative proximity to the university. In this way any difficulties occurring during the first attempt to operate the complete fieldwork programme could be ironed out, if necessary, by personal contact between the director and the research staff. The amount of time spent varied between prisons, depending largely on the number of inmates and staff (since these groups represented our sample and therefore the size of our research task).

Wherever possible, overnight accommodation was found for the research staff inside the prison, in the Officers' Mess, with obvious advantage to our aim of trying to get an 'insiders' view'. If this was not possible either because there was no Officers' Mess or because accommodation there was already booked, other accommodation was found near to the prison. Working accommodation within the prison was requested to enable research staff to store research materials, record observations and, when necessary, carry out interviews. In all cases, though with varying degrees of difficulty, accommodation was found, although in three of the six prisons the room allocated to us had to be shared with members of the prison staff. Where this was the case, a steel lockable cabinet was requested so that any information of a confidential nature could be securely stored.

At two of the closed prisons, easy accessibility to many areas was restricted since the research team were not issued with a pass key. Thus, although no parts of any prison (except for those areas directly concerned with prison security in the long-term closed prison which housed some category A offenders) were restricted from enquiries, access in and out of the main cell blocks often meant long waits until a door was unlocked.

As far as possible, research procedures were held constant

between the different prisons although certain structural differences in the prisons sometimes enforced modifications. Where, and under what circumstances, this occurred will be made apparent in later pages.

The first week or so at each prison was spent, usually with the assistance of a prison officer, meeting individually all the uniformed staff at that prison. This enabled the researcher to introduce himself and to briefly explain why the research was being carried out, and how essential their co-operation was, if the study was to be successfully completed. This also gave us an opportunity to issue them with a package containing the research instruments, including the CIES, the questionnaire and the diary. When this distribution of documents was completed, meetings were held with staff in order to explain the research and answer their questions about it. These meetings were for uniformed staff only and were not attended by the Governor or his assistants. An opportunity for the uninhibited expression of views was thereby presented, and officers made good use of this. Any staff who were not available during the first week because of sickness, detached duty or annual leave were noted and contact made with them if they returned to the prison during the fieldwork period. This meant that, since the diary required completion on three specific days, some officers returning after this time had passed were not asked to complete this instrument. Staff were asked to return their completed questionnaires, diaries and CIES response forms on or before a specified date one week before the end of the fieldwork at the prison. A collection box placed in the gate lodge or a similarly convenient location was provided so that officers could return their research instruments anonymously. None of them contained names, nor any means by which respondents could be individually identified.

Towards the end of the first stage, notices were posted on inmates' notice boards informing them of the purpose of the CIES and the dates on which some of them would be asked to complete it. The remainder of this initial period was then used to select the sample of inmates required to complete the CIES. During this period, all members of staff likely to be affected by this procedure were informed and arrangements were made concerning the rooms and equipment necessary for the group administrations of the CIES. Depending upon the size of the sample, group testing was carried out in a period of two or three days (see section on the administration of the CIES in chapter 4 for a full account of the procedures adopted).

In the following weeks, interviews were arranged with staff in all departments of the prison, in order to supplement our observations of the ongoing life of the prison. Depending on the size of the prison, interviewing lasted between one and two weeks, and interviews still outstanding after this time were left whenever possible until the end of the fieldwork period at the prison. The remaining period at each prison was spent in attempts to improve the response rate from staff to our formal research instruments, and in carrying out the inmate census. Efforts to improve the response rate were initially intended to spur on those officers who had yet to complete their forms or who, having completed them, had not at that time returned them. Reminders, both verbal and written, were issued by one of the research staff and the Governor in all prisons. This procedure was often supported by a reminder from the Prison Officers' Association local branch committee during branch meetings. It was then decided by members of the research team to carry out a second issue of the research instruments to try to achieve a further improvement in the level of response from staff. Accordingly, after other fieldwork had been completed in each prison, arrangements were made for this 'second wave' assisted by representatives of the Prison Officers' Association branch committees. As the instruments were anonymous, non-respondents could not be identified, so all staff were reissued with copies of the research instruments.

Data analysis

This commenced in March 1971, and details are given in the chapters which follow. Some preliminary issues will however be discussed at this point.

Although the research started with some tentative hypotheses about the nature of open/closed differences in regime, and staff and inmate participation in everyday affairs in the two settings, the preliminary work indicated that this approach might prove too simple to fit the facts. The patterning of differences and similarities between prisons was not always along open/closed lines. It was therefore decided to examine any and every difference between the prisons on each variable, instead of confining ourselves to the open/closed dichotomy. But this necessarily made the statistical analyses more complex.

As the problems of multiple comparison in social research have received detailed discussion elsewhere,[31] there is no need to repeat them here. However, a preliminary account of the general rationale of statistical analysis in this study is called for. (Detailed accounts of the methodological orientation, and the rationale and the procedures adopted for the statistical analysis of the data obtained from each research instrument are incorporated in the appropriate chapters.) The framework of statistical analysis included the testing of null hypotheses at two levels. First, for each variable a 'first order' null hypothesis was tested for the data from every prison included in the analysis. No further testing was undertaken in instances where this null hypothesis (i.e. that there was not a statistically significant difference between the results from all the constituent groups) was accepted. However, in cases where the 'first order' null hypothesis was rejected, 'second order' null hypotheses were tested for each constituent pair of prisons from which data were available. Other statistical procedures were adopted in addition to these when necessary, but these will be discussed at appropriate points in the succeeding chapters.

Chapters 2 and 3 contain descriptive accounts of the six prisons, based on observations and interviews completed during our field-work, and at the end of chapter 2 are also included tables containing the structural and ecological data recorded in the data collection sheets and the census, as well as summary tables of some of the research material included to facilitate comparisons. It was hoped that the 'running accounts' of chapters 2 and 3 would put 'flesh and blood' on to the skeleton provided by means of the more formal research procedures. As will be seen, the two kinds of data do support and complement each other in a number of ways. Chapter 4 contains an account of the procedures adopted in administering the CIES to staff and inmate groups in each prison, while chapter 5 sets out the results obtained. Chapters 6 to 8 study prison staffs in the light of the results obtained from the staff questionnaire and the diary, chapter 6 describing the methodology adopted and chapters 7 and 8 setting out the results. Finally, in chapter 9, the main conclusions from the study are reviewed, and an attempt is made to determine their implications for penal policy in Britain, especially in relation to open prisons.

2   The closed prisons

Although our three closed prisons were alike in being training prisons, they displayed many differences in other respects. The long-term closed prison was thus larger than the others and also possessed better educational, training and psychiatric facilities than most other prisons in this country. Also, unlike our other research prisons it contained category A (high-security) prisoners (see Table 2.6 below). Although, in accordance with the Home Office's policy of dispersing high-security prisoners among a number of institutions throughout the country rather than concentrating them on certain 'fortress' institutions as recommended in the Mountbatten Report, category A prisoners constitute less than 5 per cent of the population of the prison, it is necessarily such a group, representing the highest level of risk, who set the institution's security target. (At the beginning of 1974, segregation units were introduced into 'dispersal' prisons for the more effective containment of troublesome prisoners, thus limiting the application of the dispersal policy.) As the only prison in our sample containing category A prisoners, this was therefore the most security-conscious of them. It was also, as Table 2.1 (below) shows, the most long-term of our three closed prisons. As will be seen, the length of sentence being served has a crucial effect upon a regime.

Our second prison was the medium-term closed. As in length of sentence so also with regard to the security grading of its population, it lay nearer the centre of the spectrum than the other prisons (Table 2.6). Thus although it was distinguished from the long-term closed in having no category A prisoners, 20 per cent of its inmates were in category B as compared with 1 per cent at the short-term closed. This latter fact seems to have had less effect in differentiating regimes between this prison and the short-term closed than other (notably architectural) factors in the situation. In a prison in which the segregation of high-escape-risk prisoners is not carried out (in other words, in a prison operating the dispersal policy of the Home Office) the rule about security adumbrated above is bound to operate. Thus, even 1 per cent of category B prisoners means that the prison has to maintain category B levels of security.

The feature which seemed to influence most strongly the way in which it operated was the building. It is often argued that the main impediment to the improvement of prison methods is the fact that most of our prison buildings were constructed in the nineteenth century to give effect to the prison philosophy of the time, mainly centring on the 'separate system'. What then is one to say about a prison which was originally built as a castle in the fourteenth century, reputedly by John of Gaunt for his wife? It could hardly have been intended as a kind of princely chastity belt, in view of the security problems which it presents to those who now have to run it; it is this more than anything else which accounts for the undue preoccupation with security hinted at above. But presumably castles, being intended to keep people out rather than to keep them in, are bound to arouse anxieties about security in those who have to run them as prisons. Confined by its outer fortifications (complete with moat), this prison also suffered more from lack of space than the others.

Then there was the short-term closed prison. Its population consisted largely of category C prisoners (see Table 2.6 below), though its security conditions tended to be those of a category B prison because of the category B element (admittedly small) with which it had to cope. However, its regime had been most influenced by the fact that the prisoners whom it contains were serving short sentences. This is a factor the importance of which is not confined to the closed prisons alone. As will be seen, it cuts across the open/closed dichotomy, though not entirely eliminating its effect.

What follows is a fairly detailed account of the regimes of the three closed prisons, based upon observations made by the research staff while actually living in the prisons in question. Although concurrently carrying out a test programme, reported in later chapters, they also interviewed governors and staff both formally and informally in general conversation, talked with prisoners, and watched what was going on as they moved about the prisons in the course of their duties. Each of these periods of observation lasted for periods of up to two months. Although this period of time was relatively short, it was part of an intensive experience in which the observers spent many hours each day in the prisons, and in which they also had the opportunity of presenting themselves as neither staff nor inmates. It was hoped that they would thus obtain an all-round picture not readily available to those who, because they were more clearly identified with one side or the other, were also more caught up in the suspicion and hostility natural to a penal institution.

The following then is subjective and impressionistic. It includes all sorts of judgments made on the basis of what some of the more scientistic social scientists would call 'soft data'. Nevertheless it seems to us to have its own validity. It enables us to show how the prisons looked to a trained, experienced and impartial observer. It enables us to try to see a prison as a whole in a way which it is not easy to achieve using the kind of fragmented data which are available from the use of more objective research instruments. And seeing the institutions whole, we hope that we can discern patterns— show how the various parts of the institution's regime hang together to give it a particular character. We believe that the development of an 'ideal typology' of prisons in this way is a useful complement to the study of 'components' or 'factors' made possible by the use of the instruments described in later chapters. Of course we hope that the two aspects of the investigation will converge: that the various factors shown to be present in a particular prison will add up to the kind of overall regime which this chapter describes. To the extent that this is achieved, the validity of both aspects of the research will have been confirmed.

The long-term closed prison

This prison was built in 1847, although there has been a prison on the site very much longer. Although its date means that it is a cellular prison, it suffers less from this fact than prisons on more restricted sites. The main problem of the nineteenth-century cellular prison is of course that it was built with the intention that the prisoner should spend almost all his time in separate confinement in his cell. As a result there were no ancillary buildings for work, education or even recreation. When prison ideas changed and emphasis was placed on these latter activities, the earlier disregard of them meant that there were not only no facilities for carrying them out, but that no room had been left within the walls where such facilities could be provided. The great problem for twentieth-century penal reformers has been how, nevertheless, to make room for them. Because of its large site no such problem has arisen here. Engineering workshops, weaving and tailoring workshops, a gymnasium, a hospital, and even a hard football pitch and a grassed recreation area have been provided. This impression of spaciousness extends even to the population density of the cell blocks themselves. Almost all prisoners are in single-occupation cells, whereas in most other prisons many men share with one or often two others.

In view of the large proportion of category A prisoners in this institution, it would, however, be unrealistic to expect the free movement of prisoners around these various facilities. A rigorous procedure controls the movements of every category A prisoner. His photograph is lodged near the officers' roster board so that all officers may become familiar with his appearance, and his name is also entered into a 'category A movements book'. Whenever his surveillance is transferred from one officer to another, this is recorded in the movements book so that the responsibility for his personal supervision is established and formalised. Category A men are also dispersed as widely round the prison as possible, and every attempt is made to ensure that cliques of them do not build up.

However, it is the measures adopted along the outside wall of the prison that bring home most vividly its maximum security character. All walls, and buildings adjacent to them, are painted with a reflective white paint, which is illuminated at night by high-intensity sodium lights. Thus at all times, and in all weather conditions excepting fog, the perimeter of the prison is in perpetual 'daylight'. Along the whole length of a private lane running beside the prison wall are tall poles, upon which are mounted television cameras which gyrate in order to survey all movements, both on foot or car anywhere near the gates or wall of the prison. Cameras of this kind were also to be found within the prison, although not in the cell block itself, and are capable of scanning through a wide angle or 'zooming in' on any incident which the monitoring officer considers worthy of closer examination. The walls themselves, which were divided into numbered sections for quick identification, were topped by 'weight-sensitive wires' which were so delicately poised that even a large bird perching on one of them could activate the warning bell in the control room. Fifteen specially trained officers worked in the security monitoring room on a shift system extending over the 24 hours of the day. Finally, dogs with their handlers patrolled the prison grounds day and night.

It has never been suggested that such a system would actually prevent any escape from taking place. Nevertheless it must have been a very formidable deterrent. And although it sounds very intimidating, its concentration at the perimeter of the prison made it possible for the movement of men within the prison (category A apart) to be much freer than would otherwise have been the case. As already stated, this is a long-term institution. Two consequences seem to flow from this. One is that it has been possible to plan for a settled life within the prison, including a properly phased training programme. The other is the feeling on the part of the staff, as well as the prisoners, that a man who is serving a long sentence is entitled to rather more consideration from the institution than the man who does not have to live with it for so long. It might be noted in passing that this view has some curious implications for the retributive theory of justice, for the long-termer has presumably committed the more serious crime and therefore 'deserves' the severer punishment. This prison has always had a good training programme, but it is the long sentences being served by the men in it which makes such a programme possible.

Four vocational training courses are available: tailoring, electrician's, welding and bricklaying. Of these the tailoring course was the best integrated with subsequent experience in the prison, as men who had completed the course could go on to work in the bespoke tailoring shop. This has special value in a long-term prison as no course is likely to last for very long—most are completed in six months. A longstanding complaint about vocational training in prisons is that men are rarely able to get jobs in the trade afterwards. This still seems to be true, in this prison as elsewhere—even in tailoring. This seems to be partly because the men do not wish to work in the trade for which they have trained after leaving the prison, or because it would require a more deliberate effort to that end on the part of prisons, but another factor is undoubtedly the technological gap which often exists between the way in which a trade is taught in the prison and the way in which it is practised outside. A case in point at this prison was the welding course, which used gas welding equipment, whereas industry outside is largely going over to electrical welding. Apparently even if there were enough money available to buy new electrical welding equipment for the prison, there would not be an electrical supply suitable for operating it. Many men in any case were more interested in a 'cushy' or well-paid job (as alas is also sometimes true outside prison) than in the possible vocational implications. For example the loom shop was very popular because this was the highest paid shop in the prison, and as a result there was a long waiting list for admission.

In spite of the existence of alternative forms of work at this prison, mailbags are still used as a last resort for mopping up the unemployed, though only 74 men out of a total population of 784 were occupied in this way during the time that the research worker was in the prison. This would seem very wise: as the officer-instructor in one of the shops concerned said, 'You only have to mention mailbags, and you have six men on report straight away.' One of the shops concerned, called the 'heavy fabric shop', had the reputation of and was often referred to by the prisoners as the 'punishment shop'. Though the staff denied that it was used in this way, officers agreed that it was more closely supervised than any other shop in the prison. The prisoners also believed the 'miscellaneous shop' to have been assigned a derogatory function; they described it as being for those 'who can't cope with, or are too stupid, to do anything else'. In practice they appeared to be the rejects, employed here to save them from disrupting the other shops. At the time of our visit to this prison, 18 out of the 37 men employed in the miscellaneous shop were serving life sentences. They did a variety of things including rugmaking, hospital blankets, minor repairs and the assembling of plastic connectors for the Post Office. For the most part the work required the very minimum of skill and of imagination, but the disciplinary climate of the shop was more easy-going than most.

As in most institutions some inmates were employed on mainten-ance work around the prison. Where possible the works department employed men from the bricklaying and electrical training courses, but most of the labour force tended to be unskilled and untrained. Some men were also employed in the gardens and the greenhouses, but this involved almost unlimited mobility around the prison, and was therefore confined to redbands (trusted prisoners) and other minimum-escape-risk inmates. A few men were also employed on domestic work, as cleaners, and there was the usual kitchen team.

Apart from vocational training courses which were also under the prison's tutor organiser, there was an extensive educational pro-gramme within the prison. This was undoubtedly the best of any of the prisons in which we did research. A recent survey carried out by the tutor organiser revealed that he and his staff had contacts with 42 per cent of the prison population. Of course such contacts varied enormously, ranging from work with inmates who were taking full-time day courses to the mere supply of exercise books and pencils to men separately confined under Rule 43—a rule which provides that certain prisoners should be separated from the rest for their own protection. There were no fewer than fifty members of staff working in this educational programme. Most of them came in only once or twice a week but four were full-time and another twelve came in frequently, either during the day or in the evening to take classes. Most of the educational activities of the prison took place in the evenings. This was because of the principle adopted in the workshops of giving priority to productivity, and of resistance therefore to interruptions of the working day to attend classes, etc. It was argued that such interruptions not only led to a fall in production, but also involved something of a departure from the realistic factory atmosphere and training in regular work habits which it was hoped would stand inmates in good stead when they were eventually discharged. However, such a policy in the prison did, as we have seen, lead to an imbalance in the distribution of the workload for the staff of the education department in the evenings. Such a concentration on evenings may prove to be unavoidable in the nature of the job, but it also increases the resources, both in manpower and space, needed to maintain a given level of educational activity.

A wide range of courses were provided. There was a basic English course held, as it happens, during the daytime as well as in the evening, and intended to raise an inmate from 'illiteracy to the ability to read the *Daily Mirror*, fill in a Social Security form, and write a letter'. Although it was estimated that about 10 per cent of the population needed remedial reading instruction, they did not flock to this course. This it seemed was partly because they did not wish to be identified as illiterate; but also because in attending a day class they tended to lose working time and also the opportunity of being in a well-paid 'production shop', losing money on both counts. There was a similar basic course in mathematics. At the other extreme were the sixty inmates who had enrolled for Open University foundation courses, and others who were taking National Diploma courses in Business Studies or in Graphic Art. Others were studying advanced English, creative English, French, German, Mathematics and Bookkeeping. A wide range of more recreational activities were also provided ranging from handicraft classes to drama and music appreciation, a brass band, a poetry group and a debating society. A Braille group, which at the time of the research worked only in the evenings, produced books for local blind welfare organisations, schools for the blind, and individual blind people. There was even a course in computer studies linked with the IBM Co. Ltd, who initially were supplying both the equipment and the expertise.

There were many difficulties nevertheless surrounding the

education programme of the prison. There was the competition for the daytime hours with the industrial shops already mentioned. This was a problem in some of the other prisons, especially in a prison like the short-term closed with a similar industrial orientation. The very extensive programme also meant that, even in this prison, space for classes was at a premium. This situation was further exacerbated by the concentration of courses on the evening period which meant that the education building was not fully utilised during the day. Major difficulties also arose from the limitations understandably imposed in a maximum security prison. Because the education block was not built as a maximum security section, category A prisoners were not permitted to enter it. To deprive category A prisoners of educational opportunities seems particularly anomalous, for they, as inmates serving the longest sentences, were most likely to need and to benefit from them.

It remains to examine the general organisational framework of the prison: its structures of authority and communications, its sub-groupings and their inter-relationship with one another, and the pattern of personal relationships, both within the inmate and staff groups and between them. There appear to be two schools of thought on these matters. One is that they are solely determined by the Governor, who is the all-powerful figure, setting his personal stamp upon the institution. The other view, espoused by sociologically minded students of prisons, is that the Governor can have only a marginal effect upon his institution, which constitutes a powerful and longstanding structure of pressures and constraints, checks and balances, made up of a multitude of established expectations and vested interests. Certainly the Governor of this prison wished to produce improvements for both inmates and staff, but although he had been posted to the prison only a very short time when the research took place, he was already finding it hard going. He attributed this to 'apathy' among the staff, but it might be more accurately understood as the result of organisational resistances including those already referred to.

One such which struck the researchers with particular force was the insularity of the various wings of the prison. Both inmates and staff tended to look inwards to their own wing rather than outwards to the prison as a whole. In an institution with nearly 200 uniformed staff and 780 prisoners, it was bound to be difficult for them all to have a firm concept of the prison as a whole unless special efforts were made to try to create it. In fact the way in which the prison operated decisively frustrated such an aim.

Decisions were passed from the Governor to his assistant governors, one being attached to each wing. It was the responsibility of each assistant governor together with the principal officer for his wing to ensure not only that these policy decisions were made known to the staff on the wing, but also that they were properly implemented at the 'grassroots' level. Basic grade officers were also rarely moved from wing to wing, though this was of course necessary sometimes. The result of this seemed to be the development of a strong in-group feeling among the staff of a wing, and a certain lack of sympathy with the staff of other wings. One practical outcome was that little mutual aid passed between wings, for example at times of staff shortage. On the venerable principle that it is the exception that proves the rule, the researcher noted a contrary example. During a crisis as a result of a shortage of inmate clothing, staff of all wings co-operated in the search for hoarded items of inmate apparel. It is significant that this was considered worth remarking upon; the examples on the other side were numerous and generally recognised by the staff. They were manifested mainly in unwillingness to 'help out' in times of need. For example it would be difficult to get either the principal officer or the assistant governor in charge of a wing to allow the short-term transfer of an officer to another wing needing temporary help.

Most officers saw this as merely an annoying fact rather than something which presented a real difficulty in the organisation of the prison. Nevertheless, the effect of the restricted range of personal interactions which it produced was to increase the separateness of the various wings, reducing the already tenuous communication between them. It was not therefore surprising if their norms also began to diverge. Thus although officially each wing operated under the same policy and had to implement the same directives from the Governor, each developed its own ways of doing this. These differences seemed to be very subtle; when inmates were asked to describe them they suggested that they could only be learned by experience. It was always inmates who were most conscious of these differences—not unnaturally as the most important of them arose in the granting of various concessions by the principal officer or the assistant governor on the wing. Some wings granted these privileges much more regularly than others. Inmates were naturally impressed by the advantages derived from being on the more generous wings, but difficulties arose when they were moved and suffered the contrary effects of these differences in the informal system. But there may have been other disutilities in this situation. Knowing what to expect and how to behave is a *sine qua non* for a secure and satisfying social adjustment. Moreover, if, as it is argued, one of the disadvantages of the closed prison is the way in which it turns the motivations of its inmates inwards, producing adaptation to an artificial and highly introverted society rather than to the wider and more differentiated society outside, what can one say about a system which turns each wing within a prison in upon itself?

Many officers were however more concerned about difficulties occurring within the staff group itself, and these resulted from another form of internal differentiation within the prison. While some officers were continuously involved with prisoners and having to bear what was seen as both the stress and the animus resulting from disciplining them, others in more specialised roles such as the dog-handlers or the staff of the clothing store were free from this. A negative stereotype of the latter groups resulted. For instance, the uniformed officers argued that the clothing shortage already referred to was caused by the inability of the civilian officer who ran the clothing store to maintain discipline among the inmates. If the nature of these problems had been recognised definite steps could have been taken to provide channels of communication, in the form of meetings, etc., through which these difficulties might have been ironed out. In fact, apart from meetings which the Governor held separately in each wing (thus tending to intensify the insularity already referred to) there was only a senior staff meeting, called the Governor's Meeting. There were thus few opportunities for discipline and other basic grade staff to come together specifically for the purpose of clearing up their mutual misapprehensions.

Formal staff-inmate communication was better developed, taking the form of a series of joint consultative committees. One of these was the messing committee, which largely concerned itself with complaints and suggestions regarding the quality of food served from the kitchens. Although largely seen by both staff and inmates as a 'safety valve' through which complaints could be channelled and brought to the notice of the kitchen staff before the situation got out of hand, it did seem to have more important functions in marshalling inmate support for changes in the kitchen arrangements. The principal officer in charge of the kitchen argued that his newly developed central feeding system would have been almost impossible to introduce without the co-operation of this committee. There was also an entertainments committee responsible for organising and co-ordinating inmate shows and productions, as well as for considering inmate requests for particular types of entertainment.

But it was at the informal level, in this as in most other prisons, that really significant interactions between officers and prisoners occurred. And at this level there were many points of agreement between them. There was of course the usual consensus on where different kinds of offenders stood in the pecking order, from the 'decent rogue' at the top, to the sex offender or the psychiatric case at the bottom. There was also the usual implicit agreement between officers and inmates to 'leave each other alone' so long as all went smoothly—the 'let sleeping dogs lie' approach referred to above as the 'custodial compromise'. Only a few officers rejected this and attempted to establish some sort of dialogue on a personal basis with the prisoners. The traditional staff-inmate dissociation became virtually ostracism with respect to homosexual prisoners, reflecting a much stronger antipathy than that found in the wider community. Nevertheless a minority of officers did manage to understand these men.

Very significant in the context of this prison was the consensus between most of the staff and inmates about the special privileges due to long-term prisoners. This was partly a 'charity begins at home' attitude; long-termers made up most of the population, such short-termers as were in the prison being on temporary transfer from other institutions in order to take part in vocational training courses, or to receive psychiatric treatment or treatment in the prison's special alcoholism unit. Nevertheless a minority of the staff did disagree with this 'family first' viewpoint. Also some influence must be credited to the traditional preference of both the experienced prison officer and prisoners for the long-term prisoner who 'knows how to do bird' and is going to be a nuisance to nobody. There was also some recognition here of the point already made: that the wind ought to be tempered a little for the man who has to spend so much of his life in the already sufficiently depriving environment of the prison. Whatever its origin, this preferential attitude appeared to be a real impediment to the Governor in his efforts to ensure that all prisoners were treated alike. But like the Governor's own egalitarian policy, it is antagonistic to the individualisation of treatment which has been seen for three-quarters of a century as the approach which is likely to be most conducive to the reform of offenders. Both it and egalitarianism see these issues as concerned with 'privileges' rather than being determined by the requirements of a treatment regime tailored in each case to the personality and situation of the particular prisoner.

The 'custodial compromise' is thus well in evidence here. Living and working together in a closed institution, the staff and the inmates have to achieve some common ground. Perpetual war would be intolerable for both sides under these circumstances. What emerges is something very much in the nature of a shared culture or pattern of values and ideas, but varying in character from wing to wing. This is a far cry from the popular picture of a prison as a place in which the staff are constantly trying to communicate to the prisoners a different and better set of values than their own. At the same time one can see, in the long-term closed, a number of rifts in mutual understanding between the staff themselves. The insularity of the wings gives rise to some such. The mutual mistrust between discipline and other basic grade staff is another factor. Then there are the minority groups who challenge the established wisdom that one ought not to be friendly with prisoners, or who reject the view that one should favour the long-termers above all others.

Communication within the inmate groups seems to have been very efficient indeed. Specific items of information could be transmitted to a particular individual in a very short time. At a meeting in the Governor's office it was announced that a redband working in the education department was to be released on licence. The Governor wished himself to give this news to the inmate. Another redband cleaning the stairs to the Governor's office overheard this titbit, which he then relayed to another redband working on the yard outside the Governor's office. The latter walked around the outside of the prison to the education block, made contact through a window with the education block redband, and informed him of his impending departure. When the tutor organiser returned to his department he was greeted by an elated inmate assistant with what he had thought was strictly confidential information.

More general news travelled equally fast. As a result of the shortage of inmates' clothing, it was decided at the Governor's Meeting that a prison-wide cell-search should be undertaken in order to retrieve surplus garments and if possible identify the culprits who had been hoarding them. The Governor's Meeting finished after inmates had started their morning's work. By the time they returned for lunch, most of them already knew of the plans for the spot-search. The researcher was at the time watching inmates through the research office door as they queued up for their midday meal, and noticed a number of them carrying various items of clothing. Some of these were thrown into the research office as they went past. Indeed clothing was deposited all over the prison, and in the wells outside the cell blocks, presumably having been thrown out of cell windows. Only a minority were caught redhanded, and one of these, perhaps more through greed than lack of information, was found to be in possession of nine shirts. The researcher felt that this incident pointed very clearly to some leak through the staff to the inmates—perhaps another illustration of the communality of ideas and interests which (as might be expected) the two sides tended to develop.

Finally there is the daily routine of the prison. The early-shift staff came on duty at 6.40 a.m., so that inmates could be unlocked, and then 'slop out' their toilet buckets in the wing recess, wash and shave and be fed in time for their work, which began at 8 a.m. Prisoners then worked through until 9.50 a.m. when there was a twenty-minute morning break for exercise. The workshops closed for the midday meal on a rota basis between 11.10 and 11.30 in order to stagger the flow of inmates into the central feeding system, which would otherwise have been unable to cope with them. Afternoon work recommenced at 1.30 p.m. and continued until 2.50, when a further twenty-minute break was allowed for exercise. Only a small number of inmates were actually confined to the exercise yard for this purpose. Most drifted around outside the workshops smoking, talking and occasionally playing football. After this break, work continued until 4.30 p.m., when inmates returned to the prison for tea. Once tea had been served and eaten, the various evening activities commenced at 6 p.m. Those who did not wish to take part in educational activities could spend the evening in a more informal way in the association area on each wing, but those who did neither were locked in their cells. By 8.30 p.m. all inmates were locked up, and lights were extinguished by 10 p.m.

The medium-term closed prison

Some description has already been given of the castle in which the staff of this institution had to attempt the task of containing its prisoners, while also providing for them the kind of constructive regime appropriate to a training prison. Its many corridors, thick walls and moat strictly constraining the area, and narrow and sometimes spiral staircases presented almost unique problems for the administrator. The observer commented on a 'claustrophobic atmosphere' resulting from the sheer lack of space, and the frequency with which areas of the prison had to be artificially lit, all day long.

If there is anything in the idea that prisons ought not to turn the minds of prisoners further inwards, on the grounds that incarceration causes this kind of introversion even under the best circumstances, doubts would have to be expressed about the use of this building as a prison.

The sheer lack of space, of course, marked it out very sharply from the prison just discussed; many of its activities seemed to be restricted by the dearth of places in which to conduct them. For example, the educational programme was adversely affected by the fact that the rooms used for it were scattered in so many different parts of the prison. None of these places was used, at the time of the research, exclusively for educational purposes; each had to be vacated for some other use for part of the time. Also, because of the overall lack of space, most of the work opportunities for prisoners were outside the prison. Because taking men to these work-places represented something of a security hazard, category B prisoners could not go and were therefore limited to the very narrow range of jobs which could be provided within the prison itself. These sometimes almost petered out altogether, so that payment by results, adopted as a technique for stimulating involvement and diligence, had to be abandoned in favour of flat-rate payment—presumably in order to avoid the danger that prisoners might be so stimulated as to use up the work available to them too quickly.

Outside work opportunities consisted of three prison farms and an outside workshop. Prisoners were taken to these various centres by bus, accompanied by supervising officers. The workshop was fenced, and the number who could take advantage of what went on in it was controlled entirely by its inflexible size. The kind of task available was mainly unskilled sewing work. The three prison farms were originally intended to be labour-intensive in order that they might absorb a large number of prisoners. However, this objective seemed to have been given up in favour of more mechanised and modern forms of farming. This would appear to be a desirable thing to do: there seems little point in training men to do any kind of work in ways which nobody ever uses nowadays, quite apart from the unnecessary drudgery involved. The farm also had a market garden, and one way of legitimately increasing the labour-intensiveness of the work might have been to have turned a larger acreage over to gardening.

Inside the prison there were a number of workshops: the boot and shoe shop, at that time being run down because of the vogue for moulded shoes; the mailbag shop, often seen by inmates of this as of other prisons as a 'punishment' assignment; and the toy manufacturing shop. Although the observer felt that the mailbag shop was not really used as a punishment, it did seem to be used as a preventive billet for those who might cause trouble if placed elsewhere; however all prisoners worked there when they first arrived at the prison. The toy manufacturing shop underlined the difficulties which arise in a prison like this, where the structure of the building is so inappropriate to its purpose. This shop was located in a room at the top of a spiral staircase. The security problems here are obvious, but it has also meant that machinery could not be used, the kind of work carried on being thus limited to handwork. The general shortage of work-space in the prison also meant that plans had to be made for taking over part of the chapel as a workshop. Having regard to the longstanding religious tradition in English prisons, this must be seen as a drastic step. The canteen was used also to serve the purpose of a concert hall or cinema. In addition two vocational training courses were available: one in welding, and one in radio and television engineering.

The general educational programme compared very unfavourably with that of the long-term prison and indeed the tutor organiser himself felt that all he was able to do (in view of the rather unsuitable, scattered and restricted accommodation available to him) was to provide inmates with a couple of evening hours a week 'out of their cells'. That was apart from a daytime class for non-readers. Although, as a member of the management board of the prison, the tutor organiser was in a position to put forward the case for education in competition with other priorities, the research team felt that as a part-time member of staff he was apt to give too little regard to the observance of prison routine. The consequent inconvenience to other staff members hampered him in securing the support, particularly of officers in the prison, in developing his programme. The physical difficulties of operating an educational programme within the prison were nevertheless real enough.

The incubus of the building had its effect also upon the prison hospital. It could only be entered by ascending a flight of stone steps, passing through a steel gate, and then climbing a further three flights of narrow, steep stone stairways, each flight of which contained a hairpin bend. As a result of this it seems very reasonably to have been assumed that if an inmate became too ill to walk, it would be necessary to take him straight to the local General Hospital rather than to try to manoeuvre a stretcher up to the hospital. In fact partly for this reason and partly because there was no permanent posting of a hospital officer here, the hospital seems to have been very little used except for the conduct of the daily out-patients' clinic. A sign of its disuse was that although each bed in the hospital ward had a personal radio and a light, none of these appeared to be in working order.

There was a general lack of space for organised games. The men who worked outside could play soccer on one of the prison farms, but men who were required for security reasons to work within the prison walls were consequently also precluded from this kind of activity. Nor was there any gymnasium within the prison to compensate. These lacks must have their humanitarian and health implications, but they probably also do not ease the task of managing prisoners. Opportunities for 'letting off steam' are desirable especially for prisoners who are serving their sentences under such restricted, and presumably tension-producing conditions. Other spatial handicaps included a long trek from the kitchen to the dining room, and the fact that the clothing store was scattered over several floors.

In addition to the sheer lack of space, and the inconvenience of much of the accommodation for the purposes which it was required to serve, a building of this sort was bound to present serious security problems. The population consisted largely of category B and C men, the majority being in the latter group, but the difficulties of maintaining security meant that the low-risk category C men had to be subjected to a degree of rigour which might otherwise have been unnecessary. And of course it meant, as we have seen, that the category B men, forced to stay within the purlieu of the prison, would have very few opportunities of experiencing and learning to use freedom and personal responsibility. All this quite apart from the safeguards necessitated by spiral staircases, dark corridors, and so on. It may be for such reasons as this that one of our tests, the CIES (p. 109-10) showed this to be almost the most 'closed', i.e. institutionalised, of the prisons we studied. This was reflected in low scores for such factors as the 'personal problem orientation' of the prison, the 'autonomy' and 'involvement' of prisoners, the prison's 'clarity' of purpose, and lowest of all, its 'practical orientation', i.e. the low priority given to directing the prisoners' attention to ways of coping with practical problems which are likely to arise either while in the prison or after discharge. The research workers also felt that the geographical isolation of the prison, especially from the area east of the Pennines which provided a substantial part of its population, meant that visitors were fewer than they should have been, resulting in the prisoners becoming socially isolated, and perhaps even more institutionalised.

A specific if minor instance of the security procedure of the prison indicating the level of concern about it was that the research worker, whose office was situated on one of the cell landings, was told by a member of staff that his tape recorder and typewriter should be locked away in a steel cabinet whenever he was not himself in the room. Also if he needed to change a light bulb in the office, he was told that under no circumstances should it be thrown away, but kept until it was convenient to dispose of it securely. The security officer had a 'letter-box' on the door of his office so that inmates could deliver to him information they considered to be important without disclosing their identities—assuming, of course, that they were not seen posting it! The security officer claimed that although much of the information posted into his letter-box was incorrect, or at least unprovable, it was always followed up, and it was his impression that without such a system the prison would be in 'minor chaos'.

The previous history of this prison seems important for any attempt to understand its general climate or regime. There was a general belief among the staff that the previous regime had been too permissive. One example quoted by the staff was of an inmate who was said to have been reported to the Governor seventeen times for the same offence, receiving a caution each time. The present Governor had therefore felt obliged to tighten up discipline; the research worker felt that the Governor kept a pretty tight rein on the situation, and reported a comment by him that 'in total institutions, law and order are paramount'. A result of the staff dissatisfaction with the previous dispensation had been a feeling also on the Governor's part that he should consult the staff about any changes he might make. Although he certainly made a lot of changes, the research worker felt that these were not great in comparison with other prisons, but the staff nevertheless interpreted them very much amiss. This was felt not to be a result of the Governor's own personality but the result, in spite of his verbal support for consultation, of bad communications. However it arose, there was a general feeling of 'Whatever is he going to do next?'

In fact communication failure seems to have been the main pathology of this prison. In part this was a result of the deficiencies of the building. Because activities in the prison had to take place in so many locations throughout the institution, the staff themselves were also dispersed. Very often officers worked alone in the various areas of the prison supervising inmates, and since neither inside nor outside the prison was there any formal gathering place for them— there was not even an Officers' Club—a number of the staff tended to become somewhat 'privatised'. The only real meeting place was at the gate, when officers moved in and out of the prison at mealtimes. It was here that official announcements were made as necessary by the chief officer, and where staff could talk among themselves until they were either let out or into the prison *en masse*. This absence of a meeting place for the staff outside the dining room cropped up also as a problem for the research staff when they wanted to meet the officers as a whole to discuss the project with them. On that occasion one of the inmate association rooms had to be used. Difficulties might have been minimised if regular staff meetings had been held. The Governor did hold a weekly senior and principal officers' meeting, in the expectation that these senior grades would disseminate information received at the meeting to the basic grade officers in their charge. In fact little was passed on from these meetings. As a result all sorts of suspicions developed among basic grade officers about the kind of discussions that took place at these meetings. In spite of frequent denials, it was a commonly held belief that individual officers were discussed in secret during the meeting, and thus prevented from exercising any right of reply. The only other meeting held at the prison was that of heads of departments, attended by the Governor, deputy governor, chief officer, administration officer, farm manager, the two welfare officers and the tutor organiser. Meanwhile grievances, notably about the state of repair of staff housing, were felt by basic grade officers to receive little or no airing because of the lack of an appropriate forum in which they might be examined.

Communication between staff and inmates seemed to be no better. Apart from the general effect of the architecture, there were some special factors at work here. In order to relieve the strain on the limited amount of accommodation available for association among prisoners, a number of the dormitories had television sets. Most of the occupants therefore preferred to stay in the dormitories watching television, and to resent intrusion upon their privacy at these times, or any reorganisation of their evenings. Therefore officers tended not to mix with these inmates as much as they would if they had met them on association, and so were lost many opportunities of chatting together and getting to know each other better. In the cellular 'A' wing, with its association room, the situation was quite different. The acceptance by the staff of the inmate desire for privacy under these circumstances, while it might have appeared correctionally disadvantageous, is a rather striking example of the way in which the 'custodial compromise' operates.

The research staff also felt that this dormitory seclusion also facilitated the growth of the criminal underworld in this prison, and particularly aided the more exploitative forms of leadership among the prisoners (the so-called 'tobacco barons') to establish their hegemony. Some kind of vicious circle seemed to have been established: dormitory seclusion led to 'baroning', and 'baroning' to an even more determined exclusion of possible interference by the staff. In fact little attempt was made by the staff to penetrate these groups.

We have already seen above something of the negative attitudes engendered among the staff themselves by failures in communication. Thus although relationships within the senior staff group appeared to be quite good, this was by no means true of relationships between them and their subordinates. Even more strained, however, were those between staff and prisoners. As a comparison of Tables 2.2 and 2.8 (below) shows, there was a real generation gap between them.

Apart from this demographic factor, however, communication difficulties must have played their part in generating misunderstandings. Failure of communications between staff and prisoners means a lack of information about each other, and in such a factual vacuum the way is open for both sides to create fantasies of each other based upon their own fears and resentments. Inevitably such fantasies are going to be negative in character; a penal institution is a frustrating and resentment-producing place for both staff and inmates, and this prison has features which might well make it more so than most. So when things went wrong, the prisoners blamed it upon staff malice. On two occasions power cuts brought about by electricity strikes resulted in a decision to 'close down' the prison and lock up all the inmates. Such a decision was probably unavoidable because of the lack of natural daylight in the prison, so that a power cut meant virtual twilight even during the day. Some of the prisoners actually blamed the staff for the blackout itself, but most felt that even if the staff could not help that, they did not have to lock up the prisoners, and only did so in order to have an easy day or to 'get back' at inmates. When asked why staff should wish to 'get back' at them in this manner, they replied that the staff were 'just like that'.

Nor did these unfavourable perceptions fail to have their effect on behaviour in the prison, both on the staff and inmate sides. The research staff encountered some of this in their own work in the prison. For instance, when the research worker was advised to lock up his typewriter and tape recorder, he questioned whether prisoners would be able to hide such bulky objects if they did steal them. He was told that it was not simply a question of the articles being stolen; most of the inmates were so malicious that they would, if given a chance, simply smash them up. On the other side, prisoners needed for the research refused to leave their cells when the officer arrived to escort them to the testing room, although they co-operated quite readily later on. One inmate explained that when ordered to join in by an officer he had replied: 'If you are telling me to go then I am not going.' Incidentally only at this prison were prisoners put on report for disobeying an officer in such circumstances.

It was this of all the prisons in our sample, faced with the impasse born of such misperceptions, which displayed to the research team the highest level of staff despair. An animated gatehouse discussion on the necessity of mandatory hanging for anybody convicted again after three previous prison sentences lasted for over an hour. The topic recurred from time to time and was always proffered as a genuine solution.

Even more than in the other prisons studied, there was a staff shortage—in a prison, moreover, the physical structure of which might have justified a rather more generous staffing ratio than most. A long and frustrating working day was therefore the rule. The staff shortage also meant that the proportion of officers detached from other prisons for relief duties here was high. Their identification with the prison and involvement in its activities was consequently slight, reducing both the amount of staff contact with inmates which was possible, and the already attenuated pattern of personal interaction within the prison.

Although the special physical and social characteristics of this prison have been seen here from the negative standpoint, they did offer certain opportunities which could be taken. There was obvious scope for the development of small-group work in the 'neighbourhood' groups into which this institution was divided. Similarly, because there were only two welfare officers in the prison, they had to confine intensive casework help to very few of around 260 men in the prison. To relieve the pressure on the welfare department, officers were encouraged to write reports on inmates, and deal with many welfare applications. If they had been specially prepared for this work it could have represented something of a breakthrough in increasing social work facilities in a prison, and modifying staff-prisoner relationships. And even when the disadvantages referred to could not thus have been turned to account, many of the problems associated with them would have been alleviated if their character had been recognised and staff appropriately trained for dealing with them. This prison gave the research team its first inkling that some of the difficulties from which our prisons suffer may be the result of the concentration of staff training on general techniques and attitudes rather than upon those which are appropriate to the special features of particular institutions. This was a tentative conclusion which appears to take on a special importance in relation to our discussion below of the open prisons. Staff training at this prison hardly existed, so that any such systematic adaptation to local circumstances *in situ* was not possible.

The inmates' day at the medium-term was of much the same length as that at the long-term prison although, perhaps surprisingly in view of the lack of working facilities, their working day was longer. Their rising hour was 6.30 a.m. and, after the usual slopping-out and ablutions, breakfast was served at 7.15. A parade was held on the exercise yard at 8 a.m., which was followed by work until 11.40 with a break between 10 and 10.15. Lunch was served between noon and 1 p.m. and after another parade work continued until 4.40, with a fifteen-minute exercise break. At 4.40 inmates returned to the prison for a final parade, and tea was served at 4.45. Various inmates who did not attend the classes or go on association were locked up at 5.30. Classes were held between 6 and 8 p.m., and association between 6.30 and 8.20. Supper was at 8.30 and after this all inmates were locked up for the night, lights being switched off at 10 p.m. The three parades referred to before and after the working period were justified by the number of men going to work outside the prison, but if any abscondences from outside working parties had taken place it was likely that they would have been noticed long before these tallies occurred.

The short-term closed prison

Its short-term character seems to have a crucial effect upon the way in which this prison is organised, causing it to share many of the characteristics of a local prison, where populations are also, of course, short-term, and very transient. So, like local prisons, this institution was less tidy than the other prisons in the research, which had time to 'catch up' with domestic tasks. There are other features, also, which this prison shared with local prisons: for instance, the place was sometimes short of food or clothes. This seemed to result from the rather unpredictable intake into a short-term prison. For example, food requirements are calculated on the past week, whereas the current week may involve a very much larger intake. Similar problems are bound to arise in connection with clothing, and sometimes prevent changes taking place as frequently as would be desirable. Nor is it surprising that the prison was sometimes overcrowded.

One of the major problems of any penal system is how to develop a training programme in a short-term prison. In local prisons the organisational problem takes precedence; this is inevitable having regard to the continuous mobility of much of the population, with all the administrative processes which this sets in train. This may in part account also for the 'cosy', 'clockwork', 'smooth' regime at the short-term closed—these words were used about the institution by some of the staff during the research.

Such a highly routinised system is prone to exploitation in the sense that when life becomes so formalised, all the emphasis is placed upon superficial conformity to rules and procedures, with prison staff tending to 'let sleeping dogs lie'. As a result the inmate culture tends to grow apace. The research worker heard many stories from prisoners about gambling and 'baroning', and also about the violence surrounding these activities. Much of the gambling centred on horse-racing, but there was also gambling on the weekly inter-wing football matches. In one case it was alleged that a wing team were bribed to lose by the prison bookmakers in order that the latter might make a 'killing'. Officers were also aware of these activities, for they talked about them. It seems a most perfect example of the 'custodial compromise' in action.

This was the institution in which the staff received the research most inhospitably. There was a very small staff response to all of the instruments used, and although the director of the project went to the prison and addressed the staff, it had absolutely no effect on their willingness to co-operate. In fact his occasional slight hesitation in replying to their questions was interpreted by them as 'shifty' behaviour, proving that he and the research were instruments of some plot by the Home Office which might work to the disadvantage of the staff. Again, when the research worker himself had quite truthfully explained that he knew nothing about prisons, but later made what proved coincidentally to be a shrewd comment on the security arrangements of the prison, it was assumed that he had been lying previously, and was probably spying on the staff for the Prison Department. He believed there were two main reasons for this mistrustful attitude. One was historical: a previous research had asked inmates to make evaluations of particular officers within the prison. This had angered the officers who felt in their own words that they had no 'right of reply'. It seemed to reinforce a widely held belief that all research taking place in prisons was for the benefit of inmates and to the detriment of officers. Our own research included certain statements in a test administered to inmates asking for an evaluation of staff and staff performance, and this must have seemed very similar to the earlier research which had aroused such resentment. However, the observer felt that a more important reason was the hierarchical and tight nature of the regime. The prison actually did 'run like clockwork', and nobody wanted this peace to be disturbed. Any innovation, of which research might be seen to be a threatening harbinger, would therefore be unwelcome. A firm and predictable regime in an institution seems often to be attractive to both inmates and staff, because it relieves them of the anxieties arising from uncertainty and from having to make decisions for themselves.

Some further evidence of such hostility to change was the attitude to a newly appointed assistant governor, among whose responsibilities was staff training. He tended to emphasise more modern issues (especially those connected with welfare and therapy) rather than the normal programme of training, which had focused upon court procedure and the security and custody of inmates. The staff resented the intrusion of the new assistant governor's ideas into this area of routine activity. The research worker felt that it was very much the disturbance to the *status quo* to which they objected, and not the actual ideas which he was engaged in developing through the training programme—particularly a disturbance, as they saw it, which would bring advantages to prisoners for which they, the officers, would have to pay the price. This rivalry with prisoners occurs in other contexts, notably in the complaints about their quarters, which they felt received less official attention than accommodation for prisoners. They contrasted the failure to do necessary maintenance work on their quarters with the building of a new boilerhouse for the comfort of the inmates. There was also incidentally some feeling that, in quarters, they were living in a ghetto; in fact a number of them lived not in quarters but in municipal housing estates in the town, though admittedly adjacent to each other.

Relationships between basic grade and senior grade prison officers were also not good. The former complained that senior grade officers often took privileges for themselves which they denied to the junior staff, including for example wearing 'outside coats' into the prison, and also making modifications in their uniforms to smarten them up a little. The refusal of higher grade officers to allow these small privileges to their basic grade colleagues, while bending the rules in their own favour, was seen as 'petty'. In addition, basic grade officers felt that their seniors were unwilling to make any decisions of importance for them, leaving them as it were to carry the responsibility which ought to have been carried higher up in the hierarchy. There was very little interaction between the two groups. Even in the mess they sat separately. Their main areas of agreement seemed to be on pay—and on their hostility to research!

There were also difficulties between prison officers and members of the non-uniformed staff. Communication between officers and the mainly civilian staff of the discipline office broke down completely at times. The observer believed this to be due to the insistence by the discipline office on the use of memo sheets (known in the prison as 35s) as a rather formal medium for requesting information from officers, instead of making personal contact with them as in other institutions. This seems more likely to be a rationalisation for hostility than an explanation. As will be seen later, it is likely that the discipline office was just one more target group for a certain amount of free-floating, outwardly directed hostility on the part of the officers. Reference has already been made to similar conflicts between them and their senior officers; and there was also little liking for the welfare department. The welfare staff complained that officers displayed 'a total lack of manners' in their dealings with the department, and gave them little or no co-operation. The welfare department themselves felt that this was due to the threat that welfare poses to the role of the prison officer, and the research team could see that officers might feel the welfare department to be a threat to their traditional relationship with inmates. Certainly this antagonism, which was found only in this prison, among those studied in the present research—indeed the relationship in other prisons was often mutually appreciative and helpful—might possibly be a special case of the fear of anything which could disturb the smooth running of this 'tight ship'. But there nevertheless remained the need for scapegoats; objective complaints against senior staff, the discipline office or the welfare staff providing a justification for the choice of these particular groups as targets.

'Tight ship' it certainly was. The Governor, who was indisputably in charge, delegating very little of his responsibilities to others, had a strong personal identification with the prison which the staff also acknowledged. However, he was popular with the staff; they said he was a very good Governor and they knew where they stood in their dealings with him. This is a not unusual tribute to a dominant but fair boss. They also found him very approachable and they felt they could discuss problems with him. He had recently established an information room as a dissemination point for information pertaining to the prison, and this room was open at all times to members of the staff. All power was centralised on the Governor; the deputy and assistant governors had by comparison very limited functions.

All the space within the prison was used up, and therefore improvements meant either modifying an existing building or pulling it down; they usually took the form of modifications. Because of the lack of space, opportunities for association seemed to be very limited, being confined to two of the wings. Not even all the residents of those wings could obtain association, and any prisoners from other wings had to go on a waiting list for transfer. Because those not attending classes and not eligible for association had to stay in cells, a good deal of locking up therefore took place. Many prisoners must have spent much of their time thus immured. Incidentally, this prison had a larger proportion of double cells than the other prisons in our research; it seemed to be in the van of the new policy of 'doubling' rather than 'trebling up'. The old fear of homosexual activity seemed to have been allayed by this experience, though the Governor's instructions were that 'personality factors' were to be considered in doubling up, and no man was to be placed in a double (as distinct from a treble) cell against his will. As usual the level of security was determined by the requirements for the highest category of prisoners in the institution—in this instance a minority group of category B men. This affected other aspects of life in the prison besides 'locking up'. For example, when a football match was being held on a pitch near the walls, all the prisoners watching the game were kept well away from the walls, and as many as thirty officers would sometimes be lined up there for extra security. Where the wall was considered too low, a ditch had been built in front of it, and there were also fairly frequent routine cell-searches. Such measures make 'containment' very obtrusive.

Welfare officers were too few for the size of the institution. The prison has an inmate population of 697 (see Table 2.1), with only three basic grade welfare officers to cope with these large numbers. As a result they could not actively seek out prisoners with problems; they concentrated on those who came for help. Most inmates did not see the welfare officers during their whole stay in the prison and as a result many left with unresolved problems. A staff of six would have made it possible for them each to have a case load of a little over a hundred. The welfare department suffered possibly more than most other parts of the prison from the space problem. They shared a single interview room in the main cell block with the Roman Catholic priest, and when the research staff also began to use it, the priest just had to go elsewhere. As a result of these difficulties the welfare department could not hope to be fully effective, and some prisoners called to see the researcher in the hope that he was a kind of auxiliary welfare officer. As one inmate put it, 'The welfare officers don't so much help as try to be helpful.'

One possible supplement to the work of the welfare department were inmate discussion groups, attended also by two prison officers and providing an opportunity for inmate-officer interaction which was unique within the research. They concentrated in a non-psychiatric manner upon individual problems, especially those likely to be met with on discharge, the only restriction being that no one outside the group was to be discussed. However, there were only four of these groups in operation at the time of the research—there had been more—and their future seemed bleak in view of the shortage of staff and a proposed increase of about a hundred in inmate numbers.

There was a modified hostel scheme as well as an orthodox hostel scheme. These were not for the use of inmates of this prison, who were of course short-term prisoners, but for long-term inmates selected from other prisons. Hostels are, of course, intended to be used for precisely this purpose of re-socialising long-term offenders.

In the conventional scheme prisoners live in a hostel in the grounds of a prison and go out daily to work, but in the modified hostel scheme they live in cell blocks. Although the latter are separated from other prisoners, they are seen as something of a security problem by the staff, in that they can make telephone calls for other inmates when outside the prison. Trafficking in contraband goods was hardly likely as they were searched both on leaving and returning to the prison.

Educational facilities in general were dispersed, although all the classrooms were situated within the main cell block, the majority being on one wing. These seven classrooms were in varying states of repair, and one or two had very specific purposes, for example art and woodwork, or weaving. The equipment was usually rather elderly and sometimes a classroom had to be created by knocking two cells into one. The tutor organiser's office was shared with his clerk, and also served as a storeroom; it was really too small to serve all of these purposes. The library was run by a prison officer and three inmates, and had a close relationship with a local public library, which maintained a large stock of books in the prison, and also visited three times a week in order to take requests for special books and to advise inmates on reading in their special areas of interest. This last seems a particularly far-sighted and valuable facility.

Near the library was a small room where the monthly prison magazine was produced. Most of the contents were reprinted from other journals, such inmate contributions as there were having come, it seems, from members of the editorial board. A number of inmates claimed that their contributions had not been accepted, and this may have been because of their low standard. However, the magazine on its first page pointed out that it was printed by 'kind permission of the Governor' and there may have been an understandable tendency by the editorial staff to control what went into it. Certainly nothing of an adventurous kind was ever seen in it by the observer during his stay there.

There was a very small gymnasium with just enough room to play basketball, but no room for spectators. Otherwise facilities for physical recreation seemed to be quite good. Football however consisted largely of representative games; wider participation was not encouraged. Non-players were catered for as spectators.

The main industrial activity in the prison was the manufacture of protective clothing which had a maximum life of two years, when it had to be replaced. It thus provided a continuous outlet for some of the labour resources of the prison. There was a special training room in which men could be given such skill as was needed for making these suits. Clearly the amount of skill involved could not be great, as most of the trainees were going to spend only a relatively short time in the prison. However, the shop did represent an attempt to develop a thoroughgoing 'industrial regime' in a prison. This is shown in a number of ways. For instance, men were admitted to training for this work only after passing an aptitude test. Also during training, output standards were established for them; if they failed to maintain these in the production shop, they were returned for retraining. And the work itself was arranged on a 'production line' basis. This meant that each worker was performing a rather repetitive operation, constituting only a small part of the total productive process. As a result men found the work boring. Nevertheless there were compensations, notably that it was well paid. Meanwhile increased effort was stimulated by a system of payment by results, called an 'applied incentive scheme'. The supply of labour to the shop was also carefully planned, being maintained by a labour allocation unit consisting of a senior officer and three prisoners. The various sources of wastage for which they had to allow included discharges, and some less predictable losses through transfer, etc. Although a prison programme structured as here is in conformity with the current view that prison work programmes should make demands on prisoners similar to those which they would meet outside, they may also have other effects. In this prison they did seem to add markedly to the impression of rigidity and control in the prison as a whole.

The only other ostensibly industrially orientated shop in the prison was a large weaving shop. Unlike the department in which the protective clothing was made, it was not based on an applied incentive scheme and as a result the trade instructor in the shop felt that too many men were rather unproductively employed there. They were engaged in weaving tape, for the Prison Department of course, but also for the Ministry of Defence and the Post Office.

The remainder of the work available was on a flat-rate basis, and was organised in a rather 'non-industrial' fashion. For example, the induction shop over the prison kitchens employed all men when they first arrived. They did such things as painting miniature footballers, assembling electrical plugs, stripping wire, putting together parts of Tupperware beakers, making umbrella handles and gluing together

plastic walkie-talkie sets. Occasionally seasonal jobs were introduced, such as the manufacture of fluffy dolls for a small local firm.
None of these jobs required much skill, and both pay and production
were low. The amount of work available in the shop fluctuated and it
was often impossible to keep all the men fully occupied. In addition
to the new intake, some men were kept in the shop because they were
considered unsuitable for industrial work or work in the grounds. As
a home for the incompetent, however, it had a competitor in the
shape of the heavy textile shop, which produced mailbags. Known
around the prison as for the 'sick, lame and lazy', it had a high
standard of discipline, and most of the men in it had bad work or
discipline records. The observer considered that many of the men
suffered from various degrees of mental handicap; no special
training or work facilities existed for such prisoners. There were also
men working in the garden and the yard, and in the works and
engineers' department.

There were two outside working parties; one worked at an open
prison and the other at a remand centre. At the remand centre they
were concerned with clearing up rubbish, removing swill, road-
sweeping and tidying the gardens. At the open prison the party
worked on land reclamation or the prison farm, and were kept
separate from the open prison inmates. These out-workers were
usually approaching the end of their sentences. The remainder of
the prison labour force were employed as cleaners, or in the
domestic and service areas of the prison.

Two factors seem to be of importance in understanding the way in
which the prison operated. One of these was undoubtedly its
short-term character, leading to a regime geared for a high prisoner
turnover rather than a training programme. This is a situation in
which (in spite of the existence of inmate-participating committees
dealing with work, catering, and general purposes) decisive control
by the Governor would be encouraged, work opportunities would
tend to be relatively unskilled, and both in physical appearance and
mode of operation the prison would begin to resemble local prisons,
with their even higher turnover, rather than other training prisons.
It has been suggested that the emphasis on procedures and formal
compliance may (as in local prisons also) account for the vigorous
development of the anti-social inmate culture, with its gambling and
baroning.

A firm regime would be only one possible result of such conditions,
but the Governor's own preference was also clearly for a 'tight ship',

and this was reflected both in the daily life and relationships of the prison, and in the way in which the main industrial activity of the institution, the manufacture of protective suits, was organised. That the supportive qualities of such a firm structure were valued by both the staff and inmate populations of the prison is obvious from the resentment of anything which appeared likely to bring about changes. However, there may also be other consequences. The suspicion directed by the staff towards the research staff seemed excessive and irrational. The regime also seemed to mobilise officer hostility towards the office and welfare staff, an assistant governor, and senior officers, and towards inmates—who were seen significantly enough as getting all the attention. It is worth noting also that the 'boss' himself, the Governor, received none of this hostility. Other researches have suggested that 'controlling' institutional regimes, which thus produced dependent attitudes on the part of the controlled towards their controller, analogous to those of children towards their father, involved frustrations which generated hostility, though this was directed not towards the frustrator himself, but towards peers, as a form of sibling rivalry.[1] The peer group hostility evident in this prison could thus readily be understood as the obverse of dependence on the Governor and his firm style of government.

The daily routine for prisoners was not markedly different from those of the long-term closed and the medium-term closed, and will not therefore be described in detail.

Summary tables of demographic data

Table 2.1   Average daily population of the research prisons

Date	Long-term closed	Medium-term closed	Short-term closed	Long-term open	Medium-term open	Short-term open
1965	665	228	585	405	399	332
1966	719	244	634	391	434	339
1967	704	241	625	228	400	195
1968	716	239	639	199	373	251
1969	751	254	668	215	443	325
1970	789	263	697	218	506	282

(Source: Annual Reports of the Work of the Prison Department, 1966-71).

Table 2.2   Age distribution of inmates (years)

Age (years)	Long-term closed	Medium-term closed	Short-term closed	Long-term open	Medium-term open	Short-term open
19-23	160	120	224	15	51	46
24-28	201	89	210	35	113	99
29-36	219	28	136	74	150	97
37+	204	20	114	85	178	82
Totals	784	257	684	209	492	324
Median (years)	30	24	26	35	32	30

Table 2.3   Distribution of the number of previous court appearances of inmates

Number of previous court appearances	Long-term closed	Medium-term closed	Short-term closed	Long-term open	Medium-term open	Short-term open
0-2	268	40	54	136	111	102
3-5	192	65	125	48	88	71
6-9	142	80	168	21	120	60
10+	120	65	194	4	151	63
No information	62	7	143*	0	22	28
Total	784	257	684	209	492	324
Median	4	6	8	1	7	4

*This loss may reflect the pressures created by the rapid turnover of short-term men and at the allocation prison through which the men passed. It may also be a reflection on the efficiency of the police authorities who were responsible for the provision of this information to the prison.

Table 2.4   Distribution of offence categories of inmates

Offence category	Long-term closed		Medium-term closed		Short-term closed		Long-term open		Medium-term open		Short-term open	
	N	%	N	%	N	%	N	%	N	%	N	%
1	258	33	5	2	—	—	54	26	—	—	—	—
2	59	8	40	16	75	11	6	3	2	1	4	1
3	150	19	21	8	7	1	10	5	10	2	—	—
4	42	5	87	34	227	33	22	10	174	35	87	27
5	84	11	43	17	11	2	13	6	14	3	1	1
6	26	3	29	11	158	23	41	20	164	33	123	38
7	11	1	—	—	22	3	45	21	79	16	27	8
8	23	3	7	3	3	1	2	1	1	1	1	1
9	67	9	25	10	38	6	16	8	26	5	53*	16
No information	64	8	—	—	143	21	0	—	22	4	28	9
Total	784	100	257	101	684	101	209	100	492	100	324	101

Offence category	*Offences included*
1	Murder, attempted murder and manslaughter.
2	Offences of violence against the person, e.g. death by dangerous driving, wounding, assault.
3	Sexual offences, e.g. rape, buggery, incest, indecency, and procuration.
4	Offences against property with violence (except category 5), e.g. burglary, and taking and driving away.
5	Robbery and robbery with violence.
6	Offences against property without violence (except category 7), e.g. theft, and handling and receiving stolen goods.
7	Fraud, false accounting, forgery, embezzlement and other frauds.
8	Malicious damage to property (e.g. arson).
9	Others, including offences against the Aliens' Restrictions Acts, Dangerous Drugs Acts and mixed categories of the above.

*includes a large number of civil prisoners.

Table 2.5 Distribution of length of sentence of inmates (years)

Sentence length (months)	Long-term closed	Medium-term closed	Short-term closed	Long-term open	Medium-term open	Short-term open
1-18	5	1	667	57	1	318
19-47	59	216	4	45	450	6
48+	720*	40	13†	107**	41	0
Total	784	257	684	209	492	324
Median (months)	72	36	12	48	27	9

*Includes 33 sentences of more than 10 years and 257 life sentences.
**Includes 2 sentences of more than 10 years and 44 life sentences.
† All inmates in this category were in the hostel attached to this prison.

Table 2.6 Distribution of security categories of inmates

Security categories	Long-term closed		Medium-term closed		Short-term closed		Long-term open		Medium-term open		Short-term open	
	N	%	N	%	N	%	N	%	N	%	N	%
A	40	5	—	—	—	—	—	—	—	—	—	—
B	519	66	49	19	5	1	—	—	—	—	—	—
C	157	20	204	79	589	86	—	—	—	—	—	—
D	61	8	4	2	40	6	209	100	492	100	324	100
No information	7	1	—	—	50	7	—	—	—	—	—	—
Total	784	100	257	100	684	100	209	100	492	100	324	100

Table 2.7 Staff deployment by ranks

		Long-term closed	Medium-term closed	Short-term closed	Long-term open	Medium-term open	Short-term open
Security	BGO	36	—	—	—	—	—
	SO	6	—	—	—	—	—
Discipline	BGO	73	30	51	29	38	25
	SO	20	4	7	3	4	3
	PO	13	4	9	5	5	3
	CO	2	1	2	2	2	1
Uniformed instructor officers	OI	8	4	14	1	6	3
	SOI	1	—	1	—	1	1
Civilian instructor officer		14	6	12	9	13	1
Engineers' department	TA	16	7	12	8	6	6
	Eng. I and II	4	2	2	2	2	2
	SFOW/FOW	1	—	1	—	1	—
Kitchen	Cat O	1	1	1	1	1	2
	S Cat O	—	1	—	—	—	—
	P Cat O	1	—	1	—	—	—

Hospital	HO	7	1*	4	2	1	—
	SHO	2	—	1	—	1	1
	PHO	1	—	1	1	—	—
	CHO	1	—	—	—	—	1
Sports	PEI	2	—	2	1	2	1
	SPEI	—	—	—	—	1	—
Governor grades		6	2	3	5	3	1
Welfare department	WO	4	2	3	2	2	2
	SWO	1	—	1	1	1	1

BGO Basic Grade Officer
SO Senior Officer
PO Principal Officer
CO Chief Officer
OI Officer Instructor
TA Trade Assistant
SFOW Senior Foreman of Works
FOW Foreman of Works
HO Hospital Officer
PEI Physical Education Instructor
Cat O Catering Officer
WO Welfare Officer
SWO Senior Welfare Officer
*Detached Duty Officer from the short-term closed prison.
N.B. BGOs include Temporary Officers.

Table 2.8   Distribution of age of staff (years)

Age (years)	Long-term closed	Medium-term closed	Short-term closed	Long-term open	Medium-term open	Short-term open
22-32	65	10	18	12	23	18
33-39	63	14	28	17	15	10
40-48	46	22	32	8	20	11
49+	39	13	29	18	23	14
Total	213	59	107	55	81	53
Median (years)	38	40	41	39	40	38

Table 2.9   Distribution of length of service of staff (years)

Length of service (years)	Long-term closed	Medium-term closed	Short-term closed	Long-term open	Medium-term open	Short-term open
0-3	55	23	11	16	20	14
4-9	86	15	25	8	24	14
10-19	46	13	32	11	15	11
20+	26	8	39	20	22	14
Total	213	59	107	55	81	53
Median (years, months)	6,6	7,5	9,0	8,8	6,8	7,4

Table 2.10   Non-discipline to discipline staff ratios

	Long-term closed	Medium-term closed	Short-term closed	Long-term open	Medium-term open	Short-term open
Non-discipline to discipline staff ratio	1 : 2·7	1 : 1·2	1 : 1·4	1 : 1·6	1 : 1·8	1 : 1·9

N.B. These figures include Temporary Officers and Civilian Instructor Officers.

Table 2.11 *Staff to inmate ratios*

	Long-term closed	Medium-term closed	Short-term closed	Long-term open	Medium-term open	Short-term open
Staff to inmate ratio	1 : 3·7*	1 : 4·4	1 : 6·4	1 : 3·8	1 : 6·1	1 : 6·1

N.B. These figures include Temporary Officers.
*This ratio includes 40 officers who were wholly employed on security tasks (e.g. CCTV monitors) and who had no contact whatsoever with inmates. Excluding them, the staff to inmate ratio at this prison would be 1 : 4·5.

Table 2.12   *Percentage of inmates employed in listed occupations*

Occupation	Long-term closed	Medium-term closed	Short-term closed	Long-term open	Medium-term open	Short-term open
1	43·6	36·5	61·0	23·0	42·8	31·2
2	15·3	9·2	—	2·4	2·0	—
3	4·8	5·0	2·9	12·0	3·2	4·6
4	2·6	—	0·9	9·6	1·7	2·8
5	11·1	5·8	7·1	10·6	4·0	4·6
6	7·6	7·7	8·0	5·3	7·9	3·1
7	1·9	3·9	0·7	14·8	25·6	7·7
8	1·9	9·2	5·5	1·8	0·8	29·0
9	9·2	9·2	4·1	18·2	10·3	13·6
10	—	—	9·8	1·8	1·7	—
No information	2·0	13·5	—	0·5	—	3·4
Totals	100%	100%	100%	100%	100%	100%
N	784	257	684	209	492	324

Occupation
1	Manufacturing
2	Vocational training and full-time educational courses
3	Kitchen
4	Laundry
5	Storemen and orderlies
6	Cleaners
7	Gardening party
8	Out-party
9	Engineers' party
10	Others (including training shops/inmates in hospital)

3   The open prisons

The long-term open prison

Although this prison does not cover the largest site, it was certainly
the most spacious of all our open prisons, for it was scattered fairly
widely over its 134 acres. This was of course in striking contrast to
the very 'tight' situation of the short-term open prison, crowded on
to a very small area, or the medium-term prison, which had even
more land than the institution under discussion here, but used very
little of it so that there was, as it were, hunger in the midst of plenty.
This undoubtedly played some part in producing the relaxed
'openness' of the climate in the long-term prison. That climate was
also favoured by the absence of any obtrusive demarcation of the
boundaries of the prison, with the result that the visual and
psychological impact of the measures necessary for security was
lessened. There was no fence around the prison, of course, most of
the perimeter being marked by trees, hedges and single-strand wire.
There was not even a gate at the entrance to the prison: merely a gap
in the stone wall, and a 'Halt' marking on the tarmac road leading
in. This did not mean, of course, that the boundaries of the prison
were not strictly maintained; inmates knew what they were, and
were expected to keep to them.

The other factor which probably contributed to the general
climate of the prison was its long-term character. The quantitative
data about our three open prisons show very clearly that the
shorter-term the prison, the more it resembled the closed institutions
in our sample. Thus the short-term open was the open prison which
most clearly resembled its closed counterparts. In other words the
pressure of the routine is bound to be greater in the shorter-term
institutions, where men are being booked in and out all the time,
and where they do not stay long enough to enable preliminary
restrictions, enforced until a prison has got to know the men better,
to be lifted. In the long-term prison, all of these things could be left
behind. And in particular, blanket bureaucratic restrictions could
be replaced by an individualisation of the regime to meet the degree
of risk which one had come to discover that individual offenders

represented. Prisoners themselves also had time to 'shake down'. They would have time to learn how they fitted in—what the prison expected of them, and who they could get along with among both the officers and the inmates. Many sources of friction would thus be removed. And of course many long-term prisoners would have been in prison before, would know the ropes already. In particular they would have learned the futility of overt resistance, and that the policy likely to lead to one's serving one's sentence with minimum discomfort is that of achieving a mutually convenient compromise with the staff. This is what is known in prison as 'learning to do bird'. It is also the basis for the development of what we have elsewhere called the 'custodial compromise'.

The long-term prison has of course other advantages, and these were as apparent in the long-term closed prison as in the present open institution. A long-term prison does permit the administration to develop a training programme; prisoners are there long enough to undertake courses, and even to gain experience afterwards in putting into practice within the prison what they have learned in the course. This is particularly true of the prison work programme itself. Prison work opportunities, in a short-term prison with a constantly changing population, tend to have to be unskilled and repetitive, and therefore rather boring and uninspiring. Given more time, the prisoners can be trained for and inducted into jobs of a more demanding, but therefore of a more interesting and constructive kind.

In the event these latter advantages, at any rate, do not seem to have been realised here. On the educational side there were discussion groups, art, pottery and light handicraft groups, woodworking, a photographic studio, and (as might be expected with so much space) very good physical education facilities and programmes. There were also basic English and mathematics classes, and an A-level mathematics class for the more advanced. The education department of the prison also ran a welding class, and there was a vocational training course in painting and decorating. It is difficult to escape the conclusion in reviewing this provision that it was mainly intended to provide rewarding ways for the inmates of filling their time—the prison's contribution to helping them with their burden of 'doing bird'. There was certainly little here which might be described as part of a continuous process of training, and which would eventually enable a man to make a different kind of adaptation to society than he had done previously—by finding himself a different kind of job, or entering upon a new level of intellectual or educational activity.

This could not have been more clearly evidenced than it was by the prominence given in the prison's work programme to the laundry. This was the best-paid work within the prison, being run on a 'production line' basis, but it could have very little training value for the men who worked there. At first sight one might have expected that the printing shop would provide better training opportunities, and there was a time when men working there had been trained as machine-minders and compositors. By the time the research team had arrived in the prison, this had changed: training had taken second place to marshalling the labour force of the shop for productivity and profit. There were possibilities also in the carpentry industry within the prison, where there was a development shop in which designs for chairs and tables were produced, and which could have been part of a general programme of educational and vocational training. However, as with the printing shop, the focus was on productivity rather than on developing long-term interest or vocational skills by the men involved. The one exception was the painting and decorating course, from which men usually joined the works department and were able to take part in the repainting programme within the prison.

The great moppers-up of labour were however farming and market gardening. The market gardens proved very attractive, largely because they were rather remote from the main prison, making it possible for men to escape for a while from the prison ambience. They covered about 20 acres and grew potatoes, cabbages, carrots, salad crops and swedes, some of which were used here or in other prisons, the remainder being sold on the open market. A number of prisoners looked after the arboretum, and a number were on the farm, with its 100 pigs and 1,000 laying hens. The farm and gardens department was also responsible for maintaining the grounds around the prison. As many as thirty-three men worked on the farms and garden party during the summer, but during the winter this number dropped to about twenty. Finally there were the service departments: men engaged in the maintenance of the prison fabric and in work as clerks, orderlies, cleaners, etc.

The industrial manager saw prison work as a process of 'de-skilling', arguing that this accustomed inmates to the kind of jobs they might afterwards be able to find for themselves outside. He pointed out that it was hardly helpful to teach men to cut dovetails in the woodwork shop if afterwards they went to work in commercial joinery where joints would be cut at great speed by machine. The kinds of work available were also rather few as compared with some other prisons, but prisoners were often given a good deal of responsibility and the opportunity of initiative which meant that there were few complaints about it. On the whole they seemed to find work more satisfying than in the other prisons in the sample, and certainly more satisfying than would have been expected having regard to its character.

Security in the traditional sense appeared to be at a minimum. Although the boundaries were of course maintained, the absence of any of the usual markers even, much less barriers seemed, as we have seen, to be designed to push the containment aspect of the prison into the background, as did the 'wide open spaces' of the prison estate. This made it possible for men to go for long quiet walks—and some did just this. Reference has already been made to the preference of many men for work in the gardens because of their distance from the centre of activity in the prison. There was also a sense of informality about life in the prison. Men moved around the prison (for example, to work) without supervision and it would probably be a prisoner, and not a member of the staff who would show visitors around the prison. The Governor himself was not above a little badinage with the prisoners from time to time, and although there was a punishment block in the prison, it was in fact never used. This does not, of course, mean that there were never problem prisoners. It was simply that the Governor preferred to transfer intractable men to closed prisons rather than to mar the open climate of his prison by maintaining a lock-up within it.

This last point makes it clear that in spite of its openness, this remained a prison, in which the containment function had to be performed as in any other prison. Punishments consisted of loss of privileges, or in serious cases the kind of transfer already referred to. The Governor, however, started with a unique advantage: unlike almost any other prison in the system, he was permitted to choose his own inmate population. So he could reject men whom he felt were too unstable or incorrigible for his particular kind of regime, or who were likely to be serious escape risks. Moreover, in spite of some staff complaints that he was too soft, and did not always back up his staff, he ran an efficient operation. He knew what he wanted to achieve and was vigilant in seeing that his requirements were met, both by staff and prisoners.

Those men who did cross the boundaries of the prison were treated as absconders. It is true that when escapes did occur, it was often some time before they were discovered because of the relatively few tallies at the prison—only three during the day. However, men were always searched after visiting day to make sure that no contraband goods had been passed, and a close watch was kept on inmates' tobacco tins. A strict check was also kept on non-prison clothes worn by inmates, as these might be used in the course of an escape. They usually consisted of sports gear, and particularly cricket clothes, which inmates were allowed to keep in their possession during the summer months.

The researcher was often told stories about how prisoners would go out during the night, for example to a local pub on the A38 for a drink. It is possible that these stories were embroidered for retailing to the researcher, but there certainly seemed a number of myths abroad of these kinds in the prison. There was no factual evidence that anything of this kind had ever taken place.

It was, of course, a great advantage to the regime that the prisoners could be distributed over so much space. Congestion can lead to problems of management and to the multiplication of interpersonal frictions. This spaciousness was not simply a matter of the amount of land available; having regard to the relatively small size of the prisoner population, this prison also had a large amount of associational and recreational space. This included two television rooms, a billiards and table tennis room, a large room for more formal but unsupervised inmate recreation, such as musical appreciation or practising on the musical instruments that quite a number of the prisoners possessed. There was also a building used as an inmate theatre and cinema, but this was out of bounds except when rehearsing a play or attending a performance. There was also a good gymnasium.

The hospital also operated as a surgery, and provided very generous hours for inmates to attend for treatment. This meant that minor complaints could be dealt with immediately, as compared with other prisons where prisoners often had to wait until morning, or make a special application to see a doctor. Because so many men worked out of doors, the surgery had to deal with many minor cases of scratches, bruises and insect bites during these extended hours. Originally the research team had imagined that hospitals in open prisons might provide a sanctuary for inmates who felt persecuted by other inmates but, under the dormitory conditions prevailing, found that they could not escape from them. There may have been one case during the time of the research team's visit where this applied, but it certainly seemed to be the exception which proved the rule.

Kitchen and inmate dining rooms were adjoining, and men working in the kitchen were allowed two hours' recreation in the middle of the day. This did not represent any reduction in working hours, but merely meant that the spread of working hours was slightly different from those of others in the prison. Prisoners dined in association, sitting at small tables for four. Rather unusually for an institution, even the inmates felt that the food was good.

The arrangements for the canteen were rather different from that of most other prisons. Men placed their orders in advance and their purchases were then procured, parcelled up into little individual packages and passed out to them on canteen day. This enabled a little more variety to be introduced, but it also meant that purchases had to be made at local shops where prices were rather higher than if the canteen had been supplied in bulk from a wholesaler or large supermarket. This was probably especially important here where, in general, wages were low, and inmates had to husband their money very scrupulously each week. The system did however cause a certain amount of queueing, as most inmates had to collect their canteen purchases during the evening of the one day. Men on domestic work had certain advantages here because they could get to the canteen during the working day. Sometimes other men sought to achieve the same advantage by applying to the hospital officer for a period of 'rest in ward' on canteen day. When the purpose of this became clear, the hospital officer adroitly countered the manoeuvre by insisting that men who did succeed in this application had to rest within the confines of the hospital.

Like other open prisons most of the men were accommodated in dormitories divided up by wooden partitions into cubicles curtained across the front. A few favoured inmates had single rooms. These were usually serving the longer sentences, and they succeeded, in the rather relaxed atmosphere of this prison, in making their rooms very homely indeed. Besides a bed, bedside table and clothes storage units, each of these rooms had hot and cold water and a mains socket, and inmates were allowed a radio, bedcovers, rugs, potted plants, pictures and pin-ups, as well, if they wished, as pets. A number of them were looking after stray cats, others keeping cage birds, and some had goldfish tanks. Much the same facilities were allowed to inmates in the dormitories, except for pets. Most of the beds in the dormitories had headphones left over from the old army hospital and thus had no need for radios. Many of the men had decorated their rooms, and apart from the usual pin-ups and photographs, some had created elaborate collages on the walls. Most had managed to obtain pieces of scrap material in order to make tablecloths or curtains. The windows of these rooms, like other windows throughout the prison except the main stores and the cashier's office, were unbarred.

Near to the education block was the prison library. This was divided into two halves, one containing book stock and the other used as a reading room. A rule of silence was observed in the reading room; this room was available also for those who wished to read the daily papers or write letters. The main library was run by two inmates and an officer and consisted largely of old books with a much smaller number loaned by the County Council Library for short periods. During the day, when inmates were not permitted to use the library, it was used as the office of the prison newspaper, and one of the inmates working in the library served as the newspaper's editor.

This prison was accepted throughout the service as different from the rest. To some extent its reputation was a hangover from the past, when it was alleged to be largely under the control of intelligent white-collar prisoners who have always constituted an important part of the prison's population. Although such complete 'middle-class control' certainly no longer existed during the time the research team were at the prison, it was still generally believed to be liberal if not permissive, and to be populated by what officers called 'a better class of prisoner'. As a result prison officers generally felt that it would present few disciplinary problems and would therefore be a pleasant place in which to work. There were reservations, of course, based on the feeling that the authority of the officer might be less, and it might therefore be difficult for a prison officer to operate in the customary fashion. Protagonists of these two views probably belonged to different groups.

But what was the regime actually like? The best word to use about it is probably 'relaxed'. This relaxation was displayed in a number of ways. It arose in part from the spacious campus, and the opportunities which this presented for getting away from other people and particularly from the prison itself. Nevertheless, it was also partly a result of the Governor's policy. No doubt the bounds of the prison could have been more precisely demarcated and even fenced in—

though here again the sheer length of the boundary would have made this expensive. There were only the three 'counts' every day which most prison governors would have felt too few, but which also had the effect of reducing the pressure of the regime upon the individual inmates. But, as we have seen, neither of these relaxations prevented the security of the prison from being fairly vigilantly watched. Discipline and order seemed to be maintained without any of the shouting noticeable in other prisons. Personal relationships between inmates and staff were also more relaxed than at any of the other prisons in the research. Men often worked in small groups with members of staff, at points some distance from the centre of the prison, and this made for more informal interaction between them. The staff would often address men by their Christian names or by nicknames, and share sweets and cigarettes with them (not all officers would practise such familiarity, of course), although the asymmetrical nature of relationships in a prison was reflected in the fact that inmates could not address officers in the same casual way. When a man was about to be discharged, his neighbours in the dormitory would often hold a 'going away' party for him, and the Governor himself had been known to attend these. To that important minority of the staff who preferred more traditional ways of relating to prisoners, all this seemed very dangerous. There was indeed a definite current of cynicism about the regime among certain members of the uniformed staff.

This group also complained that the Governor did not always support them in disputes with prisoners. This kind of complaint arose from the fact that the Governor would sometimes go more deeply into the background report on a prisoner instead of taking the report by an officer at its face value, and also sometimes impose a less severe penalty than an officer thought justified. The quantitative data on punishment suggest that this did not happen as often as in the other prisons (see Table 8.20). In such circumstances it was the Governor's practice to discuss the matter with the officer in question and explain his position, but this did not always remove the sense of grievance. His main aim throughout seemed to be to increase informality and the opportunities for responsibility and self-determination within the prison. Nevertheless he remained vigilant, and although the punishment cells and dietary punishments were never used, other forms of punishment were—the withdrawal of privileges and, in particular, the attachment of prisoners' earnings. The ultimate sanction was of course removal to a closed prison. In general, the approach of the staff to the inmates was more sensitive than at some other prisons: a result partly, no doubt, of the fact that these officers had begun to establish relationships with the men as persons, rather than merely as prisoners. The Governor seemed also to be aware of the importance of symbols; thus, each of the men with a private room had a key to his door which he could lock. It remained only a symbol of privacy as far as the administration was concerned, as they, of course, also had a copy of all these keys. At the other extreme, the normal prison pattern of censorship over mail was maintained very efficiently, and in one case led to the discovery of a plan for smuggling of contraband into the prison by visitors on the prison's Open Day.

This was met by the threatened cancellation of the Open Day itself if there was further evidence that the privilege was likely to be abused. Similarly, the chief officer at one point made it plain that if inmates playing in sports matches were late or failed to attend 'counts' at any time but especially over the weekend, then the sporting activities themselves might be cancelled.

It is not known whether any of these mass punishments were ever carried into effect. As such they would normally have been the kinds of thing which would have led to widespread discontent as affecting the innocent as well as the guilty, but this does not seem to have been the case here. Perhaps the reason was that the population, specially chosen as of low security risk, were also better educated and probably therefore more sophisticated than most. It is possible also that the Governor's policy had led to the development of the 'custodial compromise' to a very high degree indeed. The researcher felt that he often turned a blind eye to some minor infringements at the prison, and this mild 'indulgency pattern'[1] seems to have produced an intelligent *quid pro quo* from the inmates. This was probably assisted by a broad value consensus between staff and the predominantly middle-class inmate population. A delegation to the research worker from the inmates to express anxieties about the research consisted of two ex-public schoolboys and one ex-stockbroker. Nevertheless, as will be seen, the prison had its own class struggle between working-class and middle-class inmates.

The peaceableness of this prison, then, may have been due to an implicit compact between the administration and inmates in which the latter were left alone so long as they behaved themselves, but met swift retribution if they stepped over the line. The prison had a long history of being managed in this way, and before the present

Governor took office there was a story of one Christmas Day when an influenza epidemic had reduced the officers on duty to two, and the inmates made themselves responsible for 'checks' and the inspection of the dormitories. The day's routine was completed smoothly. The new Governor felt that this kind of thing had gone too far, and devoted his own efforts to tightening up the 'longstops' while nevertheless leaving plenty of scope for self-respect and responsibility—but there is little doubt that the pre-existing inmate tradition was still active to some extent.

The government of the prison was the resultant of a complex process involving three separate committees. Executive control was of course in the hands of senior staff under the chairmanship of the Governor, in a management meeting. However there was also a staff consultative committee, at which other staff could make their views and grievances known to the Governor grades. Although this was the only formal contact between the Governor grades and the uniformed staff, most officers agreed that the Governor was very approachable, and sometimes spent an hour or two chatting with them in the Officers' Club.

The other institution was the Prison Council. This consisted of representatives of the dormitory units and of the various prisoner clubs. It met both in plenary session and in committees. The Council controlled the disposition of the common fund, giving grants to the clubs. Beyond this it had no decision-making power, but its terms of reference were very wide, and it could make proposals to the management meeting.

The chairman of the Council, a prisoner, was himself a member of the management meeting, able to discuss there major prison policy with the senior staff of the institution. Officers could attend the Council, but did not normally do so unless they either had a matter to raise, or their attendance was sought to deal with something about which inmates were concerned.

Generally the Council was dominated by the more articulate (and therefore middle-class) members of the inmate community. This of course is no different from the situation in political organisations in the community outside, but it often led inmates, who on the one hand criticised the Council for being (because of its lack of executive authority) a 'talking shop', at the same time to accuse it of being class-biased. The celebrated case of 'tennis versus birds' illustrates this. While refusing more money to the bird club (a working-class organisation) it had readily provided new tennis balls for the tennis club. Nevertheless the research worker felt that the periods of middle-class dominance were those when its work went most smoothly and it exercised most influence over the management meeting; while the rare occasions on which a violent climate developed in the prison were those when the Prison Council was dominated by working-class inmates.

The Governor saw the development of better relationships between inmates and staff as one of his prime aims. There seemed to be some evidence that, in the system of government as described, this was happening. One sign of goodwill on the part of the staff was the resettlement group run by the chief officer. He and other interested officers, during their off-duty periods, would take certain men near the end of their sentences out of the prison, to do voluntary work in the neighbourhood—cutting grass in churchyards, redecorating old people's houses or digging their gardens, etc. This however was an enthusiasm of the chief officer himself, and reflected a less widespread feeling of concern among the staff than did a pre-release group being formed at the time of the research to enable inmates about to be released to visit towns, factories and other places of interest in order that they could once again get into the pace of normal life. One officer described how an inmate at the end of a 15-year sentence had been taken out by him to Bristol city centre; the inmate was almost totally paralysed with fear by the traffic conditions prevailing in the city, and clutched the officer's arm, imploring him not to go away for a moment. This must have been an extreme case, but after the long sentences which many of the inmates of this prison had experienced, some process of resocialisation was undoubtedly necessary. The first meeting of staff and inmate members of the new group together showed how much those officers present appreciated the inmates' problems and wanted to help them.

The short-term open prison

Physically, this differed in a number of ways from the prison just described. First of all the campus was smaller—only 20½ acres, most of which was filled with buildings. Although it would be wrong to suggest that there were massive perimeter defences, the boundaries were nevertheless clearly demarcated in a way that was not true of the long-term open. In the main they were marked out by thick hedges, and where gaps occurred in the hedges these were filled by barbed wire. The main entrance was guarded only by a metal pole barrier, while the other entrance near the staff houses had no gate at all. It appears that respect for the boundaries was enforced very strictly indeed; the research worker was informed that any man seen on the wrong side of the hedge would be immediately transferred to a closed institution.

There was some suggestion indeed that some men did break bounds on purpose, in order to be sent back to closed conditions. If true, this may be connected with the use of this prison as an 'open special local prison'—not merely as a place to which men suitable for open training are sent, but as an overspill for overcrowded closed local prisons. This may well have meant that some men were sent here who, though in no way representing a threat to security, could themselves have felt exposed and insecure under the conditions of freer interaction and dormitory living in an open prison. Under such circumstances the only redress would be to engage in some form of mock absconding in order to ensure transfer. Certainly any interpersonal difficulties which open conditions might cause to men of a particular temperament would be exacerbated by the rather cheek-by-jowl kind of life which the relatively small size of the estate necessitated; it was easier to get away from other people at the long-term open.

The buildings consisted of the usual prefabricated blocks, usually in pairs, with a recreation area between each pair. Tenancy of the different huts was determined according to job, length of sentence, etc., but a special feature was the 'honour block', for those who were felt more likely to keep their block clean and to behave well without supervision. This block was noticeably brighter and better equipped as well as better kept than the others.

The dormitory huts were divided into cubicles, each of which usually accommodated two but in some cases only one prisoner. These cubicles had no doors, but curtains were hung over the entrances. A hut would contain twenty-four of these units. However, personal possessions seemed to be very much fewer and much less individualised than at the long-term prison. In part this may have been due to the fact that the men were staying such a short time, and therefore did not have either the same opportunity or the same motivation to develop the home-like characteristics of their cubicles.

Officers' living accommodation was similar to that in the other open prisons. The dwellings were of the same external structure as other buildings on the camp, which gave them a somewhat temporary appearance. Officers seemed more content with their state of repair than at either of the other open prisons: they were centrally heated and well planned. But there was some concern about their proximity to the prison—separated from the rest of the camp only by a wattle fence. Some officers were worried about their children playing out of doors there, but there was no suggestion that anything had ever happened to give rise to such anxiety.

The general appearance of the camp was pleasant. The huts themselves were well cared for and brightly painted in a variety of colours. In front of the administration block was a lawn which was kept meticulously mowed, with a centrepiece of a rose garden and a frame of herbaceous plants, while in one corner was an old, but gaily coloured wheelbarrow, filled with flowers.

The rest of the grounds consisted of a large playing field, and market gardens. These also were scrupulously weeded, sometimes it seems to the detriment of the crops. Much of this neatness was perhaps attributable to the fact that all of the Governor's previous experience had been in closed prisons, and this may account also for the strict adherence in the prison to rules and regulations. But this, rather like other features of the prison, was probably not unconnected with its short-term character. With a large turnover of prisoners precision and orderliness are probably an absolute pre-condition for efficient operation. The short-term closed prison displayed similar characteristics and probably for the same reason—though it could hardly have been described as neat and tidy. Appropriately enough for a prison with so many transients, the reception unit through which men passed on entry and discharge was the most modern of those in any of the six research prisons, and was organised on a kind of one-way assembly line basis.

The rather literal attitude to absconding, already mentioned, did not however stand alone. There was a widespread preoccupation with preventing escapes at this prison which, in part at least, must have been caused by the prison's rather high escape figures during the years 1968 and 1969. As a result an induction unit was established in the prison in 1970, to ensure that no unnecessary friction arose as a result of prisoners not understanding the way in which the prison ran. It was hoped that the unit would also ensure that, during the escape-prone period early in a sentence, indications of trouble could be picked up beforehand so that something could be done about possible escapes. Whether due to the induction unit or not, escapes fell from a high point of 38 in 1969 to 16 up to

September 1970. It is interesting that in this prison, as in the long-term open institution, the staff seemed to have fantasies about wanderings by prisoners outside the prison after lights out. They were believed to go to drink in local pubs and so on. All of this reflected an anxiety aroused by minimum security conditions which is not unnatural in view of the primary containment function of all prisons, apparently impressed firmly on the minds of all prison officers by their training, as well as by experience gained predominantly in closed institutions (see p. 177). In the event officers at this prison were always on the lookout for any sign around the prison, or in the behaviour of inmates, that escape attempts might be in prospect. They seemed to feel that escapes reflected upon them, and when one did take place, joined eagerly in an organised search of the surrounding countryside in the hope of finding the absentee and thus making it unnecessary to call in the police.

It is probably accidental that the punishment block in this prison is located in the very centre of the camp, but its effect, a little like that of the stocks in the medieval market place, is to represent a public and omnipresent reminder of the penalties for transgression. It consists of six cells and a fenced-in yard, where inmates under punishment were exercised in full view of any other prisoners who happened to be in the area. Of course the main purpose of such a unit in an open prison would be to hold offenders, normally absconders, securely until they could be transferred to a closed prison. The prominence given to it chimed in only too well with the anxiety about security here, so much greater than at any of the other open prisons which we studied. As with the reception unit, it was difficult to escape the architectural symbolism which seemed to be involved.

A number of the results of the short-term character of the prison are to be observed. Some are features which the prison shares with short-term closed prisons, and are probably only to be expected. They include the fact that there are no vocational training courses, and that as far as education in the more specific sense is concerned there are, in the main, only hobby classes. An impermanent floating population seems to inhibit more serious forms of study, not only because prisoners may not be in the institution long enough to benefit from them, but also because the continuous turnover of prisoners seems to monopolise everybody's attention. Another consequence seemed to be an *ad hoc* approach to their work, among the staff: a tendency to live from day to day. There were indeed not only day-to-day but often even incident-to-incident solutions to problems rather than an approach which embodied some kind of long-term policy for the prison. This was usually blamed by the staff on the Governor, but there certainly is a serious problem in giving direction to a short-term institution of this kind. One supportive influence for the staff in this inchoate and rather threatening situation was the work of the training officer, who visited each of the younger officers while they were actually on the job, and asked them if they had any particular difficulties. He pointed out to the research worker that when prisoners had questions to ask, they invariably asked their party officers, and a young and inexperienced officer in this situation might be hard put to give an answer without some support and guidance. Formal training took place mainly in the winter, when work parties were fewer and pressure on the staff therefore less, and he had developed an interesting 'project method' of instruction. The lack of any clear purpose in the prison must, however, have made it difficult for him to do more than help either in establishing routines or in dealing with immediate situations confronting them.

In effect staff were engaged in 'doing bird' in much the same way as were prisoners. Having no general objective before them, they saw their task as one of removing the immediate inconvenience which problems with prisoners represented to them rather than trying to deal with the problems as such. Very often this meant that some members of the senior staff would give orders one minute, and then if they proved unworkable, deny later that they had done anything of the kind. Officers naturally resented this and there was in fact a considerable schism between the two grades of staff. This was reflected in the fact that the Officers' Club was used by senior and older members of staff but that the basic grade officers, especially the younger, never went there, often in fact expressing derision at the very idea. This may seem trivial, but it reflected something much deeper in the social structure of the staff at this prison.

With such a failure to give a lead and accept responsibility from the top downwards, it is not surprising that each officer adopted his own opportunist policy with prisoners. They thus transferred to the inmates the confusion and frustration which they were experiencing themselves. Officers would countermand one another's orders: a duty officer would arbitrarily take away an extension of television time which had been previously granted, because of some alleged infraction, and so on. Not surprisingly, there was a retreat by inmates in upon their own group. The consequence of this will be examined later. There was one exception; as is often the case, the kitchen staff had a much friendlier and more informal relationship with their men—a situation which led to much criticism from the other officers in the prison on the grounds that it undermined discipline in the prison.

The only serious education in the prison, apart from craft classes and a car maintenance course, consisted of basic arithmetic and English classes. There were, however, good physical education facilities. A number of the sports teams were in local leagues, and were able to go out of prison to play 'away' matches as well as to receive their opponents in the prison. The library was rather small, but included a reading room for quiet activities.

The work programme included the ubiquitous laundry; an enamel shop for painting car badges; a shop which made chairbacks, and stretchers for government use; an assembly shop for those who were unable or unfit to work elsewhere and in which the work was essentially simple and repetitive (at the time of the research it consisted of manufacturing cheap novelty items such as ornamental rings and scarf rings). There was also the mat shop, which had the largest labour force of any shop in the prison and where, the work being rather unpleasant, it was believed that difficult prisoners were sent as a punishment. Certainly men were often sent into the mat shop after being punished for some infraction, and half of the men in the shop had received at least one warning for failing to meet their production targets. There was also two-thirds of an acre of market garden, and the men who tended this also looked after the lawns and flowerbeds around the prison. There were, of course, men on domestic and kitchen work, and also a large group (second in size only to the mat shop) doing maintenance work around the camp.

All other work opportunities were outside the prison; there were five which were supervised by officers, and six which were unsupervised. The latter included parties working on farms in the area, at a nearby Catholic convent, and at the village church. Prisoners in these unsupervised parties were sent off with bicycles and a packed lunch each morning, and returned to the prison in the evenings, when their bicycles were locked in a wire-netting compound near the gate, and each of them was individually searched. While one of the supervised parties travelled forty miles by coach every day to a farm owned by the prison authorities, others did maintenance and gardening work at a women's prison or went off by bicycle with a packed lunch to do maintenance work at a nearby light engineering factory, or in the Prison Officers' Club, which was situated about a mile away from the prison itself. It is difficult to imagine a more informal arrangement for a penal institution. Still another group, about twenty strong, went out each day under supervision to help on an archaeological excavation. This was greatly enjoyed by the men since it enabled them to mix with non-prisoners in a much more informal way than would normally be the case.

Thus there was an interesting range of outside work available to the prisoners in striking contrast to the prison workshops themselves. It also gave the men the opportunity of a freer atmosphere, and of accepting some responsibility for themselves. However, the number of men on outside jobs meant a work shortage in the winter when the weather was less hospitable. Also, pay was generally as poor here as at the long-term institutions, for there was little scope, with the kind of work programme provided in this prison, for the development of factory methods and an applied incentive scheme like that at the medium-term open (to be described shortly). No doubt this was seen as a further inevitable consequence of its being a short-term prison, but factories outside do manage, by breaking down their productive processes into simple repetitive units, to make effective use of transients—as indeed did our short-term closed prison. Whether it is a good thing to organise prison industry entirely for production in this way remains, of course, a debatable point. However, because of the absence of such an orientation, and the absence also therefore of the related 'applied incentive scheme', pay could not be compared with that in the medium-term open.

As in the other prisons, the welfare staff were too few to seek out problems among prisoners, or to provide the interview on reception which was supposed to be routinely available. Instead they dealt with those who came to them for help. Although it was intended to build a new visiting block, at the time of the research prisoners received their visitors in the gymnasium, though on warm days in the summer they could use the lawn in front of the Governor's office. Visits were officially supposed to last for only half an hour, but prisoners were often permitted to remain with their visitors for a full two hours, provided that the visitors arrived at the beginning of visiting time on either the Saturday or the Sunday. Although inmates were always searched before and after visits, the atmosphere was informal and supervised by only one officer, another being employed in escorting visitors from the gate to the gymnasium. But a major problem for visitors was the isolation of the prison; virtually the only way of getting there was by car.

Reference has already been made to the tendency of the inmate group to turn in on itself. What this means of course is that the inmate culture develops apace. Equally consistent with the 'quiet life' policy of the staff was their tendency to 'let sleeping dogs lie' rather than to interfere in what was happening within the inmate community. The Governor argued that there was hardly time for 'baroning' to gain a strong hold when potential barons were there such a short time. Nevertheless, it was the research workers' opinion that it was widespread. Also powerful were the bookmakers; there was a good deal of gambling on horses as at the medium-term open.

The inmate committee was the only formal means of communication between the Governor and the inmates. The committee consisted of a chairman and seven members drawn from the various working parties of the prison, and they met with the Governor every week on Sundays. At the meeting, according to the chairman of the committee, 'Complaints, suggestions and the results of last week's suggestions are read out, and then any further complaints are dealt with.' The matters discussed would include meals, laundry facilities and sometimes objection to disciplinary measures such as the withdrawal of television privileges, though these were tactfully presented by the men as proposals for improving the smooth running of the camp rather than as complaints.

The main features of life at this prison seemed to be a result mainly of its short-term character leading to an emphasis on the rules which is not very appropriate for an open prison, and also making it difficult to develop much more than a hand-to-mouth policy in the prison. To surmount these difficulties and thus give some sense of purpose and direction to his staff would call for a Governor with more commitment to the open prison idea.

The medium-term open prison

The medium-term open occupies what was originally the site of an RAF camp. The site covers a large area but the prison is concentrated on only a small part of it, the rest, out of bounds to prisoners, being littered with old buildings, roads and other signs of its earlier occupation. However, one valuable legacy from the RAF is a number of very large hangars, providing vast and airy rooms of which the prison has been able to make very good use.

These, then, are two of the physical differences between this and the other open prisons in the research. The other striking difference is the existence of a high fence all round the prison, broken only by the main gate, which is under surveillance during the day and locked every night. Such a fence of course is not an insuperable barrier to escape; this remains an open prison. Nevertheless it must be something of a disincentive to potential absconders, and certainly represents a formal recognition of the boundaries of the prison lacking at both of the other open prisons. The fence, then, is largely symbolical but as such had probably been a reassurance to the people living in the vicinity, who were originally very resistant to the idea of establishing an open prison of this size there. Local attitudes have improved over the eleven years of the prison's existence, largely because escapers seem to have been more concerned with getting out of the area than with causing trouble there. The prison's proximity to the main road must have helped them in realisation of this understandable ambition. Current apprehensions in the neighbourhood related to a proposed increase in the population of the prison from its present 500 to 750, which it was feared would lead to a 'land grab'—the compulsory acquisition by the Prison Department of land locally needed for a housing estate. In fact the expansion plans seemed to involve mainly the more intensive use of existing buildings, and in any case there was a large area of unused land on the existing site.

Apart from the hangars already referred to, the buildings were the usual hutments. Broadly speaking the layout of the camp was that administrative buildings were on one side, industrial buildings on the other, and separating these two were the prison dormitories. There was some evidence of lack of space in some sections of the prison, notably in the reception block, and for the storage of clothing; congestion under these two heads could become acute as the prison expanded its population.

The dormitories were divided, as in the other opens, into cubicles, and each dormitory contained collective washing and toilet facilities. The dormitories were, however, rather austere compared with those at the long-term prison. There were, for example, no curtains at the windows, and wall decorations seemed to be fewer and very much less adventurous. Some of the men had radios, but although they were allowed to retire to the dormitories in the evening for peace and quiet, or to write letters, etc., no games or craft materials were allowed there.

The cubicles were not perhaps barer than those at the short-term prison, but the reasons were probably different. As the inmates of the latter were going to be there for only a short time, there was hardly opportunity for them to acquire personal possessions. It might be argued that their more home-like appearance at the long-term open was a result of the same kind of cause, i.e. that men were staying for a long time, and could both accumulate possessions and expect to be allowed to keep them. In fact the differences were partly due to the nature of the regimes and the attitudes of the governors of the three prisons.

But at least the punishment block was not brandished in the centre of the prison as it seemed to be at the short-term prison. In this prison it was in a fairly secluded spot, and part of it was actually used at the time of the research for the storing of spare clothes. Another endearing example of the opportunist misuse of accommodation was the appropriation of the physiotherapy room for breeding fish for the various prison aquaria. One hastens to add that physiotherapy did not seem to suffer as a result; the room did not appear to be needed for its officially assigned purpose.

The dining room was large and the men all ate there in association. A unique feature was the washbasins at the entrance to the dining room—probably another legacy from the RAF. The kitchen had a tradition of doing elaborate confectionery, of which the staff of the kitchen were inordinately proud. A socially more useful activity was in preparing the 'meals on wheels' supplied to old people in the district.

Education in the prison was largely on a hobby basis. There were of course the usual classes in basic education for those who needed them, but these were not very popular. There seemed to be two reasons for this: the embarrassment which a man feels at admitting, for example, that he is illiterate; plus the loss of money involved in going to a class instead of a workshop during the day. This latter is bound to be a factor affecting other unremunerative activities besides education, in a prison organised like this one, on the applied incentive scheme (see below). The only other exceptions to the craft and hobby basis of the educational programme were examination-oriented courses in gardening, book-keeping, mathematics and English, and a few men who took correspondence courses. Courses in horticulture were related to the work programme in that they were taken mainly by prisoners working in the gardens. Apart from this the only part of the whole programme with direct vocational bearing seemed to be the class on book-keeping.

One could obviously criticise the educational programme on such grounds as this, but even more serious, perhaps, was the lack of involvement on the part of the discipline staff. This has not always been the case: at one time a number of the officers were directly involved in teaching in the education department, but the number who still did so was small. This seemed to be the result of what they felt to be the rather schoolmasterly and patronising attitude adopted by the tutor organiser towards officers. They resented this very much, and indeed there was a derogatory nickname for him current among the officers. Yet as an educator he did seem to have good ideas. For instance, one of the classes was in Braille, intended to lead eventually to the production by prisoners of Braille books for the use of the blind. The education centre itself was also a lively place, with newspaper cuttings, both serious and amusing, on the walls, occasional quiz competitions, and so on.

The physical educational facilities were probably as good as any in the prison service and certainly better than those at any of the other prisons in this research. The gymnasium, located in a hangar, was inherited from the RAF. It was immense, and the facilities in it had been improved since the Prison Department took over. It was used not only by the staff and inmates of this prison, but also by the Prison Service as a whole, who run officers' training courses there. Local officers used it during the day, though some prisoners were allowed also to use it at this time. At times of work shortage, activity in the gymnasium was used as a 'labour soak' and this kind of use may increase as the population of the prison rises and work for the men becomes rather more difficult to find than at present. The most popular activities were squash, badminton and weight-lifting, and some of the prisoners had even acquired their own squash rackets.

The main problem of the welfare department was the same as in other prisons; the staff were really too few to have time to seek out men with problems, but had to limit themselves to those who approached them. The senior welfare officer carried a case load of 100, and the two welfare officers 200 each. There was no routine interview of all cases at the beginning of a sentence, but all men were seen shortly before discharge. Few men came during the day because of the pay considerations already mentioned, but they were allowed to turn up without appointments for the early evening sessions. Although they did not have to do so, men often discussed their problems with their party officers first, who thus became involved in, say, telephone conversations with welfare officers about the men. This seemed a wholly desirable development likely to improve relationships all round as well as to help officers to see the men under their control as human beings in need of help. In fact relationships between officers and the welfare department were very good.

Visits of prisoners' families and friends were organised in a relaxed way, mostly at the weekend though sometimes during the week. A WRVS cafeteria was held at one end of the room. Prison officers were assigned to supervising different sections of the room and returned to that section on each visiting day. This enabled them and the visitors to get to know each other on successive visits. Rather sensibly, visits were not curtailed to the regulation period, but could extend to up to two hours if the visitor arrived early enough.

Work was given much more emphasis in the training programme of this prison than either education or welfare and was organised very much on 'industrial' lines. The men were even summoned to work by a siren. The prison's industrial manager was shared with the medium-term closed prison, with whose work programme it also had much in common. Almost all the prisoners were paid in accordance with an applied incentive scheme—a form of payment by results, the standards for which were established by a firm of management consultants. The only exceptions were two trade training courses in bricklaying and painting. These were originally 'vocational training courses', but they were converted into 'trade training courses'—a shorter process designed to supply labour for maintenance work in the prison rather than to set men on the first steps of a career ladder. As it happened there was never enough work available either in bricklaying or painting to occupy the men coming out of the trade training courses, who were therefore transferred to other work within the prison. Without the further experience which could have been gained from working in maintenance departments, it is doubtful if the very elementary training given in the courses could be of much use to them after discharge.

A third training shop was intended to assess the suitability of prisoners for work in the weaving shop, and then to train those who passed the test. The weaving shop itself was concerned with producing drill cotton, beaverteen, shirting twill, calico, terry towelling and huckaback for use within the prison itself. This shop presented a very good example of the factory-type production being aimed at here, and men complained that in order to reach the maximum wage on the basis of the production norms set by the management consultants, it was necessary to work flat out without stopping or interruption for the whole week. Although men who did work hard could receive high pay by prison standards, the work itself was repetitive, arduous and boring. Another shop produced wooden pallets for forklift-truck staging, and the storing of commodities. Both inmates and staff were of the opinion that maximum pay on the production norms in operation was virtually unachievable in the pallet shop, largely because the work study team had ignored the need for rest breaks during working periods.

Twenty-six men worked in the metal recovery unit which was responsible for cable stripping, and the sorting and weighing of the various metals recovered. This work was being done for an outside firm. There was a relatively high ratio of officers to men in this shop and this, plus the kind of work involved, caused some to argue that the shop was the prison's 'punishment' shop. Also stigmatised was the miscellaneous shop, sometimes referred to as 'Lloyds', for the 'sick, lame and lazy', and the 'Noddy' shop. These names were due to the fact that the prisoners employed there were generally men who could not be employed elsewhere because of physical disabilities, or mental incapacity. Some men however did not appear to suffer from any particular disability though all, perversely enough, appeared to enjoy the monotonous routine of the shop. The contracts carried out there varied from time to time, but at the time of the research they included manufacturing soft toys, breaking up old roller towel cabinets, and carrying out a very simple operation which required men to screw a top on to a small tube. It was hoped that in the future a contract involving the painting of miniature footballers would be brought into the shop. Although there seemed to be so little inmate dissatisfaction with the boring character of the work, the officers complained that a day spent supervising men in that shop seemed like a week anywhere else. There was also a maintenance department, concerned with both constructional and repainting work.

There was the usual laundry, where conditions were better than in any other prison in the research. This was largely due to the lofty hangar in which the work was carried out: there was much less of the steamy discomfort found in the other institutions. A particular 'perk' for men working in the laundry at this prison was the opportunity of laundering their own clothes. This was an unusual parallel to the privileges of extra food often available to men working in prison kitchens. The laundry processed articles for the prison and for two of the closed prisons in the present research, and had also a small contract with the Post Office. With the closure of the laundry at our long-term open, and the removal of its laundry equipment to this prison, there were prospects that the laundry here would expand by taking on still more outside work. The laundry was very efficiently organised on industrial lines, and this made it a very profitable operation both for the prison and (relatively) for the prisoners.

Work in the gardens was at an experimental stage. The use of polythene tunnel greenhouses was being developed in order to grow early spring vegetables and salad crops. Up to the time of the research, there had been little antagonism between local farmers and the horticultural unit at the prison, since the crops produced had either been used within the prison itself or sold to other prisons in the area. The time was rapidly approaching, however, when the increasing crop production would exceed the needs of these prisons, making it necessary to sell produce on the open market. One suggestion was that a cleaning and packaging plant should then be set up within the prison, and that goods thus processed should be supplied direct to the Co-operative Wholesale Society at competitive market prices. There were also three traditional greenhouses, which were used to propagate plants and ornamental flowers for transplantation to flowerbeds throughout the prison. It seemed likely that the gardens would expand their operations as more land was cleared by a land reclamation unit, which acted also as a labour 'pool' for the prison, and at the time of the research amounted to some 66 men. This was hard work and, in the exposed conditions of this prison, was also cold and uncomfortable. The discomfort involved had led to a number of strikes during the previous year.

As at the medium-term closed prison, a labour control unit had been established to feed information on the location of inmates within the prison industries to the industrial manager. Plans for the future included the appointment of a full-time industrial manager (at present he was shared with our medium-term closed), the establishing of the cleaning and packaging plant already referred to, further developments within the weaving industry, the expansion of the pallet shop, and the possible introduction of a tailoring shop. Bearing in mind the plans for a 50 per cent increase in the population of the prison, this seemed a rather modest and unimaginative programme.

A number of important consequences for the prison as a whole seemed to have flowed from the way in which the work programme was arranged. They were mainly the result of the applied incentive scheme, which itself seemed to be intended to reproduce factory-type conditions in the prison workshops. Such conditions have been advocated a good deal by penal reformers in recent years as giving offenders the kinds of work experience they are likely to meet in the world outside after discharge.[2] The profitability of workshops organised in this way is probably also not unimportant, though no doubt the prison authorities would say this was a by-product rather than the aim of the system. However, there was a price to be paid at this prison, and it is worth while asking whether that price is justified.

First of all prison officers, especially those with constructive attitudes towards the training of prisoners, were dissatisfied with it. They felt that an impersonal applied incentive scheme made it impossible for them to use rewards as an individualised aid to rehabilitation. The system regarded results rather than effort, whereas a more flexible system would have made it possible to discriminate according to ability, stamina, the need for encouragement, and so on. Of course discretion in the hands of prison officers, or anybody else, is not necessarily going to be used solely in the interests of rehabilitation. One of the advantages of an impersonal, standardised system is that it prevents arbitrary action and petty persecution, to which those, like prisoners, who are under other people's control, are very likely to be subject. This has always been a basic problem in prisons: how far you need to protect the rights of prisoners by restricting the powers of prison staffs to discriminate between them. But when you do this you also prevent staffs from adapting the programme to individual needs and capacities.

However, the inmates also had their own complaints about the system under which they worked. Reference has already been made to the routine and monotonous character of much of the work, a disadvantage which the prisoners shared with many workers in modern factories. However, the production norms set by the industrial management consultants also seemed to be very severe. This may have meant that conditions in the workshops were not entirely realistic when compared with factories outside; also they lacked the minor relaxations and indulgences which trade union activity and public opinion have won for most workers. However, probably even more important was the effect which possibly any system of payment by results had upon the men's attitude to their work. It had become for the most of them merely a way of making money, reducing both its value as a form of personal satisfaction, and any value it might have as a training and character-building medium in the broader sense. And it was largely responsible for the fact that men were so reluctant to leave the workshops to engage in welfare interviews, basic educational classes, or in any activities outside the workshop which were likely to reduce their pay at the end of the week. It must be a bad thing if the work programme of a prison comes to dominate what goes on in it to such an extent that possibly rehabilitative or educational activities are hampered in this way. Oddly enough, the men were not unwilling to come to be interviewed by the research workers during the day; they seemed to see it as something of a change from the monotony of their work. They did not see the non-industrial activities of the prison itself in the same light.

It is interesting also to observe the emergence of strikes: a previously unheard-of feature of prison work programmes. Presumably if the prison authorities are in search of industrial reality, they must take the rough with the smooth. A more ominous aspect of this was the emergence within the prison also of industrial sabotage. Mysterious fires had occurred in the shops: once in the weaving shop, and twice in the pallet shop. The former was attributed to an electrical fault, but prisoners believed that it had been deliberately started. There seemed to be a general assumption that the fires in the pallet shop were arson attempts by dissatisfied prisoners. Certainly there had been a good deal of unrest in this shop in the past, including threats to stop work during the winter months when the hangar in use was very cold.

The relatively high rates of pay were reflected in the wide range of often expensive goods on sale in the canteen. They included toys, Christmas cards, a variety of toilet articles, and large boxes of chocolates. Though a little ironical, it would seem a very good thing that men in prison could buy presents for their wives and families in this way. The canteen was open no fewer than four times during the week, and turnover averaged £400 a week—about 30p per head more than most prisons.

The library was the best in any of the prisons in the research. It contained 7,000 books of which 1,000, supplied by the County Library, were changed every month. Even the officers found it worthwhile borrowing. The library was also responsible for the circulation of newspapers: a daily and a Sunday newspaper were supplied to each dormitory in the prison. One can imagine the horror and astonishment with which old lags on either side of the bars in traditional prisons would look upon this innovation.

Yet it remains a prison. Reference has already been made to the perimeter fence; and dormitory doors were locked at night. There were no other formal restraints—for example, as at the long-term open men walked unescorted back and forth to work. However, the selection of prisoners, in common with the other open prisons, would be such as to reject the more obvious escapers, and the prison itself had the right to reject any violent, sex or drug offenders, car stealers or potential absconders if they nevertheless did find their way there. This prison shared in the wave of escapes in 1966 which led to the establishment of the Mountbatten Committee, and the eventual tightening up of security in all British prisons. Since then, as at the short-term open, an induction unit had been set up to assist in the smooth adaptation of incoming prisoners to the institution with the idea thus of removing some of the unnecessary frictions between prisoners and institution which might provoke escapes. During this initial period, industrial tests were applied and men attended interviews and boards to assess their welfare and work needs. Meanwhile they were housed in separate wards from other prisoners, which like the other dormitories were locked at night. When the induction period was completed, inmates were allocated to a work unit, and to a dormitory in which they would normally live for the rest of their sentences.

The research worker noted that if there was some evidence that any prisoner seemed likely to escape, the security officer would speak to him personally in an attempt, as the officer saw it, 'to sort out his problems', but if this conversation did not reassure the officer that the danger was past, the man concerned was often put under observation in the punishment block. As it was generally agreed in the prison that most inmates absconded for family reasons (for example, domestic difficulties), or at or around Christmas time, this locking-up technique, though effective, seemed a little insensitive. As in other open prisons, officers were very security conscious, and dormitory huts were almost constantly being searched in order to find contraband goods, or to catch men card-playing, which it was well known went on in the cubicles of the dormitories. However, an efficient internal telegraph system made sure that when officers interrupted what they expected to be a game of cards, they usually found a 'cosy chat' in progress. Another security problem lay in the proximity of the prison to the main road. This made it very easy for outsiders to throw goods in packages into the prison, usually into the gardening area from passing cars. These were hastily retrieved by any inmate who noticed them, and then delivered to the prisoner to whom they were addressed. Although officers made every attempt to prevent this activity, it seemed that all too often the goods had been distributed by the time they heard about them. Of course any attempt to escape was usually immediately followed by removal to a closed prison.

Training innovations, then, were confined very largely to the industrial programme of the prison. The educational programme was recreational in character, being designed in the main to enable men to pass their time in the prison rather than to form part of a planned programme of rehabilitation. Welfare work also we have seen to be limited by the lack of enough welfare officers. The attitude of party officers towards welfare work seemed positive, and this might have been capitalised upon further by involving them more directly in the work of the welfare department. No actively rehabilitative or attitude-forming techniques, such as group counselling, were operating within the prison.

There was a pre-release scheme in operation, but participation was voluntary, and attendance therefore very erratic. The period of six weeks during which the course ran began with an interview in which inmates discussed with the staff of the unit what they felt to be their needs upon release. The officers involved were then supposed to evaluate these and, if desirable, see how they might be realised. Usually, this amounted merely to organising home leave for a man and arranging for him, while at home, to see employers. Indeed, the research worker felt that most of the time of the unit staff was taken up with writing letters to potential employers. As resettlement is probably the most critical problem for prisoners, a real opportunity seemed to be being missed here. Although courses on the resettlement of ex-prisoners were run at the Prison Service Staff College, the officer in charge of this unit had never attended such a course. One feature of the discharge situation seemed particularly open to criticism. The high rates of pay ought to have had the advantage that men could save money for use when they were discharged. In fact the £4 release grant which they received from the Supplementary Benefits Commission was docked if they had any money of their own on discharge. Although the sum involved may be very small, it is important to prisoners, who have in any case been earning only small sums while in prison, and in whose minds short-term deprivations of this kind loomed very large as compared with the longer view of the future which the rehabilitative process might attempt to inculcate.

Staff attitudes towards the prison and towards its administration were not very favourable. Staff housing was in purpose-built accommodation adjoining the prison, and many of the officers disliked the ghetto which they felt this represented. There was also much dissatisfaction because of the delay in building a new Staff Club. 'If it had been something for the prisoners, it would have been finished by now', was a frequent comment on this. All of this, however, was a symptom of deeper rooted dissatisfactions. And, as also seemed to be the case with the short-term prison, it appeared to be nurtured by the lack of any clear conception about the nature of an open prison on the part of the Governor.

The Governor saw himself as a progressive and democratic man, but to the officers he appeared inconsistent and autocratic. A number of factors can be identified which may account for their attitude towards him. One of these was his tendency to 'distance' people. This was experienced by the research team themselves on their first day at the prison, when they went to introduce themselves to the Governor. He showed no sign of recognition, although they had met him on a previous occasion and had exchanged many letters with him about the research. His almost theatrical reception of them was 'Come into this office and explain yourselves.' When they followed him into his office, he disappeared for some time into an annexe behind it, although upon re-emergence he formally welcomed them to the prison—while suggesting that they shouldn't bother him too much unless 'something important came up'. A number of the staff commented upon how frustrating they also found this kind of technique. It took a number of forms: for instance, he would not accept reports against inmates if they were either spelled incorrectly or used bad grammar.

Even more unacceptable to the officers, used to the certainties of closed institutions, was what they perceived as his inconsistency. As they put it 'What is right one day is wrong the next'. This was particularly noticed in connection with the kind of punishments given out for two prisoners. For example, it was complained that an inmate in illegal possession of two tomatoes from the greenhouse would be punished more severely than an inmate who had been insolent to an officer—a serious fall from grace indeed by the Governor. On another occasion both charges would be dismissed. The relative weight given to the crime of insolence towards an officer shows clearly where their concern really lay. They felt that he did not support them against prisoners, and indeed often 'showed them up'. Thus in deciding whether or not to report an inmate they had to decide not whether the infraction justified a report, but what the

Governor's view of it might be, in a situation where they saw that view as fluctuating wildly from day to day.

The uncertainty resulting from this spread downwards throughout the authority structure of the prison. Imitating the Governor's style, the principal officers had become largely desk-bound, delegating much of their power to basic grade officers. The latter valued these opportunities, but felt that making use of them was often a very hazardous thing, as the principal officer concerned would often accept no responsibility for the outcome.

As an example of how this worked, an officer was asked one day by the assistant governor, the senior works officer, and a principal officer to take a party of men 'out of bounds' in order to tidy up some rubbish. While this operation was being carried out under the supervision of the officer, the Governor on his afternoon round noticed that both officer and men were 'out of bounds'. The officer was brought before the Governor and reprimanded on the spot, and apparently further disciplinary action was being contemplated. The officer reported all this to the branch secretary of the Prison Officers' Association, and on investigation it became clear that none of the three people who had given the officer the task of carrying out this work was willing to support him by accepting some responsibility for what he had been doing. Few basic grade officers are going to be willing to assume responsibility when they see things like this happening. Thus the instructor in the miscellaneous shop, finding that there was no work available for his men, phoned through to the assistant governor to find out what he should do. The assistant governor suggested that he let them either play cards or read books. In the end he did neither, for fear that the Governor would find out and blame him.

It was suggested that part of the problem arose from principal officers themselves who had had little experience of open prison work and in any case had little interest in the prison as most of them were awaiting either retirement or promotion. It seems more likely that the lack of structure itself, emanating from the behaviour of the Governor, was the real villain of the piece. If he could have been 'nearer' to the staff and also been clearer about his policy, the implementation of which he had then ensured through a well-defined command structure, few of these difficulties would probably have arisen.

In the event the basic grade officers felt themselves threatened by the hierarchy, and in classical Marxist fashion developed a strong 'consciousness of class' and a high level of solidarity. The officer peer group at this prison were stronger than in any of the other prisons. Surprisingly, the research was received very well in this institution. Because the staff for the project presented it as being as much concerned with the problems of officers as of prisoners, they felt that, at least to us, they mattered. The usual comment was, 'It won't do any harm, and it might do some good', presumably in throwing light upon some of their problems and difficulties.

But the most important effect of all this uncertainty was in producing a situation in which, as the research worker put it, 'prison officer activity was almost imperceptible'. If doing almost anything is likely to get you into trouble, the only safe thing to do is nothing. So life tended to be easy but purposeless. When officers were transferred from this prison to another, the first thing they then noticed usually was an increase in the tempo of work.

So this was very much a prison for 'doing bird'. Not only the men but also the officers tried to 'keep their noses clean'. Education was directed towards tension reduction, and work towards productivity rather than vocational training. And even if officers had wanted to establish constructive social relationships with prisoners, this would not have been very welcome to the prisoners themselves, who were preoccupied most of the time with meeting their work targets.

As in other prisons, therefore, inmates turned in on their own community life. And, as in the short-term open, there was a good deal of gambling, mostly on horses, though some officers contended that the men were prepared to gamble on anything, 'even on the direction in which an officer walks'. Gambling seemed to play an even larger part here than in our other prisons. There were a number of bookmakers, and an even larger number of bookmakers' runners, responsible not only for the placing of bets, but also for the collecting of debts and the dispersal of the tobacco that formed the gambling medium. Raids on huts also, as we have seen, disclosed many packs of cards, though oddly enough hardly any card players.

Needless to say there were no inmate representative committees or councils at the prison, and only one discussion group run by an officer, who predictably had to assume sole responsibility for it himself; altogether a mutual withdrawal from rehabilitative contact on the part of both the staff and the prisoners. Perhaps the final comment on the prison is to be found in its lack of any real staff training, in spite of the fact that one of the principal officers had taken a course on this at the Staff College. Before one can train staff effectively, one has to know what it is one is training them to do.

4   The measurement of prison regimes

The Moos Correctional Institutions Environment Scale

The CIES is one of a number of similar instruments which were developed in the USA during the 1960s in response to a fairly general recognition that behaviour in organisations is as much the product of how participating individuals perceive their situation as of formal organisational aims. In giving expression to this idea, the CIES and similar tests have followed the lead of those theories which assert that personality and setting, and the interaction of these two, all contribute to producing the range of behaviour found in an organisation. In particular, the CIES relies on Henry A. Murray's theory of personality.[1] From this theory Moos concluded that, by asking both staff and residents individually about the usual pattern of behaviour in an organisation, it would be possible to obtain information about environmental *press*. *Press*, in this sense, refers to the phenomenological world of the individual, that is, the private perception that each individual has of events in which he participates. Murray, however, maintained that there is a point at which the private world of each individual merges with that of others, that people tend to share common interpretations of the events in which they participate. He called this *beta press*. Moos claims that group mean scores on his subscales provide measures of some of the dimensions of this consensual *beta press*.

As the 'social climate scale', what became the CIES was originally a 140-item list of statements which yielded twelve 10-item subscales each measuring one postulated dimension of social climate. In addition, the test yielded a further two 10-item scales which measured the tendency of respondents to subscribe to exaggerated positive or negative statements. These were used to exclude such respondents from the analysis of results, on the grounds that they seemed prone to deviant judgments, rather than the kind of consensual judgments which one would be seeking in a study of a social system which displays some degree of unity. During the period in which the present study was undertaken, this 140-item form B of the test was extensively revised and a shorter 86-item form C was developed. Although data for the present study were originally collected using the longer version of the test, it was decided to report the results of our use of the test using the later form C version. This decision was made because the form C (now called the 'correctional institutions environment scale') excluded many features of the form B version about which we were doubtful.

For example, the original form B was designed to measure the social climates of psychiatric hospital wards,[2] and the initial item pool for the development of the test incorporated items derived mainly from the literature on the psychiatric hospital and the therapeutic community. Although the test was separately applied by its author to juvenile correctional institutions,[3] it had not been adapted for use in this setting. A test designed thus for the study of the social climates of psychiatric hospital wards is hardly likely to be appropriate for the study of prisons. In fact, initial claims concerning the potentiality of the test for valid application in adult correctional environments were based only on the evidence that it did differentiate empirically between the different juvenile correctional units in which it was administered. Thus, although the basic rationale of the CIES met the requirements of the present study, it was apparent from the outset that our use of it would necessitate a separate assessment of its reliability and validity. An additional requirement to revise the wording of some items in order to produce a form of the test which was meaningful in a British prison context made this even more necessary. Some of our other misgivings about the scope and appropriateness of the CIES were relieved by the revisions introduced in form C. These included the removal of both redundant items and redundant subscales. It was also separately validated on adult correctional institutions. Test data collected during this study were accordingly transferred from form B to form C, and it is this material which will be reported here. However, we are also concerned that the possibility of further refinement should not be overlooked, and such possibilities are being pursued at the present time. (The form C revision was perhaps too limited in scope, as it did not question in any way the relevance of the initial item pool which, it will be recalled, was assembled in order to assess therapeutic environments. It is, therefore, possible that some fundamental dimensions of prison social climates or regimes are not being assessed by the test. The literature on the prison suggests, for instance, that the degree of inmate solidarity, and the extent to which there is communication between the prison and society outside, are both crucial determinants of behaviour in prisons, but neither aspect is taken account of in the CIES. While this criticism is admittedly conjectural and its relevance can only be established by re-examining the appropriate literature, assembling a new item pool and reconstructing the test from ground up, it does serve to indicate ways in which to increase the scope and relevance of the test. This apart, it was considered that form C assessed a number of dimensions of regime which are central for behaviour in prisons, and it was used for this reason.)

As already mentioned, form B, on which the data were originally collected, was modified in collaboration with its author, in order to make it more suitable for use in Britain. This involved both changes in language and in the items used in the test. A change in terminology was required in order that the vocabulary in use might be meaningful in British prisons and for British respondents. For instance, it was necessary to substitute the term 'prisoner' for 'resident' and the term 'welfare officer' for 'counsellor'. Terms like 'schedule', 'gripe' and 'unit' were replaced by the terms 'routine', 'grumble' and 'wing' or 'prison' respectively. A different reason lay behind the substitution of items: to remove from the test any items which referred to behaviour not normally found in a British prison situation. For example the items 'Residents can wear what they want' and 'Residents can leave the unit whenever they want to' are in no way applicable to British prisons. In fact, it transpired that such items were found not to be relevant to American prisons either! Every item for which a substitution was made by us in the preparation of the anglicised version of form B was subsequently (and presumably consequently) dropped from the American form C version—an indication that perhaps insufficient thought had been given to the applicability of form B to the prison situations in which it was administered. The most significant of our alterations involved the replacement of the term 'unit' by the term 'wing' or 'prison'. The purpose of this alteration was to shift the attention of respondents to the larger institutional unit. Such a change was necessary because there appeared to be no smaller organisational subdivision, in the British training prisons selected for study, that was comparable in size and autonomy to the units studied by Moos. And those organisational subdivisions which did exist often took different forms in open as against closed prisons. Moreover, even within each prison there were a number of, often overlapping subdivisions: one for example based upon where prisoners worked and another on their cell locations. These latter facts would have made sub-unit comparison very complex. Finally, our interest was in any case in the comparison of total environments.

The CIES form C is, then, an 86-item list of statements also adapted for British conditions, which yields five 10-item subscales and four 9-item subscales. A detailed list of the anglicised items on each subscale is included in Appendix 1. Subscale labels, and definitions of what they are intended to measure, are listed below.

1   INVOLVEMENT: measures how active and energetic prisoners are in the day-to-day functioning of the programme, i.e. interacting socially with other prisoners, doing things on their own initiative, and developing pride and group spirit in the programme.

2   SUPPORT: measures the extent to which prisoners are encouraged to be helpful and supportive towards other prisoners, and how supportive the staff is towards prisoners.

3   EXPRESSIVENESS: measures the extent to which the programme encourages the open expression of feelings (including angry feelings) by prisoners and staff.

4   AUTONOMY: assesses the extent to which prisoners are encouraged to take initiative in planning activities and take leadership in the prison.

5   PRACTICAL ORIENTATION: assesses the extent to which the prisoner's environment orients him towards preparing himself for release from the programme. Such things as training for new kinds of jobs, looking to the future, and setting and working towards goals are considered.

6   PERSONAL PROBLEM ORIENTATION: measures the extent to which prisoners are encouraged to be concerned with their personal problems and feelings and to seek to understand them.

7   ORDER AND ORGANISATION: measures how important order and organisation is in the programme, in terms of prisoners (how they look), staff (what they do to encourage order) and the prison itself (how well it is kept).

8   CLARITY: measures the extent to which the prisoner or staff knows what to expect in the day-to-day routine of the programme and how explicit the programme rules and procedures are.

9   STAFF CONTROL: assesses the extent to which the staff use measures to keep prisoners under necessary controls, i.e. in the formulation of rules, the scheduling of activities, and in the relationships between prisoners and staff.

These subscales are not conceived of as totally independent entities; Moos maintains[4] that they are interrelated. The first three, involvement, support and expressiveness, which assess the types and intensity of personal relationships in the prison between prisoners and among prisoners and staff, are grouped together as *relationship variables*. The next three, autonomy, personal problem orientation and practical orientation, are called *treatment programme variables*. Order and organisation, clarity and staff control, the last three subscales, are regarded as 'system-oriented' in that they are all related to the functions required to keep institutions running in an orderly, organised, clear and coherent manner. They are, therefore, described as *system maintenance variables*. Items from each scale are interspersed throughout the test among items from other scales. Respondents are required to record whether the statement contained in each item is generally true or false concerning the institution in which they currently work or are being held as prisoners.

Administration of the test

The CIES was administered to both staff and inmates in each of the six prisons. As the method of applying the test differed as between staff and inmate groups, a detailed account follows of the procedures adopted.

The CIES was administered to all members of the uniformed staff at each prison up to and including the rank of chief officer. An updated list of all members of staff in post at the time of the research was used for this purpose. Except for those officers on annual leave, sick leave, or on periods of detached duty in other prisons, all persons on this list were approached personally by a member of the research team and issued with a copy of the test booklet, instructions for its completion and a response form. Two other research instruments, the prison officer's questionnaire and diary, were issued at the same time (these are discussed in a later chapter). Staff were requested to complete these instruments privately and in their own time and to return them unsigned to a centrally located collecting box on or before a specified date (normally three weeks from the date of issue). Although respondents' anonymity was ensured by this procedure, one result of using it was that subsequent attempts to improve the response rate could not concentrate on known defaulters, but had to be directed at the whole population.

As for inmates, because populations ranged in size from approximately 200 to 700, it was decided to use a variable ratio sampling strategy in order to produce a minimum sample base of 100 in each prison. The sampling fractions, which varied from 1 : 2 to 1 : 7, are reported together with other sampling data in Table 4.1 below. In each prison, the populations sampled were drawn from the updated 'unit roll board', the register of all inmates currently housed in each wing or unit of the prison. Information obtained in this way included each inmate's name, number, cell or dormitory location and place of work. Samples were stratified according to wing or dormitory to ensure representation of all locations, and the individuals in each such stratum were selected in random fashion with the aid of random number tables. It was to be expected that some of those selected would not respond and, in order to test whether those who did were a representative sample, data about 'age', 'number of previous court appearances' and 'length of sentence' were obtained for all inmates from the discipline office card index and prisoners' records. In this way it was possible to make a statistical comparison between respondents and non-respondents in each institution.

At the pilot stage of the project, the CIES was administered to inmate groups of varying sizes and using different methods of presentation. As a result of this experimentation it was decided to administer the test in the main study through the playback of test items from a pre-recorded tape to groups of about 15-20 inmates. The procedure adopted was as follows.

An officer in each prison was delegated to escort inmates between their places of work and the test-room. Lists of the inmates selected for inclusion had previously been circulated to relevant personnel. The officer was required to collect together the men (normally from a single work location) who were scheduled to complete the test at a particular time and make a list of those of them who were for some reason unavailable. He was requested by the research team not to regard refusal to attend as a 'failure to obey an order' (a punishable offence under prison rules) but rather to ask reluctant inmates to attend and listen to the researchers' explanation of the purpose of the research before deciding whether or not to participate. Having attended and had their say, they often did ultimately complete the test. Once the men were assembled, the officer left the room. In no case was an officer in attendance during the administration of the test. The pre-recorded list of CIES statements took 25 minutes to play back to each group. Thus, in every 45-minute session, 20 minutes were available for the introduction (see Appendix 1), instructions and the answering of questions. Usually a classroom in the prison was used for this work; where this was not possible,

Table 4.1 *Moos CIES sampling statistics—inmate samples*

Prison	Long-term closed	Medium-term closed	Short-term closed	Short-term open	Medium-term open	Long-term open
Date of administration	Jan. 1971	Dec. 1970	Sept. 1970	Sept. 1970	Nov. 1970	July 1970
Prison population	741	255	641	300	500	203
Sampling fraction	1:7	1:2	1:6	1:3	1:4	1:2
Size of sampling frame	112	127	120	113	125	105
No. of inmates sampled	109	114	118	109	124	89
No. of groups	8	5	7	7	5	7
Average group size	14	23	17	16	25	13

another room of suitable size and with a power point for the tape recorder was found. Sometimes the classification of the prison made it necessary that the room met the special security requirements prescribed for category A and B inmates, but we have no reason to believe that this in any way affected the results. At the end of each session, response forms were collected and the room prepared for the next group.

Whenever possible, groups were assembled for testing on weekdays and during normal working hours, in the hope that prisoners would then be more willing to participate. However, difficulties were encountered in operating this policy in the medium-term closed and short-term open prisons where a large number of inmates were employed in outside working parties. In these prisons the test was administered to the men concerned during the evening. Another problem might well have arisen at the short-term closed and medium-term open prisons where an applied incentive earning scheme was operated. This scheme, as a method of payment by results, penalised men who left the workshops for reasons other than those stipulated in Home Office regulations. Although in principle inmate respondents at these prisons ought not to have been paid for the hour during which they were absent from work completing our test, it would seem that none did have pay deducted for this reason. But for this co-operative gesture on the part of these prisons there could have been a strong monetary disincentive against participation by prisoners who were expecting to be docked. For our part, every effort was made to ensure that the timing of groups caused the minimum disruption of routine, and shop supervisors were always consulted about the removal of men from shops. Administrative issues apart, the main consideration in the timing of this programme was the avoidance of test 'contamination'. This was expected to occur if the period of testing lasted too long. In order to reduce this risk the programme was, therefore, completed as speedily as possible.

It is possible that our response rates, and therefore the characteristics of our sample, were affected by illiteracy. Tutor organisers in our research prisons, however, were in agreement that illiteracy rates of 2 to 3 per cent were fairly constant from prison to prison. Inter-prison comparisons were, therefore, unlikely to be affected. In any case, response forms required only a minimal level of literacy. As regards comprehension, apart from a very small number who did not understand any English, the great majority readily understood the language used in the CIES. Indeed, care was taken when piloting the test to verify this. Nevertheless, the more abstract statements caused confusion for a few. Where such difficulties were encountered, respondents were instructed to seek clarification when the test period in question was over.

Sampling

The generally low response rates from the staff groups were a source of concern (Table 4.2). In three cases, they either fail to meet or barely meet the minimum acceptable level for a mail questionnaire return. (The latter is usually assumed to be between 40 and 50 per cent. There are, however, obvious reasons for being doubtful about such low returns, and steps ought always to be taken to ensure that returns are forthcoming at a much higher rate than this.)[5] With the co-operation of the local branch committees of the Prison Officers' Association (POA) the test procedure with staff was repeated, but failed to boost response rates by more than 5 per cent. In some cases it failed to produce any further response at all. In addition, a public plea made to the assembled staffs at the prisons with the lowest returns also failed to bring about any improvement. Indeed, at the short-term closed prison (and only at this prison), the result of holding such a meeting was what appeared to be organised silent opposition. In contrast, at the medium-term open and the medium-term closed prisons, from which the highest staff response rates were obtained, we were greeted 'at the gate' by local POA branch committee members who offered guarantees of full co-operation from their members. Thus it appears that there were significant differences in attitudes towards the project at this level, despite the voluntary intervention of the general secretary of the POA who

Table 4.2 Moos CIES—response rates

Prison	Long-term closed	Medium-term closed	Short-term closed	Short-term open	Medium-term open	Long-term open
Staff samples						
No. distributed	181	54	106	47	66	52
No. completed	52	37	34	20	45	34
Response rate	28·7%	68·5%	32·1%	42·6%	68·2%	65·4%
Inmate samples						
No. sampled	109	114	118	109	124	89
No. completed	77	81	110	93	102	76
Response rate	70·6%	71·1%	93·2%	85·3%	82·3%	85·4%

attached his seal of approval to the project through a letter to all the branch committees concerned. Not surprisingly, the expression both publicly and privately by uniformed staff of feelings of anxiety, hostility and, occasionally, disbelief of our expressed motives, occurred in those prisons with the lowest response rates. Our experience in this matter underlines the crucial importance of obtaining co-operation from staff from the outset in research in this field. Our experience does not suggest that this will ever be an easy task in the special circumstances and under the special stresses imposed by prison work. And it will always be influenced (as it seems to have been in our case) by the current state of employer-worker relationships in the Prison Service.

The question of whether our staff samples were representative had therefore to be tackled. In the absence of a way of directly measuring any attitudinal biases which might exist in the samples, it was assumed (although there are obviously many objections that can be raised to arguments of this kind) that attitudes would be related to such variables as 'age', 'rank' and 'length of service', an assumption which a typological comparison of the prison officers' questionnaire returns (see chapter 7) tends to support. If there were such statistically significant differences in 'age', 'rank' and 'length of service' between respondents and non-respondents, biases might be inferred in the low response samples. Accordingly, this information was collected in respect of each member of the uniformed staff in post at each prison, and respondents and non-respondents were compared on each variable using chi-squared. When this was done, significant differences were found in five out of eighteen cases, indicating the non-representative nature of the staff respondents at the long-term and short-term closed prisons. Results from these two staff groups were, therefore, excluded from subsequent statistical analyses of the data. However, mean raw score data from these two prisons will be presented later for the purpose of comparison.

The rate of response to the CIES from inmates was uniformly higher. The representativeness of these samples also was nevertheless tested by comparing respondents with other inmates in each prison for 'age', 'sentence length' and 'number of previous court appearances'. Data for this comparison were made available by a census taken from discipline office card indexes and the prisoners' records in each prison; chi-squared statistics were computed for the distributions of respondents and the remainder of the inmate population on the semi-interquartile range distribution of the variables 'age', 'sentence length' and 'number of previous court appearances'. Significant differences for these characteristics were found in only three out of eighteen cases. These were (i) at the short-term open prison on the variable 'sentence length', indicating that the more transient, civil prisoner population was not proportionately represented in our sample; (ii) at the medium-term closed prison where a slightly larger proportion of men serving shorter sentences was included in the CIES sample; and (iii) at the medium-term open prison where younger prisoners were slightly under-represented in the CIES sample. As these differences were only slight, and because no sample was unrepresentative on more than one out of three measures, it was assumed that the samples could be regarded as random and representative for the purposes of subsequent statistical analysis.

The overall response rate for prisoners was 81 per cent as compared with only 62 per cent for staff, even excluding the two prisons from which unrepresentative staff returns were obtained. In addition to being fewer in number, fewer of those staff responses to the CIES which were actually received were usable. 5·5 per cent as compared with 1·7 per cent for inmates were rejected under the rules for the administration of the test. It is possible that this latter difference partly reflects the different techniques used in administering the CIES to staff as compared with inmates.

Scoring procedures for the test were extremely simple. First, the scores of each individual on each of the nine subscales were computed. These individual scores were then totalled and averaged, to provide a mean raw score on each subscale for all the inmates or all the staff of each prison. Each of these mean raw scores constituted an assessment of staff or inmate perceptions of the regime in their prisons, in respect of the dimension measured in the subscale—in Moos terminology, *beta press.* They were then used to construct profiles for each regime and formed the basis for a first rough statistical comparison.

The profiles for all six inmate groups and all six staff groups are presented in Figures 1 and 2. Although these profiles provide an immediate visual comparison of inmate and staff perceptions of regime, it was thought that such a comparison of raw data, i.e. of data unqualified by the customary statistical safeguards, could be misleading. For instance; Figures 1 and 2 suggest a greater variation between prisons in staff perceptions of regimes as compared with inmate perceptions of the same regimes, but the underlying pattern

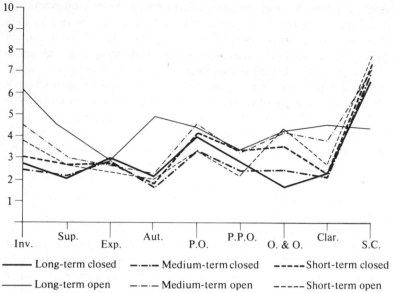

Figure 1   Moos CIES (inmate samples): mean raw score profiles. (Data from which these profiles have been drawn are presented in Table 5.2.)

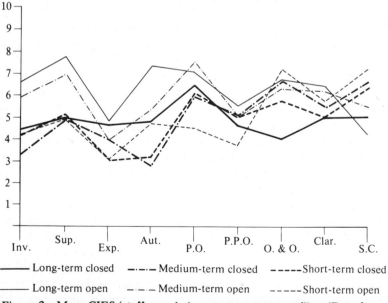

Figure 2   Moos CIES (staff samples): mean raw score profiles. (Data from which these profiles have been drawn are presented in Table 5.1.)

of statistically significant differences may be different from this. Whenever two group means are compared, the emergence of statistically significant differences between them (assuming that the variance is similar for the two groups) depends on the number of cases included in each group. Low numbers require larger differences between the means in order for a difference to be statistically significant. In this instance, there were many fewer cases included in staff than in inmate samples, so that the larger variation in staff perceptions shown in Figures 1 and 2 may actually be less meaningful than the overall differences shown between inmates. It was, therefore, decided not to place too much reliance upon the visual comparison afforded by the mean raw score profiles, and to undertake a statistical analysis of the pattern of differences in both the staff and inmate data.

However, a hint may be obtained from these raw score comparisons of some of the issues on which a more elaborate statistical analysis might be concentrated. For instance, there are the differences referred to above between staff and inmate perceptions as well as a further such difference in that staff appeared consistently to make more positive assessments on some subscales, and more negative assessments on others. There is also the point that although the long-term open prison appeared to be outstandingly different from all other prisons on most subscales, both for staff and prisoners, there were few such systematic differences overall between open and closed regimes as such. Thus the situation seems to be more complex than a simple open-closed comparison would imply; differences within each of these two categories may also be important. Limitation to the open-closed comparison would also have ignored the full descriptive potential of the research instrument. In these circumstances it was decided to go on to analyse the differences and similarities between all regimes irrespective of whether they were open or closed. This meant a subscale-by-subscale comparison for all possible (i.e. fifteen) combinations in the six inmate samples and, separately, for all six possible combinations in the four staff samples in which the criteria of representativeness had been met. As a result of this decision, however, two further methodological problems arose.

The first of these problems related to the fact that by the laws of probability, a paired-comparisons procedure of this kind (using, for example, *t*-tests) could be expected to produce a number of significant differences by chance (one in twenty at the 5 per cent level of probability). Unless such differences occur at a rate in excess of one in twenty, there is therefore no reasonable way of deciding whether or not even the larger among the differences so found are simply fortuitous. Unless we prefaced such a programme with a composite test (for example, analysis of variance) which would test for the occurrence of non-chance variations among every set of results of each CIES subscale we should thus run the risk of making *type I errors*[6] (i.e. rejecting the null hypothesis when it is true or asserting that there are statistically significant differences between samples when there are not). We elected for caution in this matter and sought to minimise the possibility of such errors. There are two ways of doing this. Either one can opt to accept a higher confidence level (say, 1 per cent) or, as has been suggested above, one can opt for a composite test. The latter course was chosen because it is more appropriate to situations in which more than two samples are being compared. There was a further reason for this choice. If each sample pair was treated separately, the resulting estimate of population variance would be based on data for those two samples only. By using a composite test, the null hypothesis (that all samples arise from random sampling in the same population) is made to apply to *all* samples and, as a result, a much more stable estimate of population variance is obtained.

The second methodological issue raised for consideration stemmed directly from a shortcoming in the procedures adopted to deal with the first. The subscale-by-subscale comparisons permitted by the first approach to CIES data analysis could not take into account any overlap which might exist between subscales. In other words, such comparisons had to be based on an assumption that the subscales were independent. Previous work on the CIES, however, has shown a moderate degree of subscale intercorrelation, sufficient at least to query any assumption about subscale independence. Given these circumstances, it seemed worthwhile attempting a more refined analysis in which it would be possible for any such overlap between subscales to be taken into account. Partly for this reason, multi-variate procedures to be discussed later were adopted. However, we did not feel that this consideration necessarily invalidated the detailed subscale-by-subscale comparison as, overlapping or not, the subscales did seem to represent realistic and recognisable aspects of prison life.

Because of the first problem referred to above, then, the explora-tion of differences between pairs of sample means was preceded by the application of a composite test. We embarked at the first stage on the testing of null hypotheses at two levels. First, the null hypothesis that all samples were drawn from the same population (i.e. that there were no overall significant differences) was tested using a one-way analysis of variance for each set of subscale scores. Second, in all cases where these 'first order' null hypotheses were rejected, a 'second order' null hypothesis was tested by means of a *t*-test for each of the fifteen constituent paired sets of data from the six inmate samples and each of the six sets from the four staff samples, in order to ascertain how many or which particular paired sets of data gave statistically significant differences. The statistical convention observed here was therefore that rejection of the null hypothesis on the basis of a composite test automatically involves rejection of the null hypothesis for all the contributing pairs of sample means, including those with the largest differences. The data met all the assumptions required for these procedures: samples were drawn randomly from normally distributed populations, the variance was homogeneous and the samples were independent.

At the second stage, as already pointed out, we needed to apply a method of analysis which would take any subscale overlap into account. While providing a test of any and every difference between the four staff or the six inmate groups, the technique used had to ensure, therefore, that the variance of each subscale did not count more than once in the analysis. To do this it would be necessary to assess the relative contribution of the variance of each subscale to an optimum differentiation of the groups included in the analysis. It is possible to accomplish this only by adopting a stepwise procedure starting with that subscale which (on the basis of a one-way analysis of variance) most strongly differentiates between the groups. Having allowed for the degree of intercorrelation with other subscales, the proportion of the total variance accounted for by that subscale is then calculated. This done, the next step involves selecting from the remaining subscales the one which, given the degree of inter-correlation between subscales, next most strongly differentiates between the groups included in the analysis. When the proportion of the total variance accounted for by this subscale has been calculated and subtracted from the total, the process is repeated for each remaining subscale until all the variance between the groups included in the analysis is accounted for. These are in fact the procedures followed in the operation of a method of statistical analysis known as a stepwise canonical discriminant function analysis.[7] This statistical procedure, along with another known as an analysis of dispersion, was employed in the second stage of the analysis of CIES results. Separate analyses were made of the staff and inmate data using these methods.

The statistical rationale of a stepwise canonical discriminant function analysis is as follows. A discriminant function allots weights to variables (in this case CIES subscales) according to their power to differentiate between the groups included in the analysis. To this end, standardised canonical variates are extracted for each set of data. In the procedures we followed, this meant that standardised scores for each staff or inmate sample in each prison were calculated for the two subscales which, allowing for subscale intercorrelation, most strongly differentiated between the constituent groups and which thus accounted for the highest proportions of the total variance between the groups. This procedure, therefore, assessed the differences between the constituent groups in such a way that the major sources of discrepancy (i.e. subscales) between inmate samples or between staff samples in their respective perceptions of regimes were sorted out. As is usual, we followed up the discriminant analysis with another statistical procedure, an analysis of dispersion. An analysis of dispersion involves the allocation of each set of scores, regardless of its group or sample of origin, to that group in the analysis to which it is mathematically closest. In other words, it tests the assumption that the responses of a particular group, say, inmates in a particular prison, are similar enough and different enough from the responses of other groups, to make them genuinely distinct. Because it is built on to the discriminant analysis, the analysis of dispersion does this, moreover, while controlling for overall multivariate differences in the grouped data. In view of all this, it was generally felt that this second stage in the analysis of CIES data provided a reasonably reliable estimation of the 'separateness' of each prison regime as it was perceived by staff and inmates respectively.

Thus, to summarise, the first and second stages in the analysis of the CIES described above were intended to reveal the nature of differences between prison regimes. This analysis, however, does not take into account the indication already observed in the mean raw score data that there might be consistent differences between staff and inmates in their assessment of the regimes within which they operated.

As an approach to the study of this, the third stage in the analysis of CIES data was focused on a comparison of staff-inmate perceptions of the same regimes. It was, therefore, concerned with within-prison differences in each of the four prisons where staff-inmate comparison was possible. First a number of indicators of staff-inmate agreement were examined. While these revealed an underlying agreement in the patterning of differences between regimes, the discrepancy already mentioned in the level of subscale assessments (i.e. that staff made consistently higher or lower evaluations on certain subscales) was confirmed. Second, closer examination of the raw scores for the staff respondents also revealed a similar difference in the mean levels of subscale response between higher grade and basic grade uniformed staff members in each prison. It was decided, therefore, to take this difference into account in analysing within-prison differences. Thus, two staff groups (higher and lower grades) were compared with the inmate group in each prison. (It proved impossible to do this with the data from the short-term open prison because of the small staff sample. In this case, combined staff scores were compared with the inmate scores.) The statistical procedures adopted here were the same as those employed in the second stage of CIES data analysis. A stepwise canonical discriminant function analysis was computed for the three groups of data from each prison followed by an analysis of dispersion. The discriminant analyses revealed those dimensions of regime (subscales) over which the biggest discrepancies between the perceptions of the two staff groups and the inmate group occurred. The analyses of dispersion revealed the degree of overlap in the perceptions of each regime by the three constituent groups, and thus the extent to which the different grades of staff and the inmates shared similar perceptions of regime in the different prisons compared in this study. This latter aspect, it will be recalled, is of some importance to an evaluation of open prisons, given the expectation that such sharing would be more likely to occur in open rather than closed situations.

Finally some work was completed towards a reassessment of the reliability and validity of the CIES. This work will be reported in Appendix 5.

5   How the regimes are perceived

Staff and inmate cultures

Do our prisons differ in the way in which their staff and inmates see them, and if so in what respect? This is the question which we now want to answer, with the aid of the Correctional Institutions Environment Scale. And an important early question is whether a more refined analysis of CIES results supports the impression given by the raw data (see Figures 1 and 2, p. 120 and Tables 5.1 and 5.2, from which these profiles were drawn) that there was greater variability between staff perceptions of regimes than between inmate perceptions of the same regimes. This is potentially a very important point for the understanding of the prison community. Much has been written about the inmate culture of the prison, and of the pressure for conformity which this exerts on individual prisoners. It is this which is said to account in fact for the criminalising process in prisons. The profiles do imply that the inmate society of the prison is distinguished from the staff by this kind of normative consensus. How far does more refined statistical analysis also support this view?

The first stage of our further analysis of the data permitted this conclusion to be tested in two ways. First, if the raw data are correct then the one-way analyses of variance should produce a larger number of significant differences between staff in different prisons than between inmates. Inspection of the right-hand column of Tables 5.1 and 5.2 reveals that this is' not the çase. Whereas statistically significant differences are found for inmates in respect of each of the nine subscale variables, they were found in only seven out of the nine cases in respect of the staff. Inmates seem, in other words, to show more rather than less variability than staff.

Similarly at the following stage, when all the research prisons were compared in pairs for each of the Moos subscales. In this case the staff unity was even more marked as compared with that of inmates. Statistically significant differences (see Tables 5.3 and 5.4) totalled 87 out of 135 possible cases (or 64 per cent) for staff, as compared with 26 out of 54 (or 48 per cent), for prisoners. We are faced with the

Table 5.1 Moos CIES mean subscale scores and one-way analysis of variance results—staff samples

Subscale	Prison						All groups** combined	F ratio**
	Long-term closed	Medium-term closed	Short-term closed	Short-term open	Medium-term open	Long-term open		
Involvement	4.4	3.2	4.1	4.2	5.9	6.6	5.1	16.743*
Support	4.9	4.8	5.1	4.9	7.0	7.7	6.3	16.841*
Expressiveness	4.6	4.0	3.1	3.0	4.0	4.8	4.1	3.908*
Autonomy	4.8	2.8	3.2	4.7	5.4	7.3	5.1	47.587*
Practical orientation	6.4	6.0	6.0	4.5	7.5	7.0	6.5	8.249*
Personal problem orientation	4.6	5.1	5.0	3.7	5.2	5.5	5.0	4.494*
Order and organisation	4.0	6.6	5.8	7.2	6.3	6.7	6.4	1.849
Clarity	5.0	5.5	5.1	5.8	6.2	6.4	6.0	1.654
Staff control	5.0	6.6	6.3	6.7	5.5	4.2	5.6	16.241*
N	41	33	32	18	42	31	124	*Degrees of freedom* Between 3, Within 120, Total 123

*Significant at 0·01 level.
**Excluding results from the long-term and short-term closed prisons.

Table 5.2 *Moos CIES mean subscale scores and one-way analysis of variance results—inmate samples*

Subscale	Prison						All groups combined	F ratio
	Long-term closed	Medium-term closed	Short-term closed	Short-term open	Medium-term open	Long-term open		
Involvement	2·7	2·4	3·0	3·8	4·5	6·1	3·7	38·982**
Support	2·0	2·1	2·6	2·6	3·0	4·5	2·8	18·449**
Expressiveness	2·9	2·8	2·7	2·3	2·4	2·8	2·6	2·434*
Autonomy	2·1	1·6	1·8	1·9	2·2	4·9	2·4	50·262**
Practical orientation	3·9	3·2	4·1	3·3	4·5	4·3	3·9	6·157**
Personal problem orientation	2·7	2·4	3·3	2·6	3·2	3·3	2·9	5·925**
Order and organisation	1·6	2·4	3·5	4·3	4·2	4·2	3·4	23·383**
Clarity	2·3	2·1	2·3	2·6	3·8	4·5	2·9	29·305**
Staff control	6·5	6·9	7·5	7·6	7·0	4·3	6·8	58·650**
N	76	79	107	89	102	75	528	

Degrees of freedom
Between   5
Within   522
Total   527

*Significant at 0·05 level.
**Significant at 0·01 level.

Table 5.3 *Moos CIES summary table of t-test analysis—inmate samples*

Subscale	(LC/ MC)	(LC/ SC)	(LC/ LO)	(LC/ MO)	(LC/ SO)	(MC/ SC)	(MC/ LO)	(MC/ MO)	(MC/ SO)	(SC/ LO)	(SC/ MO)	(SC/ SO)	(LO/ MO)	(LO/ SO)	(MO/ SO)
Involvement	+ 0·05		− 0·001	− 0·001	− 0·001	− 0·05	− 0·001	− 0·001	− 0·001	− 0·001	− 0·001	− 0·01	+ 0·001	+ 0·001	+ 0·05
Support		− 0·05	− 0·001	− 0·001	− 0·05		− 0·001	− 0·01		− 0·001			+ 0·001	+ 0·001	
Expressiveness				+ 0·05	+ 0·05			+ 0·05	+ 0·05			+ 0·05		+ 0·05	
Autonomy	+ 0·05		− 0·001			− 0·01	− 0·001	− 0·01		− 0·001			+ 0·001	+ 0·001	
Practical orientation			− 0·01	− 0·05	+ 0·05	− 0·01	− 0·01	− 0·001				+ 0·01		+ 0·01	+ 0·001
Personal problem orientation		− 0·01	− 0·001	− 0·05	− 0·001		− 0·001	− 0·001				+ 0·01		+ 0·01	+ 0·01
Order and organisation	− 0·01	− 0·001	− 0·001	− 0·001	− 0·001	− 0·001	− 0·001	− 0·001	− 0·001	− 0·05	− 0·05				
Clarity				− 0·001		+ 0·001	− 0·001	− 0·001	− 0·05	− 0·001	− 0·001	− 0·01	+ 0·01	+ 0·001	+ 0·001
Staff control		− 0·001	+ 0·001	− 0·05			+ 0·001		− 0·001	+ 0·001	+ 0·01		− 0·001	− 0·001	− 0·001
Total no. of differences	3	4	7	8	6	5	8	8	5	6	4	5	5	8	5

Key:

	Long-term	Medium-term	Short-term
Closed	LC	MC	SC
Open	LO	MO	SO

+ First prison in the comparison pair significantly higher.
− First prison in the comparison pair significantly lower.

Table 5.4 *Moos CIES summary table of t-test analysis—staff samples*

Subscale	Prisons					
	(MC/LO)	(MC/MO)	(MC/SO)	(LO/MO)	(LO/SO)	(MO/SO)
Involvement	− 0·001	− 0·001			+ 0·01	− 0·05
Support	− 0·001	− 0·001			+ 0·001	+ 0·001
Expressiveness					+ 0·01	
Autonomy	− 0·001	− 0·001	− 0·001	+ 0·001	+ 0·001	
Practical orientation		− 0·01	+ 0·05		+ 0·01	+ 0·001
Personal problem orientation			+ 0·01		+ 0·01	+ 0·05
Order and organisation						
Clarity						
Staff control	+ 0·001	+ 0·01		− 0·01	− 0·001	− 0·05
Total no. of differences	4	5	3	2	7	5

Key:	Long-term	Medium-term	Short-term	+ First prison in the comparison pair significantly higher.
Closed		MC	SO	− First prison in the comparison pair significantly lower.
Open	LO	MO		

interesting possibility that the staff culture in prisons may be even stronger and more monolithic than that of inmates.

Before making a detailed subscale-by-subscale comparison of the two sets of data from staff and inmate samples respectively, it is worth concentrating, if briefly, on this general preliminary finding. First, the fact that there is less variability between staff perceptions of regimes than between inmate perceptions of the same regimes is in accord with earlier work on the CIES and on the versions of it used in other institutional settings.[1] For example, a similar finding was forthcoming from the very first attempt to apply the test in a correctional setting—in juvenile institutions.[2] Second, this finding also has some bearing on evidence (from the questionnaire administered to prison officers) to be presented later concerning the existence of a 'custodial' staff culture which is transmitted to all prisons and which appears to work against attempts to create regimes like open prisons which claimed to embody departures from traditional custodial practices. In this respect, it is of interest to note that the two subscales, order and organisation, and clarity, for which 'first order' null hypotheses were accepted (i.e. on which there were no statistically significant differences on the analyses of variance between the four staff samples) were both *system maintenance variables*. This would suggest that staff in both open and closed regimes differ very little in their perceptions of how to keep institutions running in an orderly, organised, clear and coherent manner. Still further confirmation for this finding is obtained from the staff diaries (see Chapter 8) which enabled a detailed comparison of 'routines' to be made. The diaries showed that, while there were some differences between prison officers' work in open and closed prisons there was, overall, a strong resemblance between the ordering of priorities and the apportioning of time to the carrying out of particular duties in both situations. Thus, the first general conclusion to be reached is that the impression of greater variability in staff perceptions of regimes given in the visual presentation of raw data is misleading, and that on the contrary the evidence of the CIES results confirmed by data from the questionnaire and staff diary is of the existence of a staff culture relating particularly to 'system maintenance' which influences the attitudes and behaviour of prison staff, regardless of the kinds of institutions in which they work. As there is some evidence of a similarly (if slightly weaker) monolithic culture among prisoners, it becomes a matter of some importance (to be explored later in this chapter) to determine whether they operate in the same direction, strengthening the drive towards uniform prison regimes, or whether they are at variance with one another.

Differences between prisons

The prison-by-prison comparisons for scores on each subscale are set out in Tables 5.3 and 5.4 and revealed no fewer than 113 significant differences. The differences which emerged, however, were by no means restricted to the open-closed comparison which provided the original point of departure for this study. In fact, 57 out of the 87 (65·5 per cent) significant differences in the inmate analysis were of this kind. As open-closed pairs represent 9 out of the 15 comparisons, i.e. 60 per cent, and the proportion of significant differences attributable to them is 65·5 per cent, they seem barely more important than the other comparisons. This is of course only a very crude test, as it takes no account of the size of the differences involved. With such a number of differences between prisons in both sets of data, it was necessary to find a way of summarising the data in order that any overall pattern might emerge. Table 5.5 was therefore constructed—again, however, overlooking variations in the size of the significant differences in question.

If one adds to the overall picture given by Table 5.5 the more detailed information in Tables 5.3 and 5.4 a number of interesting features emerge.

Reference has already been made to the fact that the open-closed comparison is rather less than overwhelming in its import. Only in the case of two inmate subscales—those for Involvement, and Order and organisation—are there consistent open-closed differences. In both these cases the scores for the open prisons were significantly higher. The higher score for Involvement would presumably have been predicted in view of the basis on which open prisons are usually advocated, but the Order and organisation score is somewhat unexpected and will be discussed shortly.

The staff for their part, it seems, see matters in only a broadly similar way to inmates. Only Autonomy gives significant open-closed differences across the board for staff—a subscale which does not emerge anything like as clearly among inmates. It is only to be expected, of course, that there would be differences in the perceptions of even the same situations, by people occupying such different points of vantage as the staff and inmates of a prison.

Table 5.5 Moos CIES frequency of significant differences in t-test analysis ($P = <0.05$)

	Medium-term closed	Short-term closed	Prisons Short-term open	Medium-term open	Long-term open
			Inmate samples		
Long-term closed	3	4	6	8	7
Medium-term closed		5	5	8	8
Short-term closed			5	4	6
Short-term open				5	8
Medium-term open					5
			Staff samples		
Medium-term closed			3	5	4
Short-term open				5	7
Medium-term open					2

Open and closed prisons are, as we have seen, distinguished from one another by the former's higher inmate scores for Involvement, and Order and Organisation. Increased involvement in open prisons (with all the rehabilitative and humanitarian benefits expected to occur from this) is seemingly acceptable to the institution (at any rate as inmates see it) only if there is a compensating emphasis on the overall regulation of inmate activity, such as rules about dress, tidiness and orderliness. We begin to have some confirmation here of the ambivalence of prisons towards 'openness' which consideration of the basic containment role of prisons had earlier made us begin to expect.

This receives support from other data open to us, particularly from the observational phase of our research. For example, inmates at the medium-term open camp were confined by a chain-link fence. Each day for inmates at the short-term open prison, and to a lesser extent at the medium-term open prison, was interrupted by a series of counts, checks and parades. That prison staff see liberalising or rehabilitative measures (such as those which are expected to follow from increased inmate involvement) only in the context of steps to increase security, or their sense of being in control, was also evident in the staff questionnaire data on discipline and security (p. 202) and in their feeling of being the victims of 'conflicting instructions', especially in open prisons where the ideology and the 'containment function' are so much at odds. Also, the ambivalence felt by most staff over greater 'openness' and a treatment or training orientation on the one hand and the need to feel 'in control' on the other, probably accounts, in the absence of more subtle ways of achieving and monitoring such control, for the otherwise inexplicable emphasis on inmate supervision and security duties in open prisons as revealed by the diary. Thus, it is apparent that open and closed prison regimes differ in both expected and unexpected ways. In the case of the short-term open prison which, interestingly, was as we have seen designated as a 'special local' by the Prison Department, it would seem that scores for Order and organisation are high enough to completely undermine the advantages of increased Involvement. Although a similar effect was less strong in the medium-term open prison and least of all in the long-term open camp, there was none the less some evidence for it in these two. In the long-term open, as our observational material shows, this ambivalence actually took the form of a polarisation of staff into a 'pro' group and an 'anti' group according to their feelings about these issues. Obviously, a lot still remains to be done to modify such a 'closed prison' outlook among open prison staff if the potential of open prisons is ever to be fully realised.

Overall, then, open-closed differences are modest, and seem to be overlaid by two other kinds of distinction: the uniqueness of the long-term open, and a difference based on length of sentence.

To take first the relationship between length of sentence and regime: a greater degree of intelligibility and co-operativeness appears to enter into a regime, the longer the sentence which is being served. This is shown by progressively higher scores at a significant level for Involvement and Clarity, as one moves from short term to medium and long term. There is a similar rising gradient for Support, Expressiveness, Autonomy and Personal problem orientation, although the differences between short and medium term in these cases are not statistically significant. Equally meaningful is a parallel statistically significant decline with increase in length of sentence in the more discipline-oriented subscale of Staff control. The exceptions to the general rule are practical orientation—in which the medium-term open stands high—and Order and organisation—where there is nothing to choose between the open prisons.

The same trend is observable among the closed institutions—though less marked, possibly because of the deleterious effect of architecture on the medium-term closed, and also the narrower differences, in any case, between the closed prisons. Only in the case of Order and organisation is there an across-the-board statistically significant gradient, but differences in the predicted direction are found for Expressiveness (upwards with sentence length), and Staff control (downwards with sentence length).

Finally there is the interesting special case of the short-term open prison. It shows a lower score than any of the closed prisons for the 'tolerant' subscales of Expressiveness (even the medium-term open shows up unfavourably here when compared, revealingly enough, with the 'longer-term' long-term closed). Similarly with Personal problem orientation and Practical orientation. The short-term open's scores for the 'positive' factor of Involvement and Support, and the 'negative' factor of Staff control are more similar to those of the closed than of the other open prisons. And it has a lower score for Autonomy than the long-term closed, and higher scores than any prison in the sample for Order and organisation.

As the small response rate from closed prison staff limited analysis to the three opens and one closed (the medium-term closed), the utility of Tables 5.2 and 5.4 is not great. Nevertheless there is some trace of the same factor at work here also. Although there were many non-significant results, only one of the significant differences shown for the staff was inconsistent with the hypothesis. This was the higher score for Autonomy shown by the short-term open as compared with the medium-term closed prison.

What accounts for this relationship between CIES scores and length of sentence? Our field observations in these prisons may give two clues towards an answer. One is the tendency on the part of both prison systems as a whole, and prison staff in particular, to develop more sympathetic regimes in longer-term institutions. This is partly a favourable reaction to the more tractable behaviour of longer-term prisoners, who have got over the first trauma of incarceration and have learned to 'do bird' in a peaceable way. And it is partly an acknowledgment that a so-called 'tonic' regime cannot be sustained over longer periods as prisoners and officers get to know each other better; and that it is inhumane to subject men to stringent discipline for a substantial part of their lives.

The second clue diverts our attention to the other end of the scale—towards short-term prisons. Perusal of Table 5.5 shows that there is less difference between the regimes of the various closed prisons than between the open, an average of four significant differences compared with six for the open. This greater similarity between closed prisons might have been expected, in view of the fact that they are necessarily run so much 'by the book'. Open prisons, one would think, would be freed from some of these limitations. However, the short-term open, from its very nature, cannot be so very different. Its prisoners are there too short a time for the staff to get to know them or for the men to settle down. An active training programme would be felt to be impossible with such a transient population, most of the time being taken up in any case with the routine chores of checking men in and out. The effect of all this was bound to be exacerbated in the case of our short-term open by its part use as an overflow local prison, increasing inmate mobility even more. Hence the anomalous CIES scores of the short-term open. Thus, with the tolerance of long-termers at one end and the situational restrictions of the short-term open at the other end, one can readily also understand how the familiar gradient has emerged.

It is now possible to attempt an explanation of the very different character of the regime in the long-term open, for it is both an open prison and at the long-term end of our gradient. The limited significance of 'openness' in itself, however, has already been demonstrated, and both observational evidence and data from the diary and the staff questionnaires together with that just reviewed suggest that the long-term open is a rather different kind of open prison from the rest. In particular the Governor seems to have had a clearer conception of what constitutes an open prison, and to have been able to communicate it to both prisoners and staff. (An important advantage in achieving this which could not be available to all open prison governors was his right, unique within the prison system, to select his own prisoner intake, but this was only an aid to the implementation of his policy. The policy had to exist first.) In the staff questionnaire this is shown by the fact that so few staff felt that they suffered from 'conflicting instructions'—as they might well do in the formally unstructured situation of an open prison if the Governor was not himself clear about his objectives. The corresponding CIES subscale is that of Clarity, and here also the long-term open inmate scores are significantly higher than those of any of the other prisons. Although Clarity has a length-of-sentence gradient upwards among the open prisons, this is clearly not the only factor, as is shown by the low score in the long-term closed (which ought to show a high Clarity score if the length-of-sentence factor was the only determinant) and indeed the absence of any definite closed prison gradient. Apparently the closed prison regime is always 'clear' enough. Staff differences are not significant, but follow broadly the same trend.

So the riddle of the long-term open prison begins to solve itself. Because it is a long-term institution it is more tolerant, and because it has a definite 'open' character, it can give expression to the positive values usually seen as associated with 'openness' in a way which cannot happen in an institution in which being an open prison has no definite meaning except the lack of certain formal restraints. (As suggested in our observational account of the prison, its spacious physical characteristics must also have helped in producing a relaxed atmosphere.)

Not that the Clarity scores are thus fully explained. Why do all the open prisons score higher (though not always significantly so) than the closed institutions on this subscale, if 'openness' does produce the anomaly and confusion suggested? But this matter must be taken up again when the data from the questionnaire can also be brought to bear on the question.

In the course of the discussion about the anomalous position of the short-term open, reference was made to the greater similarity between themselves, of the closed prisons as compared with the open. The main reason for this is almost certainly that already given: that closed prisons, being more hedged about by rules (and by correspondingly restrictive architectural features), have less scope for variation, especially in the absence of any clear consensus by the Home Office or the governors as to what constitutes an open prison. However, there may also be other, contributing factors. Thus the selection process for open prisons is likely to ensure that their inmates are demographically different from their closed counterparts, and indeed open prison populations are not only more varied but also show some consistent overall differences from those in closed prisons (Tables 2.2 and 2.3). Open prisoners were older and had fewer previous convictions. The last point is likely to be particularly relevant, in view of the well-known tendency of old lags to know the rules and adhere rigidly to them. As further evidence of the relevance of inmate characteristics, it is worth noting that these differences were most marked in the case of the population of the long-term open, which we have described as the most 'open' of the open prisons.

The greater variation in open regimes may also partly reflect a similar greater variation in staff attitudes and behaviour. There is some evidence for this view in the results of the staff questionnaire and diary, though the absence of systematic differences in the kinds of staff recruited to the different prisons (see p. 210) suggests that such variations as we have found have emerged as reactions to service in the open prisons, i.e. have developed as part of the regime-forming process, rather than having been brought in on recruitment as initial attitudes. Again, staff attitudes and ways of deploying staff were most different in the long-term, although there were many more similarities than differences in the four prisons compared.

Between-prison comparisons: multivariate analysis

Finally we have to embark on a discriminant analysis designed to ascertain which subscales account for most of the range of differences (the variance) between prisons, found in the data. The method adopted is one which favours the big battalions. Beginning with the subscales which are the largest contributors to the variance, we shall move downwards until virtually all the variance has been accounted for. This means that parts of the variance which significantly overlap between different subscales will be appropriated to the largest scale and thus be lost to the smaller scales which arrive later in the analysis. This should not matter, as it leads to an explanation of the variance based on the fewest number of entirely discrete scales—and parsimony is always a desirable scientific objective.

Table 5.6 summarises the results of this analysis up to the point at which the total variance was accounted for (see final column). It will be seen that differences in scores on the subscale assessing Staff control accounted for 70 per cent of the total variance between inmate samples, and scores on the Involvement subscale accounted for a further 20 per cent. The first two canonical variables between them, therefore, accounted for 90 per cent of the total variance. As for the staff analysis, the subscale measuring Autonomy accounted for 83 per cent of the total variance between the four staff groups,

Table 5.6   Moos CIES: discriminant function analyses for six inmate samples and four staff samples—summary tables

Step number	Variable	F values	U-statistic	Cumulative proportion of total dispersion
		Inmate samples		
1	Staff control	58·655	0·640	0·700
2	Involvement	28·267	0·504	0·895
3	Order and organisation	13·427	0·446	0·964
4	Autonomy	11·625	0·401	0·994
5	Practical orientation	11·473	0·361	1·000
		Staff samples		
1	Autonomy	47·588	0·457	0·828
2	Practical orientation	7·158	0·387	0·965
3	Staff control	6·033	0·335	1·000

and that assessing Practical orientation accounted for a further 14 per cent. In all then the first two canonical variables in the staff analysis counted for 97 per cent of the total variance between the constituent groups. It may be concluded, therefore, that the major source of discrepancies between inmate perceptions of regime is attributable to perceived differences in the degree of staff control in their respective prisons. The major source of discrepancies in staff perceptions of regime results from perceived differences in the degree of Autonomy allowed to inmates in their everyday behaviour. These may be seen as different ways of looking at the same facts: to the prisoners it is Staff control that is most obtrusive while to staff it is inmate Autonomy. One could not hope for a better demonstration of the phenomenologist's claim that much depends on the point of vantage from which people observe the social situation. This connection between the scales which predominate respectively in inmate and staff results tends to be borne out by a statistical exploration of their interrelationships. There is probably a more definite relationship between Staff control and Autonomy than between any other subscales in the test. In both inmate and staff data the highest negative correlation occurred between these two subscales. Moreover, in both cases the correlation was statistically significant (inmates $r = -0.31$, d.f. $= 527$, $p < 0.01$; staff $r = -0.20$, d.f. $= 127$, $p < 0.05$). Given this, albeit imperfect, negative relationship between these subscales, it is only right to expect that some of the variance accounted for by the one would also be accounted for by the other. Thus, as an inspection of Tables 5.1 and 5.2 shows, both subscales were among those producing the highest F ratios in the one-way analyses of variance conducted for each set of subscale scores in both staff and inmate data. It may be concluded then that there are grounds for accepting that Staff control and Autonomy are assessing similar aspects and that there is much more complementarity, or 'similarity in opposition', between staff and inmate perceptions of regimes than might seem at first sight to be the case. In other words, as indicated above, inmates tend to see all the manifestations of Staff control, and staff all the evidence for prisoner Autonomy.

The main purpose in utilising multivariate statistical techniques in this second stage of CIES data analysis, however, was to produce an assessment of the 'separateness' of each regime. It does this in two complementary ways. It will be recalled from our earlier discussion of discriminant analysis that standardised scores are calculated for those canonical variables which account in turn for the largest proportion of the total variance between those groups included in the analysis. Figure 3 presents diagrammatically the results of this analysis for the six sets of inmate data.

It will be seen that the long-term open is widely separated from the others by the low score for Staff control, but that the long-term closed is also fairly clearly distinguished by the factor of Involvement. This seems to be in conformity with the length-of-sentence hypothesis, as does the rather more favourable position of the long-term, as compared with other closed prisons, with regard to Staff control. The similarity between the short-term open and the closed prison in the factor of Staff control also emerges clearly.

It will be recalled that in the analysis of dispersion which was to be built on to the discriminant analysis, each individual staff or inmate set of CIES scores would be compared with those in its group of origin as well as with those in each of the other four staff or six inmate groups included in the analysis. After this comparison, it would then be allocated to that group, regardless of its group of origin, which its responses to CIES questions most closely resembled. In this way it is possible to determine the degree to which perceptions of regimes overlapped. The results of analyses of dispersion con-

Prison	First canonical variable (Staff control)	Second canonical variable (Involvement)
(A) Long-term closed	− 0.20	1.05
(B) Medium-term closed	− 0.61	0.52
(C) Short-term closed	− 0.90	− 0.11
(D) Short-term open	− 0.44	− 0.73
(E) Medium-term open	0.07	− 0.47
(F) Long-term open	2.54	0.04

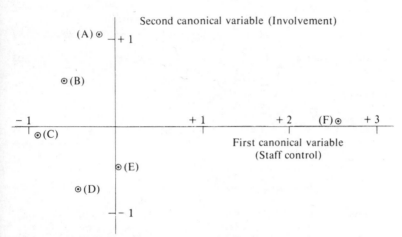

Figure 3 Moos CIES (inmate samples): group means on the first and second canonical variables, discriminant function analysis.

ducted separately on inmate and staff data are presented in Table 5.7.

The results for inmates show some degree of overlap between prisons although overlap obviously varies from one paired comparison to another. In fact only in the case of the long-term open prison were a majority of the prisoners classified as having perceptions of regime which were most characteristic of the prison in which they were held. There was less overlap in the case of the staff.

Overlap in inmate perceptions in the long-term open (as we have come by this time to expect) is so small as to be almost non-existent. At the other extreme the highest degree of overlap is found in the two short-term prisons, a large part being overlap between themselves, underlying once again the similar identity of short-term institutions, whether open or closed. The essentially 'closed' nature

Table 5.7   Moos CIES: results of analyses of dispersion

	Number of respondents classified as belonging to each group Inmate samples						
	Prison of origin						
Classified as	Long-term closed	Medium-term closed	Short-term closed	Short-term open	Medium-term open	Long-term open	*N*
Long-term closed	41	17	7	3	4	4	76
Medium-term closed	17	34	12	10	6	0	79
Short-term closed	13	19	43	16	15	1	107
Short-term open	4	12	21	38	12	2	89
Medium-term open	10	9	14	18	45	6	102
Long-term open	3	1	1	2	9	59	75

	Number of respondents classified as belonging to each group Staff samples				
	Prison of origin				
Classified as	Medium-term closed	Short-term open	Medium-term open	Long-term open	*N*
Medium-term closed	25	4	4	0	33
Short-term open	1	13	2	2	18
Medium-term open	2	6	26	8	42
Long-term open	0	1	4	26	31

of this identity is shown by the fact that the short-term open does share more overlap with the closed than with the other open prisons in our sample.

There is clearly more overlap overall between the closed prisons than between the opens, confirming the earlier conclusion of greater variation among the opens.

Finally there is the bearing of this material on the length-of-sentence hypothesis. This seems to be confirmed for the open prison by the gradient in degree of separateness from the closed institutions. The percentages of total respondents represented by those crossing the open-closed frontier are as follows: long-term closed: 19·3; long-term open: 6·9; medium-term closed: 23·9; medium-term open: 27·5; short-term closed: 36·7; short-term open: 33·3.

The hypothesis would imply a diminishing degree of 'overlap with closed' on the part of opens, as sentence length is increased. This is indicated by the data. However the hypothesis seems to be refuted by the closed prison data. It would require an increasing degree of 'overlap with opens' with increase in length of sentence, and this is the reverse of the situation shown above. However, the gradient in the closed prisons does seem to be obscured by the anomalous position of the short-term open, attracting overlap from the short-term closed, and to a lesser extent the medium-term closed institutions.

However, even if the short-term open is removed from the analysis, the gradient is not restored among the closed prisons. What of course we have here is only a crude representation of the gradient. The results are affected not only by differences according to length of sentence, but also by the high level of overlap between open and closed prisons anyway.

Perhaps this is the most significant deduction from the table: the support it gives to our earlier conclusion that open and closed prisons are not markedly distinguished from each other (see percentages above). So far as conclusions can be drawn from the restricted data from the staff, they tend to support all of the above inferences, though on the basis of less overlap than for prisoners. The exception is the long-term open, and as we have seen, the main reason for this seems to have been the lack of any agreed concept of the open prison, leading (except in the long-term open) to a policy vacuum filled variously and ambivalently by on the one hand ideas about Involvement, and on the other ideas springing from an overriding prison staff culture about Order and organisation.

Summary of between-prison differences

The analysis so far completed permits the following conclusions to be drawn.

(*a*) There are fewer differences between staff perceptions of regimes than between those of prisoners, raising the possibility of an even more powerful prison staff culture than the more widely discussed inmate culture. This staff agreement is particularly marked on the 'system maintenance' variables of Order and organisation, and Clarity.

(b) Perceptions of open and closed regimes as such are not markedly different, but differ for staff in respect of Autonomy; and for inmates in respect of Involvement, and Order and organisation. The prominence of the latter subscales among the responses of inmates of open prisons suggests an ambivalence about 'openness' in these institutions which is supported by other kinds of data. The emphasis given to Autonomy by the staff (but not the prisoners) indicates that they at least have absorbed something of the ideology if not the practice of open prisons.

(c) There is also greater variation between the perceptions of different open regimes than there is between those of the closed.

(d) There is an underlying pattern in the perceptions of regimes: what has been described as the 'length-of-sentence gradient'. This is to the effect that in both open and closed regimes (though less markedly in the latter because of (c) above), training-oriented variables increase, and discipline-oriented variables decrease with an increase in the length of sentence. As a result the short-term open bears a striking resemblance in a number of respects to the closed prisons. The exception to this gradient, possibly for reasons of physical structure, is the medium-term open.

(e) The long-term open prison is distinct from all other regimes, and this may be partly a result of its long-term character ((d) above), but also because it seems to have evolved identity as an open prison.

Comparisons of staff and inmate perceptions

One of the aims of penal administrators in the establishment of open regimes was (as we have seen) to create a social situation in which the traditional barriers between staff and prisoners might be reduced. It was argued that the raising of some of the restrictions on movement and communication within the prison would create a more mutually accepting climate, and opportunities for greater staff-inmate interaction, with the outcome of a more general acceptance of the formal goals of the prison within the inmate community. In other words, greater staff-inmate interaction would weaken the inmate contra-culture and allow some inmates to share law-abiding staff values, thus coming to share, also, presumed staff attitudes towards treatment or training. If this ambition were achieved in British open prisons, it ought to be manifested in a greater measurable overlap between staff and inmate perceptions in open prison situations than in closed situations. In what follows we shall explore by means of our CIES data both the extent to which staff and inmates have similar perceptions of their prison regimes and also the source of such divergencies as exist. Table 5.8 gives the results of a subscale-by-subscale statistical comparison (using *t*-tests) of staff-inmate differences in each of the four prisons where representative sampling enabled such comparisons to be undertaken. These differences will be further analysed in what follows. Meanwhile, examination of the raw score staff data reveals what appear to be systematic differences between higher and lower grade uniformed staff, the latter's perceptions being closer to those of inmates. Consequently, three groups have been compared in the following pages: higher grade uniformed staff (i.e. senior, principal and chief officers), basic grade staff and inmates.

The statistical procedures to be followed are similar to those adopted in the multivariate analysis of *between*-prison differences. Data from the two staff groups and the inmate group from each prison were subjected to a step-wise discriminant function analysis, followed by an analysis of dispersion. The discriminant analysis was expected to reveal the subscales which were principally responsible for the discrepancies between staff and inmate perceptions of each regime. In other words, it would show the main sources of *within* prison differences at each of the four prisons included in the analysis (the three open prisons and the medium-term closed prison). The analysis of dispersion was expected to show the degree of overlap between staff and inmate perception and would, therefore, give some assessment of the degree to which staff and inmates in each prison shared similar perceptions of regime. Moreover, comparison of the degree of overlap in perceptions in each prison would provide a further stage in the study undertaken above of between-prison differences.

First of all, one-way analyses of variance were computed for the two grades of staff and for inmates on each CIES subscale. The results, showing where differences are statistically significant, together with the mean raw scores for each group, are given in Table 5.9. Comparative profiles of each group's scores at each prison have been drawn from these data and are presented in Figures 4-7. Inspection of Table 5.9 and these profiles give some indication of the broad distribution of scores between the constituent groups at each

Table 5.8 *Moos CIES t-test analysis of staff-inmate differences*

		Prison							
		Medium-term closed		Short-term open		Medium-term open		Long-term open	
Subscale		Staff	Inmate	Staff	Inmate	Staff	Inmate	Staff	Inmate
	N	33	79	18	89	42	102	31	75
Involvement	Mean score	3.2	2.4	4.2	3.8	5.9	4.5	6.6	6.1
	t	2.42		0.60		3.38		1.18	
	p	0.05		N.S.		0.001		N.S.	
Support	Mean score	4.8	2.1	4.9	2.6	7.0	3.0	7.7	4.5
	t	7.12		5.46		11.09		7.47	
	p	0.01		0.001		0.001		0.001	
Expressiveness	Mean score	4.0	2.8	3.0	2.3	4.0	2.4	4.8	2.8
	t	3.27		1.70		5.62		6.52	
	p	0.01		N.S.		0.001		0.001	
Autonomy	Mean score	2.8	1.6	4.7	1.9	5.4	2.2	7.3	4.9
	t	3.97		7.48		11.77		5.86	
	p	0.001		0.001		0.001		0.001	
Practical orientation	Mean score	6.0	3.2	4.5	3.3	7.5	4.5	7.0	4.3
	t	6.12		2.56		8.02		4.83	
	p	0.001		0.05		0.001		0.001	
Personal problem orientation	Mean score	5.1	2.4	3.7	2.6	5.2	3.2	5.5	3.3
	t	8.66		2.83		5.96		5.96	
	p	0.001		0.01		0.001		0.001	
Order and organisation	Mean score	6.6	2.4	7.2	4.3	6.3	4.2	6.7	4.2
	t	10.60		5.33		5.32		2.95	
	p	0.001		0.001		0.001		0.01	
Clarity	Mean score	5.5	2.1	5.8	2.6	6.2	3.8	6.4	4.5
	t	10.14		7.21		6.88		4.45	
	p	0.001		0.001		0.001		0.001	
Staff control	Mean score	6.6	6.9	6.7	7.6	5.5	7.0	4.2	4.3
	t	1.20		3.47		6.58		0.49	

Table 5.9   Moos CIES mean subscale scores and one-way analysis of variance results for staff subgroups and inmate groups in each prison

Subscale	Uniformed staff— Senior officer and above	Uniformed staff— Basic grade	Inmates	All groups combined	F ratio
			Medium-term closed		
Involvement	3·6	3·1	2·4	2·7	3·369*
Support	5·7	4·4	2·1	2·9	28·449**
Expressiveness	4·3	3·9	2·8	3·2	5·691**
Autonomy	2·8	2·8	1·6	1·9	7·921**
Practical orientation	7·1	5·5	3·2	4·0	21·428**
Personal problem orientation	5·3	5·0	2·4	3·2	39·807**
Order and organisation	7·2	6·3	2·4	3·7	58·070**
Clarity	6·1	5·2	2·1	3·1	50·779**
Staff control	6·9	6·5	6·9	6·8	1·035

*Significant at 0·05 level.
**Significant at 0·01 level.

Degrees of freedom
Between   2
Within   109
Total   111

			Medium-term open		
Involvement	6·2	5·8	4·5	4·9	5·837**
Support	7·8	6·7	3·0	4·1	64·492**
Expressiveness	4·1	4·0	2·4	2·9	15·779**
Autonomy	5·7	5·3	2·2	3·1	70·317**
Practical orientation	8·1	7·3	4·5	5·4	33·576**
Personal problem orientation	4·5	5·4	3·2	3·8	19·069**
Order and organisation	7·3	5·9	4·2	4·8	16·160**
Clarity	7·0	5·9	3·8	4·5	33·504**
Staff control	6·7	5·1	7·0	6·6	24·377**

*Significant at 0·05 level.
**Significant at 0·01 level.

Degrees of freedom
Between   2
Within   141
Total   143

Table 5.9 continued

Subscale	Uniformed staff— Senior officer and above	Uniformed staff— Basic grade	Inmates	All groups combined	*F* ratio
			Group		
			Long-term open		
Involvement	7·8	6·1	6·1	6·2	2·269
Support	9·3	7·2	4·5	5·4	32·096**
Expressiveness	5·9	4·4	2·8	3·3	24·251**
Autonomy	7·5	7·2	4·9	5·6	16·614**
Practical orientation	8·8	6·2	4·3	5·1	14·523**
Personal problem orientation	6·3	5·2	3·3	3·9	17·870**
Order and organisation	6·3	5·4	4·2	4·6	4·122*
Clarity	7·6	5·8	4·5	5·0	14·435**
Staff control	4·8	4·0	4·3	4·3	0·493

*Significant at 0·05 level.
**Significant at 0·01 level.

Degrees of freedom
Between　2
Within　103
Total　105

Subscale	All staff	Inmates	All groups combined	*F* ratio
	Short-term open (Both staff groups combined)			
Involvement	4·2	3·8	3·9	0·362
Support	4·9	2·6	3·0	29·739**
Expressiveness	3·0	2·3	2·4	3·591
Autonomy	4·7	1·9	2·4	56·840**
Practical orientation	4·5	3·3	3·5	6·730*
Personal problem orientation	3·7	2·6	2·8	8·240**
Order and organisation	7·2	4·3	4·8	28·869**
Clarity	5·8	2·6	3·2	53·031**
Staff control	6·7	7·6	7·5	12·372**

*Significant at 0·05 level.
**Significant at 0·01 level.

Degrees of freedom
Between　1
Within　105
Total　106

prison. In particular, it should be noted that, except for the scores on the subscale assessing Staff control, inmate profiles show a lower assessment than both staff profiles in every case. In addition, in the three prisons where further comparison between higher and lower grade staff groups has been carried out (staff scores from the short-term open prison were combined because of the small

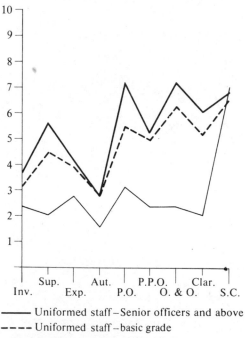

Uniformed staff – Senior officers and above
Uniformed staff – basic grade
Inmates

Figure 4 Moos CIES staff and inmate mean score profiles—medium-term closed prison. (The data from which these profiles have been drawn are presented in Table 5.9. 'S.C.' was not statistically significant.)

numbers involved), the latter's assessments are always lower than those of higher grade staff, with the solitary exception of Personal problem orientation at the medium-term open prison. Higher grade staff perceptions of each regime, therefore, are generally the more different from inmate perceptions.

There can be no gainsaying the importance of higher grade officers (particularly wing-officers) in shaping the climate within which prisoners (and lower grade officers) have to live. We were made aware of this fact continually in the course of our observational work in these prisons. Examples are given in the chapters dealing with this aspect of our research. Any attempt to narrow the gap between staff and inmates must fail, therefore, unless it takes account of this fact, by directing special efforts towards senior

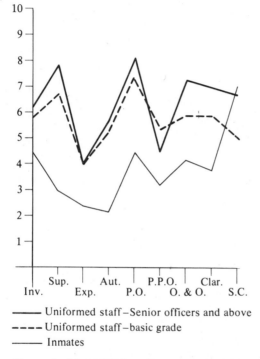

——— Uniformed staff–Senior officers and above
– – – – Uniformed staff–basic grade
——— Inmates

Figure 5 Moos CIES staff and inmate mean score profiles—medium-term open prison. (The data from which these profiles have been drawn are presented in Table 5.9. 'S.C.' was not statistically significant.)

officers and above. A first step must be to determine whether their attitudes are a result of the kinds of people they are (the result of a particular kind of promotion procedure), the experience of long years of socialisation within the prison staff culture referred to earlier, or a consequence of the situational pressures to which their jobs cause them to be subjected in the prison.

Although some of the F ratios in Table 5.9 fall below the

minimum level for statistical significance, those which are significant give some hints at the major sources of discrepancy between the staff groups and inmate groups within each prison. However, their patterns are somewhat complex and in order to clarify them the *F* ratios for each subscale in each prison were ranked according to size, and a mean calculated from these for all prisons in respect of each subscale. The result is presented in Table 5.10. If rank

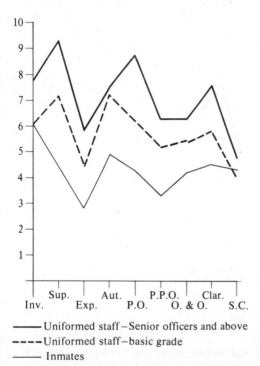

———— Uniformed staff—Senior officers and above
– – – – Uniformed staff—basic grade
———— Inmates

Figure 6   Moos CIES staff and inmate mean score profiles—long-term open prison. (The data from which these profiles have been drawn are presented in Table 5.9. 'Inv.' and 'S.C.' were not statistically significant.)

differences were random, the average rank of each subscale would be approximately 5·0, viz. the average rank for the nine subscales. Inspection of Table 5.10 reveals wide divergences from this average. The major sources of discrepancy between staff and inmate perceptions of regime are now seen to be Support, Autonomy, Clarity and Personal problem orientation, staff in all cases having the higher scores. With the single exception of Clarity, these categories belong to what might be called the 'liberal' or 'progressive' group of subscales. Clearly staff see their prisons as more progressive than do prisoners—and senior staff (as we have seen) even more so. And although Clarity is of course a 'system maintenance' factor, it has a crucial role in the development of any particular kind of regime.

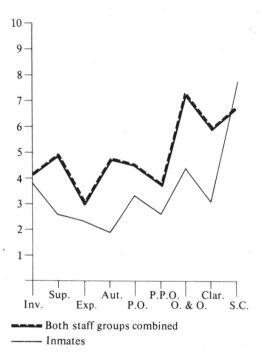

Figure 7 Moos CIES staff and inmate mean score profiles—short-term open prison. (The data from which these profiles have been drawn are presented in Table 5.9. 'Inv.' and 'S.C.' were not statistically significant.)

Reducing perceptual differences in prisons represents a formidable problem, not lessened by the effect in retarding change which the apparently divergent staff and inmate cultures are bound to have.

The results for the long-term open, as possibly the jumping-off point for newer, more 'open' regimes, justify a further word. The higher Clarity scores found earlier for inmates of this prison are seen now to be accompanied, exceptionally, by a better-than-average

Table 5.10   Moos CIES average rank of F ratios on each subscale

Subscale	Medium-term closed	Short-term open	Prison Medium-term open	Long-term open	Mean rank
Support	4	3	2	1	2·5
Autonomy	6	1	1	4	3·0
Clarity	2	2	4	6	3·5
Personal problem orientation	3	6	6	3	4·5
Order and organisation	1	4	7	7	4·8
Practical orientation	5	7	3	3	5·0
Expressiveness	7	8	8	2	6·3
Staff control	9	5	5	9	7·0
Involvement	8	9	9	8	8·5

degree of concurrence on Clarity by the prison's inmates and staff, confirming this Governor's unique success in communicating his conception of the open prison to them all.

The preceding pages have focused on the sources of staff-inmate or senior staff-junior staff dissensus as shown in the scores on the particular CIES subscales. But how much overall dissensus is there? This was studied by means of an analysis of dispersion. Table 5.11 gives the results of this, showing the numbers of discrete or overlapping perceptions as between senior staff, basic grade staff, and inmates, for each prison.

Table 5.11 shows that overall there is comparatively little overlap between the constituent groups in each prison. Extremely few staff respondents, whether higher or lower grade, in any prison produced perceptions which were classified as inmate-like, and there was not much more overlap between the higher and lower grade uniformed staff groups. This latter fact is remarkable and underlines the point already made about the necessity for doing something about it in any attempt at further penal reform. What we have is a three-dimensional disagreement, and not merely (as usually seems to be assumed) between officers and prisoners. There were, however, differences in the proportion of inmates whose perceptions of regime were classified as staff-like at each prison. For the most part, then,

Table 5.11   Moos CIES analysis of dispersion results for the staff subgroups and inmate group in each prison

| | Medium-term closed | | | | Short-term open | |
	a′	b′	c′		a′+b′	c′
a	6	3	0	a+b	15	3
b	7 .	15	2	c	6	83
c	2	7	70			

| | Medium-term open | | | | Long-term open | | |
	a′	b′	c′		a′	b′	c′
a	8	2	1	a	7	2	0
b	6	23	2	b	4	16	2
c	6	9	87	c	1	13	61

Key
a   Uniformed staff—senior officer and above
b   Uniformed staff—basic grade
c   Inmates
a′   Perceptions of regime classified as being characteristic of senior officers and above
b′   Perceptions of regime classified as being characteristic of basic grade staff
c′   Perceptions of regime classified as being characteristic of inmates

these results may be taken as confirmation of that image of the social organisation of the prison provided in the sociological accounts of, for instance, Sykes[3], the Morrises[4] and Howard Jones[5] in which staff and inmate societies are viewed as largely separate with very little informal contact and sharing of attitudes, values and perceptions. However, while the overall level of overlap between staff and inmate perceptions of regime is uniformly low, such differences as do exist ought not to be overlooked. The percentage of inmates in each prison whose perceptions were classified as staff-like (i.e. like either basic grade or higher grade uniformed staff) is reported in Table 5.12.

The greatest degree of overlap between inmate and staff perceptions (19 per cent) occurred at the long-term open camp, the next greatest (15 per cent) at the medium-term open prison. Such overlap was least (7 per cent) at the short-term open prison and only slightly more (11 per cent) at the medium-term closed prison, the long-term open regime being most different from the closed prison. All of which shows that the length of sentence pattern elicited in our earlier analyses holds also when tested by the degree of consensus found between staff and prisoners. One might almost see the present

Table 5.12   Moos CIES: the percentage of inmates in each prison whose perceptions of regime were classified as 'staff-like'

Prison	Medium-term closed	Short-term open	Medium-term open	Long-term open
Percentage of 'staff-like' inmate respondents	11	7	15	19

results as evidence of the effect which the different regime characteristics discovered ealier have in shaping inmate and staff attitudes. There does in fact seem to be some evidence in the long-term open (the most 'open' of our prisons) of progress towards that staff-inmate consensus which we saw at the beginning of this section as likely to result from the freer communication of the open regime. It is important not to exaggerate. Even in this prison, only 1 in 5 inmates produced perceptions of regime which were classified as staff-like, offering only very limited support to our view. Our contention that open prisons, being part of a containment system, operate within a hostile ideological and institutional environment, may account for some of the problems of our long-term open, and thus for even its very modest achievements in producing the greater sharing of attitudes, values and perceptions between staff and inmates. This point will be taken up again in the final chapter of this book.

There is in any case a qualification to these results in our inability to exercise control over such sources of variation as the composition of inmate populations. An approach to achieving this is reported in Appendix 5.

Summary of staff-inmate differences

(a) In all cases except, significantly enough, Staff control, staff give higher scores on CIES subscales than prisoners, higher grade staff giving responses which are even more different from those of inmates than basic grade staff. The main areas of staff-inmate disagreement are (in descending order): Support, Autonomy, Clarity and Personal problem orientation. These might all be regarded as training or treatment-relevant variables; staff see their prisons as more progressive than do inmates. These results indicate the kind of cognitive gulf which penal reform measures have to bridge, especially between inmates and the powerful higher grade staff.

(*b*) The Clarity scores for the long-term open prison represent an exception to the above pattern in displaying a higher-than-average degree of consensus between staff and inmates. This supports the view expressed earlier that the Governor of this prison does seem to have been able to communicate his clear conception of an open prison to both officers and prisoners.

(*c*) An analysis of dispersion shows that there is very little overlap in the overall perceptions of CIES regime characteristics between inmates, basic grade officers and higher grade staff. Two points here are worthy of special note. The first is a confirmation of the clear demarcation of senior grade staff from their more junior colleagues, already noted above; and the greater overlap of staff and inmate attitudes displayed in the long-term open prison. But even here overlap was limited, showing the strength of containment pressures.

6   Studying prison staffs

Prison officers frequently express regret that prison studies and the mass media fail to provide any detailed, sympathetic consideration of their work, the problems and frustrations which it engenders, and their point of view. The tendency to concentrate upon inmate problems provides some justification for their feelings. Not, however, that the staff side has been completely overlooked. For instance, there are the sociological analyses of organisational constraints on staff behaviour and their effect on staff-inmate relationships provided, among others, by Goffman[1] and Sykes[2]; the contributions from social scientists and prison staff alike to the rapidly accumulating literature on the problems confronting prison personnel as a result of proposed changes of some penal institutions from predominantly custodial to training or therapeutic objectives[3]; the studies which have provided information about the personal and social characteristics of prison officers and their work;[4] the autobiographical contributions of prison officers themselves;[5] and the publicisation of aspects of their work by the Prison Officers' Association. Clearly the neglect of the staff side of the story has been relative rather than absolute. Nevertheless, there has been an imbalance, which this section of our report is intended to remedy.

The feelings of neglect expressed by prison officers seem to arise out of three main causes. First, research is directed towards the problems of prison inmates and is undertaken, for the most part, without involving the staff. Second, the prison officer does not have sufficient access to the results of researches implicating him. For instance, most British prison officers seem to be unaware of the results of the sociological studies of the problems of staff referred to above. The results of academic research in penal institutions tend to be published in journals and books which are not generally available; research undertaken by the Home Office tends as a rule to be regarded by them as providing information for management, and is therefore not usually communicated to prison personnel below the rank of Governor. The one valuable exception is material published in the pages of the *Prison Service Journal*. Third, the results of research often tend to be worded (not always of necessity) in a way which seems critical of the officer and his work. Prison staff still 'remember' *Pentonville*; while some prison staff who have read the study regard the Morrises' strictures on prison officers as fair and the discussion impartial, an overwhelming majority, most of whom are familiar with the book only by reputation, have become hostile not only to that study but to research more generally. It has been the writers' experience that, even after ten years, the reverberations of *Pentonville* were still greatly in evidence, reflected in a sensitivity of prison staff to criticism of any kind. Other subsequent studies have tended to confirm them in their view of researchers as 'anti-prison officer'. Such sensitivity may have been encouraged also by the insular 'prison world' within which many officers and their families live their lives, and also by the relative non-involvement of officers in prison management or penal research. On the well-established principle that negative examples are always noticed first, officers have thus become most familiar with studies in which their work has been criticised, making them feel both resentful of researchers and generally hostile and non-co-operative towards research. Our own low staff response rates show the adverse influence exerted on research by these attitudes.

In his reflections on the prison research activities of sociologists, Thomas Mathiesen,[6] the author of a number of Scandinavian prison studies, offers reasons for the relative neglect of the staff perspective. In particular, he draws attention to the tendency of sociologists to concentrate on the informal rather than the formal aspects of the social structure of prisons, the major focus of such research being the informal inmate social system. While it is evident that this social system exists and exerts influence on prison inmates, it does not, Mathiesen argues, exist in isolation. It probably owes part of its origin to the major structural cleavage[7] in the prison between staff and inmate groups leading to a need for inmates to mitigate the 'pains of imprisonment'.[8] If these wider origins of the inmate culture are thus overlooked, the staff role is bound to be neglected. Mathiesen also pointed out that, in the main, sociologists have been interested in the similarities between prisons rather than in differences between them. This is probably one of the consequences of their excessive preoccupation with generalisation—with models of prisons seeking their common characteristics, in a situation where relevant differences, largely concerned with the activities of the staff, nevertheless do exist.

Another consequence of this over-generalising tendency in sociological prison studies is that they have been conducted mainly in maximum security or custodially oriented institutions, because these are seen as representing the essence of what a prison really is. The relatively few studies undertaken in treatment, training or therapeutically oriented prisons[9] are bound to raise doubts about the image of the social organisation of prison which has been usually presented, including ideas about the origin and maintenance of the inmate culture, staff-inmate interaction and communication, the effects of imprisonment and the relationship between the prison and society.[10] This kind of criticism of current researches has had less impact than it deserves, particularly among those whose interest is in practical penological rather than theoretical issues and who might therefore be expected to have some stake in having research carried out at a rather lower level of abstraction.

In the debate about the relative importance of treatment and custody as organisational objectives,[11] it is generally held that, for a change from the custodial emphasis in prison management to be effective, a considerable alteration in the traditional organisational character of such institutions is required. For instance, it has been contended that they could not become more reformative or rehabilitative until there had been fundamental changes in the patterns of staff-inmate communication, authority relationships and social interaction, away from those assumed to be characteristic of the traditional custodial prison. More specifically, increased reformative or rehabilitative effectiveness can perhaps follow only from a reduction in the staff-inmate divide found in closed, custodially oriented prisons, with the consequent opening up of better channels for communication between prisoners and staff. This might at least improve mutual understanding, though it could do more: open up channels for the exercise of rehabilitative influence by the staff, as well as creating opportunities for greater inmate autonomy and self-discipline.

The extent to which the open prison (or indeed any other departure from traditional custodial styles in prison management) is successful, may also prove to be dependent upon the extent to which both staff and inmate behaviour has been adapted to meet the new organisational requirements. The conception of open prisons demands not only an increase in staff-inmate interaction and the development of different styles of interpersonal relations but also, from the staff perspective, considerable changes in their pattern of work and in the allocation of priority to different tasks. An evaluation of the open prison system, therefore, clearly requires a more detailed consideration of staff work, attitudes and behaviour in both open and closed settings than has usually been the case.

In this project it was considered essential to obtain as wide a range as possible of information about prison officers' duties, social characteristics and attitudes. Three principal methods were used for the collection of such data. First, day-to-day staff and inmate behaviour in each prison was observed and recorded over a period. Second, two research instruments, a prison officer's questionnaire and a prison officer's diary, were developed and administered to all uniformed members of staff in each prison. These research instruments are discussed in later sections.

The prison officer's questionnaire

As indicated, a thorough evaluation of the open prison system requires more than, for example, a comparison of the recidivism rates for similar categories of offender discharged from closed and open institutions. Where such an approach has been adopted[12] the results, for reasons such as the difficulty of obtaining matched groups, have been inconclusive. In any case, it seemed always to be assumed that the establishment of open prisons in the physical sense would in itself lead to the development of a new kind of regime of a more rehabilitative kind. That this cannot be taken for granted is clearly apparent from the CIES results already presented. So a comparison based simply on the fact of openness or not is bound to be insufficiently informative, unless supplemented by a study of regimes as such. The Moos CIES[13] we have seen to provide one approach to this, but there are others. Thus it seemed essential to supplement the data derived from the Moos by data of a more direct kind. An important example is information on differences between prisons in officers' work routines and attitudes towards work.

While the relevance of much of the information collected by means of the questionnaire and the diary (for instance attitudes towards work) will be evident from the preceding discussion, it is perhaps necessary to clarify the reasons for collecting data which is less obviously relevant. In later sections it will be shown that prison officers differ with regard to biographical and social characteristics and their previous service experience. Such factors as these may influence the way they perceive and perform their work; it is possible that any variation between prisons in work and attitudes to work may simply reflect the existence of different types of officer in them. Biographical and career information was obtained in order to provide some check on this possibility.

There was another reason for collecting this information. Prison officers' work and attitudes to work, in whatever institution they serve, are only going to be fully understood if seen in the broader context of a sociological analysis of their occupation. Sociological investigations of the Prison Service as an occupation have been very infrequently undertaken: the most recent appeared as long ago as 1963.[14] It was therefore decided to collect up-to-date information within the framework of this research. For instance, earlier studies have suggested the existence of a strong correlation between the choice of a Prison Service career and a background in military service. These studies, however, were conducted at a time when, because of the Second World War, persons in many occupational groups would have had an extended military service experience; how far prison officers differed from other occupational groups in this respect is not clear. The present research commenced at a time when, owing to the cessation of national service, there was a generation of entrants to the Prison Service for whom a period in military service was no longer obligatory. The extent to which the correlation between choosing a Prison Service career and a military background still holds is clearly an interesting question, both in relation to our research and for the development of an occupational sociology of the prison officer.

The questionnaire was designed to produce information about five aspects of the life and work of the prison officer.
1. Basic biographical data such as the age, rank and length of service of each respondent.
2. Information about socio-economic background and pre-Prison Service socialisation experience. This included rather obvious facts such as fathers' occupations and details of respondents' educational and occupational histories, as well as some, less obvious, which reflect variables likely to be important in the choice of the Prison Service as a career, such as respondents' military or cadet corps service.
3. Prison career information such as age joined, reasons for joining, the kinds of training received and opinions about training, the kinds of establishments served in, movement between establishments and reasons for movement, promotion and attitudes to promotion.
4. The effect of Prison Service work and domestic and social life on

each other, including variables such as marital status, family size, residential circumstances, leisure activities and associates.

5. A section inviting attitudes and opinions about the job. In this section respondents were asked about changes in the Prison Service in which such aspects as discipline, welfare and the status of officers were considered, the effect of the Mountbatten Inquiry, such problems of the prison officer as pay, hours, overcrowding and communications in prisons, and their attitudes to such issues as the punishment of prison inmates and the use of initiative and discretion in their work. (See Appendix 2 for a copy of the actual questionnaire used.)

The prison officer's diary

This was designed to produce information about the kind of work undertaken in each prison and the proportion of time spent on the performance of the various duties. It was felt initially that the daily staff duty roster in each prison would furnish the required information. However, on investigation, it was found that although the roster provided information about what staff were detailed to do, they were often, if not doing something entirely different, engaged in tasks which were varied enough to make the roster designation a rather vague and uncertain indication. It became apparent, therefore, that to obtain an accurate record of staff activity it was essential to ask officers to record their activities systematically over a period. Only in this way could the amount of time spent on different activities be assessed.

Prior to the start of this project the Home Office had completed the fieldwork stage of an investigation of manpower utilisation in prisons. Hopes that information from this survey, based on 'activity sampling' and the use of a booklet in which officers recorded their activities over a two-week period might, if released to us, have provided the necessary information for this project, were quickly dashed. The survey had not been carried out in open prisons and, in any case, only discipline officers had been involved. The diary used in this project was modelled on the manpower utilisation survey booklets, although categories of activity were condensed or expanded in line with the requirements of the present study. The majority of the staff in the closed prisons in the study had, of course, already completed the Home Office study; preliminary meetings held with them indicated that they were unhappy about the prospect of repeating the operation within the space of twelve to eighteen months. Given these circumstances, it was decided that sufficient accuracy would result from the administration of our diary over a much shorter period of three days. This period was chosen because it was expected that it would maximise co-operation and produce a reasonably accurate portrayal of the range and proportionate distribution of staff activities.

The diary was prefaced by an introduction, instructions for its completion and descriptions of the job categories. The introduction emphasised that the diary was in no way a measure of personal performance or a 'time and motion' study. The importance of accuracy in completion and the confidential handling of results by the research staff were also stressed. Instructions for completion were accompanied, where possible, by examples. Respondents were required to mark off in the diary, whichever of eleven job categories applied to their work during each successive half-hourly period, during the three days. Job categories were 'supervision', 'security', 'staff supervision', 'observation, classification and legal aid', 'court duty', 'rehabilitation', 'staff discussion', 'staff training', 'administration', 'other duties' and 'meal breaks'. (Fuller descriptions of each job category are provided in Appendix 3.) As indicated earlier, these categories do not coincide entirely with those used in the manpower utilisation survey, because our aims were different. We were interested in such questions as the part taken by staff in the rehabilitation of inmates, differences in the emphasis on supervision and security existing in open and closed settings, and differences in the opportunities for staff training and participation. During the pilot stage of the work with the diary it was found that officers spent a not inconsiderable proportion of their time completing various forms, reports and dockets. In order to prevent this activity disappearing into the category 'other duties', it was allocated a separate heading.

Administration of the questionnaire and diary

Copies of the questionnaire and diary were handed individually to all uniformed members of the staff at each prison in the study, along with Moos 'Correctional Institutions Environment Scale' instruction booklets and response forms and an envelope for their anonymous return. Respondents were instructed to post completed research instruments in a collection box provided for this purpose and situated in a convenient place, for instance the gatehouse, in each prison. Individual distribution was thought to be desirable for two reasons: such a method ensured personal contact with every member of staff, enabling the researcher to answer questions staff might have about the instruments and to allay suspicions and anxieties about the project. Assembled groups of staff had been introduced to the aims of the research and the research instruments at meetings held earlier in each prison, and the need for such individual contact became apparent at those meetings. Staff completed the questionnaire at their leisure, but were requested to complete the diary during the three working days covered by the investigation, so that the results might not be affected by fading or faulty recollection.

The extremely low response rates for these two instruments at the long-term and short-term closed prisons have already been mentioned (p. 99). Results from these two prisons, being unrepresentative, have been excluded except where indicated, in the analysis which follows. The results given, therefore, are from the medium-term only among the closed prisons, plus the three open prisons. In these four, 219 copies of both the questionnaire and the diary were distributed. A hundred and forty questionnaires were completed and returned (an overall response rate of 64 per cent) and 127 diaries (an overall response rate of 60 per cent). Table 6.1 presents the response rates for each of the four prisons.

It is evident that the relative shortfall in diary as compared with questionnaire returns is mainly attributable to non-response in the

Table 6.1. Prison officer's questionnaire and prison officer's diary-response rates

	Medium-term closed	Short-term open	Medium-term open	Long-term open
Questionnaire				
No. distributed	54	47	66	52
No. returned	38	23	45	34
Response rate	70·4%	48·9%	68·2%	65·4%
Diary				
No. distributed	54	47	66	52
No. returned	31	22	40	34
Response rate	57·4%	46·8%	60·6%	65·4%

closed prison. (Although the relative deficiency in responses to the diary is less in the short-term open, this prison gave a much lower rate of response to both questionnaire and diary than any other prison in the research.) It is of note that this was the only prison out of the four in which the Home Office manpower utilisation survey had been undertaken. It may be concluded that we were correct in anticipating that participation in this earlier survey would influence completion of the prison officer's diary, and our decision to reduce to three days the period of diary administration would appear to have been justified.

The representativeness of samples was tested for both instruments by comparing respondents and non-respondents in each prison on a number of variables. (Semi-interquartile range distributions of 'age' and 'length of service' and the distribution 'above' (and 'including') and 'below' the rank of senior officer. Chi-squared statistics were computed for the distribution of respondents and non-respondents on each of the three variables.) The results of this exercise were to the effect that there were no significant differences between the two groups for each of the four prisons included in Table 6.1; i.e. that the respondents were representative of the whole group to which the questionnaire and diary were administered on the variables for which representativeness was tested. Comparison of all respondents against all non-respondents in the four prisons combined indicated representativeness in this case also. Similar calculations for the long-term and short-term closed prisons where there were extremely low response rates (questionnaire 30·4 and 34 per cent respectively: diary 28·2 and 28·3 per cent respectively) as already stated, showed them to be not representative of the total populations of their institutions, and they were therefore excluded.

The analysis of questionnaire results

The analysis of questionnaire returns proceeded in two ways. First, in testing for differences between the responses at each of the four prisons included in the analysis, a similar approach was adopted to that followed with the Moos CIES data on prison regimes. That is to say, the analysis was prefaced by a composite test of a 'first order' null hypothesis for each variable across all four sets of data. In instances where no significant differences between prisons did emerge no further analysis was made. Where the results of this first stage indicated such differences a 'second order' analysis was undertaken in the form of paired comparisons for the six constituent sets of data, in order to determine which factors were responsible for the differences indicated at the first stage. (Because all questionnaire data was discrete both 'first' and 'second order' hypotheses were tested by comparing response frequencies. Chi-squared statistics were used.)

However, there are limitations in this approach. The use of chi-squared requires certain minimum cell frequencies. (It is generally agreed that Yates' correction should be applied when expected frequencies drop below 10 and that it is unwise to use the statistic when expected frequencies fall below 5.) Not all the questionnaire data met this requirement. Consequently, it was not always possible to compare results statistically. In such cases the percentages or the raw data have nevertheless been given. Other than this, the convention adopted in the following presentation has been to provide combined figures for the four prisons for those data, displaying no significant 'first order' inter-prison differences, and to present separate distributions for each prison in cases where there are such differences justifying their separate exploration.

The second approach to the analysis of questionnaire data arose from the need to control for the high degree of variation in the social characteristics and Prison Service experience of the officers who responded. In the first place, some control was needed against the possibility that any differences found between prisons might simply be attributable to the presence in them of different types of prison officer. Second, there were questionnaire items which required viewpoints to be expressed and it was expected that such judgments, for instance about the desirability of changes in prisons, would vary according to 'age', 'length of service' or 'rank'. In straightforward comparisons between prisons it is not possible to operate controls for these potential sources of variation because the further subdivision of the data in accordance with such variables would have reduced the numbers concerned below a satisfactory level for statistical analysis. Furthermore, even if such a strategy had been practicable, it would not have been possible to control for the influence of more than one variable at a time except where two or more variables were highly correlated. It was clearly preferable to operate concurrent control for a number of variables. When the possibility of doing this was examined, it became apparent that it would be best achieved by constructing a matrix from such variables and then allocating each respondent to a prison officer 'type' according to the particular collection of these attributes which he displayed. These types could then be the bases for further comparison in studying officer attitudes, etc. It was decided to use the questionnaire data to construct the typology as follows.

The Prison Officer typology

The questionnaire data was scrutinised and provisionally broken down using one variable at a time in order to select those for which the operation of concurrent control seemed desirable. The following subdivisions were chosen for inclusion in the matrix.

1. Whether or not there had been promotion from basic grade officer status.
2. Whether or not there was evidence of post-school leaving age educational experience.
3. Above or below median age.
4. Above or below median length of service.

The inclusion of the further variable 'present establishment' in an attempt to control for the type of prison in which respondents currently worked was also considered, but was rejected because its inclusion would have expanded the number of matrix categories from sixteen to sixty-four. This was considered to be too many and would have prevented cell frequencies of sufficient size for statistical analysis to be undertaken. As some control for this source of variation was inherent in the inter-prison comparisons already described and as, in any case, the possibility of testing for differences in the distribution of officer types in each prison remained, it was excluded from further consideration.

This decision allowed us to consider the case for including in the typology, respondents from the two prisons which were excluded from the first approach to the analysis of questionnaire data because of their low response rates and non-representative character. After examining the arguments for and against, it was decided to include them. It was felt that individual and not institutional characteristics were being considered and, therefore, that these cases might be included, so as to increase the number in each category and thus the likelihood of obtaining groups of sufficient size for statistical comparison to be made. Thus, in all, 225 respondents from six prisons rather than 140 from four prisons were allocated to matrix categories; 4 cases were excluded because there was insufficient information available to classify them.

Not all the matrix categories were filled. Four were without any allocation whatsoever because there were no examples of prison officers who had been promoted with less than eight years (the median) service. Of allocations to the twelve remaining matrix categories, the majority (153 or 68 per cent) went to four principal categories. In addition, there were four less distinct categories, which accounted for a further 22 per cent of the respondents and the remaining four categories were barely filled (see the detailed matrix in Appendix 4). Only the four main categories were therefore included in the typological comparison. Two of these combined 'above median age' (40 years) with 'above median length of service' (8 years) and were distinguished from each other in that one group had (Type 3) and the other had not (Type 4) been promoted. The other two groups were below both 'median age' and 'median length of service' but were distinguished in that one had (Type 2) and one had not any (Type 1) further educational experience after leaving school. The remaining eight categories were treated as a miscellaneous group. The main defining characteristics of the four groups are set out in Table 6.2 below.

The rationale for the statistical analysis of differences between the four main typological groups was similar to that for the first approach concerning differences between institutions. Chi-squared statistics were used to test for differences in the distributions of responses across the four groups and, where this composite test indicated such differences, 'second order' hypotheses were tested for

Table 6.2 Main characteristics of the four prison officer types

	Type 1	Type 2	Type 3	Type 4
Mean age (years)	31·8	30·0	50·2	49·7
Mean length of service (years)	3·2	3·2	20·8	15·7
Mean age at joining (years)	28·6	26·8	29·4	34·1
Rank	Basic grade	Basic grade	Senior officer and above	Basic grade
Post school-leaving age educational experience	No	Yes	No	No
N	28	51	42	32

each of the six constituent paired sets of data in order to determine which of the factors were responsible for the differences already found. The 'miscellaneous category' was excluded from this analysis.

To summarise, the principal aim in constructing the prison officer typology was to obtain some measure of control over the wide variations found in respondents' social characteristics and Prison Service experience. Such control was essential to gaining an understanding not only of the question of whether any differences found between prisons were simply attributable to the presence in them of different types of officer, but also to a fuller understanding of those responses to the questionnaire which required judgments to be made from particular standpoints. In addition, the adoption of a typological approach could have a valuable descriptive potential, throwing into relief some of the characteristics which distinguish officers at different stages of their Prison Service careers. It might be expected, for example, to produce information about the influence on prison officers' attitudes and behaviour of further educational experience and promotion. Therefore, in addition to the comparison of differences between prisons, a large part of the questionnaire data was analysed from this typological perspective. However, the adoption of this dual approach to the analysis of questionnaire data makes it essential to consider how far the two approaches are applicable.

The questions we needed to ask were whether differences found between prisons depended not on regimes, but on the existence in the prisons of different types of officers, and conversely whether differences in the attitudes of different types of officer might be due to the way they are distributed between (and therefore influenced by) different kinds of regime. These issues could be settled by testing for differences in the distribution of officer types in the four prisons. The result of such an analysis is presented in Table 6.3. Although Type 1 officers (younger men without further educational experience) appear to be under-represented in the medium-term closed and long-term open prisons, and Type 3 officers (older men who have gained promotion) appear to be under-represented in the short-term open prison, such differences in the distribution of officer types in each prison do not occur at a statistically significant level. There is, therefore, no strong suggestion that any differences found between the prisons are mainly attributable to the presence within them of different types of officer or vice versa. In this way, the

Table 6.3   The distribution of officer types by prison

	Medium-term closed	Short-term open	Medium-term open	Long-term open
Type 1	2	6	7	2
Type 2	12	9	11	8
Type 3	6	3	6	9
Type 4	4	3	5	7
Totals	24	21	29	26

Chi-squared (Yates' correction applied) 9 d.f. = 10·345 N.S.

validity of the two approaches to the analysis of questionnaire data is supported and the potential control value of the typological approach is established.

Analysis of Diary results

The analysis of the results of the prison officer's diary was a much simpler matter. The aim of the diary was to produce a portrait of the average working day in each prison: the length of the working day, the proportion of that day spent by officers on each listed activity, any differences in the daily distribution of activities as between different levels of seniority among uniformed staff. No other sub-division of the data was thought to be necessary. The average day was computed by summing the time spent on each activity (in hours) and dividing these totals by the number of days worked by diary respondents. Days covered by sick leave, annual leave and detached duty were not counted. Time spent on meal breaks was also excluded from consideration.

A means of measuring statistical correlation was needed to assess how far the working day in each open prison was similar to that of the medium-term closed prison, the only closed prison whose sample of respondents was considered to be representative, as well as the degree of similarity between the open prisons. The proportionate amount of time shown in the diaries as devoted to the various activities in each prison was therefore assigned rank orders, and Kendall's rank correlation coefficient (tau) was used to provide an approximate measure of the degree of concordance between the rankings of activities in each of the prisons, compared two at a time. No further statistical analysis of diary data was considered necessary.

7   The social backgrounds of prison officers

At first sight, an enquiry into the social backgrounds of prison staff may seem an unjustified intrusion into their private lives, and some of the prison officers in our sample took this view of the matter. Resentment of this section of our staff questionnaire was probably one of the reasons why the response rate by staff to the questionnaire was not better than it proved to be. And certainly, if the information we were collecting were to be personalised, there would have been no doubt in our minds that these complaints were justified.

In fact, however, there was no way in which respondents to the questionnaire could have been identified. Also, as will be seen from the pages which follow, our concern was with groups of staff (for example, particular age, education or skill groups), or even with the activities of officers as a whole (for example with regard to use of leisure time, or 'taking the prison home') and not with individuals.

And we did have (as we believe) two very good reasons for seeking this kind of information. One was to put prison officers, for once, in the centre of the picture: to call attention to their problems and point of view in a way which they justifiably argue rarely occurs in research on prisons. The second reason is the influence which social background and earlier life experiences may be expected to have on the way in which people perform their jobs—prison officers are not seen as any different in this respect from other people.

Both of these motives lie behind our expressed intention to make a contribution in this chapter to an occupational sociology of prison officers. We shall begin our attempt at this by an examination of their general social characteristics, and then later turn to aspects of their prison service careers.

Social characteristics

The distribution of age and length of service of prison officers at the four prisons from which representative data was obtained are presented in Tables 7.1 and 7.2. It will be recalled that there were no statistically significant differences on these variables between respondents and non-respondents (p. 147) and between officers below and at or above the rank of senior officer. Table 7.1 shows that there is a higher proportion of younger men at the short-term open prison, particularly as compared with the medium-term closed prison. It also shows that there is a higher proportion of men aged 40 to 48 years at the medium-term closed prison in comparison with the open prisons. However, such differences as these do not occur at a statistically significant level over the range of all four prisons. Similarly, although there is (Table 7.2) a concentration of men with very little service, and proportionately fewer men with more than 20 years' service in the medium-term closed prison, these differences also are not statistically significant when evaluated over all four prisons.

Table 7.1   Age of officers

Age (years)	Medium-term closed	Short-term open	Medium-term open	Long-term open
21-32	10	18	23	12
33-39	14	10	15	17
40-48	22	11	20	8
49+	13	14	23	18
Totals	59	53	81	55

Chi-squared, 9 d.f., $= 14 \cdot 069$ (N.S.)

The age distribution of the total sample remains wide. Approximately one-fifth were 30 years and under (8 per cent were under 25); two-fifths, the predominant category, were between 31 and 40 years; one-fifth more between 41 and 50 years and a further fifth over 51 years. However, within this last group, less than 5 per cent were more than 55 years old. The picture presented, therefore, is of an occupation consisting largely of mature adults rather than the very young or the very old.

The social class background of prison officers was ascertained in the usual way by reference to the variable, 'father's main occupation'. In addition, an indication of occupational mobility was provided by comparing prison officers' first jobs after school and their last job before joining the Prison Service with their fathers' main occupations. Finally, educational and military service ex-

Table 7.2   *Officers' length of service*

Length of service (years)	Medium-term closed	Short-term open	Medium-term open	Long-term open
0-3	23	14	20	16
4-9	15	14	24	8
10-19	13	11	15	11
20+	8	14	22	20
Totals	59	53	81	55

Chi-squared, 9 d.f., = 11·885 (N.S.)

perience were examined in order to see whether or not they influenced the patterns of occupational choice and mobility evident in the preceding data. As no significant differences were found between the four prisons on any of these variables, only combined figures for all prisons will be presented (Table 7.3).

The distribution of parental employment indicates that, as a group, the prison officers came mainly from a representative cross-section of working-class backgrounds. Thus, within the manual labour range it does not differ markedly from the national pattern as indicated, for instance, by Rose in his review of studies of the working class.[1] The distribution of respondents' first jobs, however, presents a different picture. None of the prison officers was initially employed in work classified as high as social class II (intermediate occupations) as compared with 11·4 per cent of their fathers. In addition, while similar proportions (30 and 32·9 per cent) were in skilled craft occupations, almost twice as many prison officers as compared with their fathers moved into service occupations. The latter were almost exclusively non-clerical, being mainly sales and distribution occupations. The most outstanding feature of prison officers' last jobs before joining is that almost one-fifth (19·3 per cent) entered the Prison Service directly from the armed forces. Many more entered from this background after only a brief interlude in civilian occupations, mostly from class III (service occupations) or class IV (semi-skilled) varieties. As 27·1 per cent still entered the Prison Service from class III (craft) occupations—only a slightly lower proportion than that for entry into class III occupations after school—it is possible that the majority entering this way had been in

Table 7.3   A comparison of fathers' main occupations and respondents' first and last jobs before joining*

Job classification	Fathers' main occupations %	Respondents' first jobs %	Respondents' last jobs %
Social class II	11·4	—	4·3
Social class III (craft skills)	30·0	32·9	27·1
Social class III (service occupations)	10·7	20·0	14·3
Social class IV (semi-skilled)	25·7	29·3	25·7
Social class V (unskilled)	7·1	5·0	4·3
H.M. Forces	7·9	7·1	19·3
No response	7·1	5·7	5·0
Totals	99·9%	100%	100%
N	140	140	140

*All jobs have been coded with reference to the Registrar General's *Classification of Occupations*.[2] Social class III (skilled occupations), however, has been further subdivided into (i) those occupations which involve prolonged apprenticeships and the acquisition of craft skills and (ii) those occupations classified as social class III but not involving such skills. The latter category includes both non-manual class III work such as clerical and sales occupations and skilled jobs in transport and allied fields which do not involve similar apprenticeship schemes. In other words, this subdivision of class III occupations distinguishes between craft skills and service skills.

such occupations fairly continuously. If this is so (and data from the typological comparison to be discussed later suggests that it is—see p. 161) a definite pattern of occupational mobility and choice is suggested for the remainder. The prominent features of their career pattern are entry from school into service or semi-skilled occupations followed by military service.

Generally, this would suggest a trend of, if not downward mobility, sideways movement into 'dead-end' jobs for this group as compared with their fathers. It would also suggest that military service (and, possibly, the later choice of the Prison Service) are perceived as providing escape routes from such jobs and compensation for any earlier downward mobility in their careers. Certainly the evidence of 'alternative career preferences' (see Table 7.4) would seem to endorse this interpretation. Very few men (14·3 per cent) listed skilled work as their preference. Indeed, comparatively few had been trained for such work. At the same time, only 1 in 4 of men formerly in semi-skilled and unskilled manual occupations had considered continuing at this level. The great majority of our prison officers it appears were either looking to the Police as a way out of their present circumstances (25·7 per cent) or saw no alternative to the Prison Service (32·9 per cent).

Table 7.4   Prison officers' alternative career preferences

Job classification	% preference
Social class II	5·0
Social class III (skilled)	14·3
Social class III (services)	31·4*
Social class IV (semi-skilled)	40·0†
Social class V (unskilled)	0·7
H.M. Forces	2·9
No response	5·7
Totals	100%
N	140

*25·7% of the total choice was for the Police.
†32·9% of the total expressed no alternative other than the Prison service.

The educational experience of prison officers (Table 7.5) tends to confirm this picture of limited accomplishments. The vast majority of prison officers left elementary or secondary modern education at the earliest opportunity, that is at 14 or 15 years of age. Comparison of formal educational qualifications obtained during and after full-time education (Table 7.5) reveals, despite the high non-response rate, the paucity of educational attainment. This is particularly so if it is realised that, in the main, the 'Forces qualifications' refer, not to academic, technical or trade qualifications, but to tests of basic competence in reading, writing and arithmetic. Thus, with respect to formal measures of educational attainment, prison officers emerge as an occupational group characterised by only a basic level of educational accomplishment—though it should be realised that limited formal educational attainments in a predominantly working-class group may not necessarily be proof of lack of ability. The implications of this state of affairs for the issue of training are discussed in the final chapter of this book.

The third aspect of the pre-Prison Service socialisation experience of prison officers covered in the questionnaire concerned the extent to which they had served in the armed forces or had been members of such organisations as army cadet corps. In their study of Pentonville prison, the Morrises[3] found that the majority of officers interviewed by them had completed regular service engagements of more than

Table 7.5   A comparison of prison officers' educational attainment during and after full-time education

Qualifications	In school %	After school %
None	82·9	36·4
Less than 5 'O' levels	3·6	—
More than 5 'O' levels	—	0·7
Professional/commercial	—	0·7
Trade qualifications	—	14·3
Forces qualifications	—	27·1
Other academic qualifications	—	0·7
Other	—	0·7
No response	13·6	19·3
Totals	100·1%	99·9%
N	140	140

seven years and that, in addition, many had entered the Prison Service directly from discharge or after a very short period in which they had tried to follow a civilian occupation. More generally, it has been claimed that the para-military character of the Prison Service offers a more positive inducement to the ex-serviceman than do the more flexible organisational forms of civilian occupations. A particular implication is that certain kinds of personality are attracted to service in disciplined organisations like the Armed Forces and the Prison Service. However, as we have stated earlier (see p. 143), it is difficult to clarify the role played by compulsory military service in all this. As conscription no longer exists, and military service is chosen freely by those who undertake it, the picture may eventually be clearer. Meanwhile we must make the best of the data that historical circumstances allow to us.

The results in Table 7.6 indicate that, although comparatively few prison officers had joined a cadet corps during their youth, the

Table 7.6   Prior membership of military organisations

	Cadet corps	Armed forces
Yes	23·6	71·4
No	65·0	27·1
No response	11·4	1·4
Totals	100%	99·9%
N	140	140

substantial majority (71·4 per cent) had completed military service. Nevertheless the effect of compulsory service during and after the Second World War must still be allowed for. It was possible to determine how many officers had served for only two years or less (the national service period) and how many had completed engagements of more than seven years (thus enabling a comparison to be made between respondents in this study and those interviewed by the Morrises). Also it is likely that professional commitment to service in the armed forces would be indicated by evidence of promotion. Tables 7.7 and 7.8 show that, of those completing military service, only a small proportion completed engagements of two years or less, and therefore that the majority had, at some time, voluntarily elected to join the services for an extended period. These tables also

Table 7.7   Armed forces: length of engagement

Service (months)	%
Less than 12	1·4
13-24	15·7
25-36	5·7
37-48	5·7
49-60	9·3
61-72	8·6
73-84	3·6
85+	20·0
Not in services	27·1
No response	2·9
Total	100%
N	140

Table 7.8   Armed forces: rank obtained

Rank (or equivalent)	%
Private	17·9
Lance-corporal	12·1
Corporal	15·0
Sergeant	14·3
Warrant Officer or above	7·9
No information	0·7
Not in services	27·1
No response	5·0
Total	100%
N	140

reveal that the majority of these men obtained promotion above the rank of private (63 per cent) or lance-corporal (55 per cent). These are not the figures to be expected for a national service group and must be accepted as evidence of the high degree of full-time professional commitment to military service in members of this group of prison officers.

Comparison with the results of T. and P. Morris brings to light an interesting discrepancy. In the present group, only 20 per cent of those completing military service engagements had served for more than seven years compared with 58 per cent of the sample interviewed ten years previously by the Morrises. Although wartime military service would not often have extended to over seven years, the existence of conscription and, therefore, of widespread military experience, must have increased the number of such long-term commitments entered into by those studied during the Morrises' research period. So the decline from 58 to 28 per cent may not reflect any change in the extent of ex-service recruitment to the Prison Service. Nevertheless the high degree of voluntary enrolment in the armed forces both then and now, evident among prison officers, must surely differentiate them from other, socio-economically similar, occupational groups. It seems plausible to suggest that such a voluntary career choice of professional military service, like those of the police and the Prison Service itself, may reflect some kind of decision by prison officers in favour of the status, security and discipline offered by these uniformed services.

Thus, to summarise, there were no differences between the four prison staffs with respect to their social backgrounds or pre-Prison Service socialisation experience. More generally, prison officers come from predominantly working-class backgrounds; exhibit a comparatively low degree of formal educational attainment; make initial career choices which, as compared with their fathers, indicate either downward mobility, sideways movement into 'dead-end' occupations or both; and appear to seek to reverse this trend by seeking alternative careers in such 'secure' and 'respectable' occupations as the armed forces, police work and, ultimately, the Prison Service.

The typological comparison supports this picture. Evidence of further educational experience and attainment, the choice of skilled manual occupations and opting out of military service characterise only one group (type 2 officers: younger men with further educational experience). The remaining three types are totally lacking in similar educational experience and attainment, tending to choose 'dead-end' semi-skilled or unskilled manual occupations more frequently and to move from these occupations into professional military service. As a result, they joined the Prison Service at a later stage in their careers (see Table 6.2).

Because evidence of post-school-leaving age educational experience was one of the four dichotomous variables upon which the typology was based, type 2 officers accounted for the whole of the recorded incidence of such experience. There were two other ways in which type 2 officers differed from other types. First, as the information presented in Table 7.9 shows, this group accounts for 53 per cent of all the initial career choices for skilled manual craft occupations and only 17 per cent of all initial career preferences for semi-skilled and unskilled work. These figures distinguish type 2 quite markedly from the others.

Table 7.9   Comparison of prison officer types on the variable 'respondent's first job'

Job classification	Type 1	Type 2	Type 3	Type 4
Social class III (skilled)	6	23	11	7
Social class III (service)	4	12	12	3
Social classes IV + V (semi-skilled and unskilled)	12	8	13	15
Totals	22	43	36	25

Chi-squared (Yates' correction applied), 6 d.f., $= 16\cdot958$ ($p < 0\cdot01$).

The other way in which type 2 officers differ from the other types is related to their previous experience of military service. Although they account for 20 per cent of all cases where there is a service background, the engagements were in the main of two years which were, presumably, national service periods. And this same group accounts for 64 per cent of all cases where a period has not been spent in military service. Thus, while generally there is evidence of a pattern of prison officers having opted for military service; and while, as may be expected from the cessation of conscription, the pattern is less obvious for the two younger groups, the experience of type 2 officers is very much against the overall trend.

Table 7.10   Comparison of prison officer types on the variable 'previous military service'

	Type 1	Type 2	Type 3	Type 4
Yes	17	21	38	30
No	11	30	4	2
Totals	28	51	42	32

Chi-squared (Yates' correction applied), 3 d.f., $= 37 \cdot 761$ ($p < 0 \cdot 001$).

The suggested relationship between occupational trend and the choice of professional military service, therefore, received considerable support from this evidence. In other words, type 2 officers tend to choose skilled occupations, follow apprenticeships, avoid military service, continue their pre-Prison Service careers in industry and enter the Service at a younger age. Other types, however, tend to opt for different occupations which, on the face of things, appear to be less rewarding or satisfying, leave such employments at a comparatively young age in order to follow careers as professionals in the armed forces and enter the Prison Service more or less directly from the armed forces.

It would be surprising if these two distinct career patterns before entry to the Prison Service did not have some implications for their occupational socialisation within the Service. Thus, although the emergence of these distinct subgroups of prison officers may not present problems for the comparison of differences between prisons (there was not a statistically significant difference in the distribution of types between the staffs of the four prisons), it clearly poses important overall considerations for such issues as staff training and the attitudes which officers hold about their work. Data on these aspects, therefore, will also be examined from a typological perspective.

Prison service careers

Just as there were no differences between the staffs in the medium-term closed prison and the three open prisons with regard to social background and pre-Prison Service socialisation experience, so there were no statistically significant differences between them on Prison Service career variables. An overall picture for all prisons combined will, therefore, be presented in the following discussion. In addition, there were no statistically significant differences on these variables between the four typological groups, and such a comparison has therefore also been omitted from this section. The preceding analysis has suggested some possible motives for joining the Prison Service. For instance, there was a suggestion that its paramilitary structure might appeal to ex-servicemen: that it afforded an environment in which they felt at ease and in which they could exercise man-management skills acquired during military service. Moreover, as it appeared that disenchantment with the civilian occupations which they took up after school may have been a reason for entering the armed forces, it is likely that they wished to avoid such occupations, if possible, after their discharge from military service. Many officers joined directly from the forces and many more spent only brief interludes in such occupations before applying for the Prison Service. Prison officers' perceptions of alternative career possibilities available to them at the time of joining and their reasons for joining provide further evidence on these points.

Alternative career choices have already been discussed. For the majority of officers there was either no alternative, or only the police force. A senior officer at a closed prison, whose comments were typical of many older officers, summed up his own situation in this way:

'As a serving soldier at the end of the war and with no trade the only course was to join the police or Prison Service. Married in 1944 with no prospect of a house in normal circumstances, I chose the Prison Service where there was a possibility of quarters. The Prison Service was a job which after army training was easily dovetailed together.'

The choice of police work partly reflects its high prestige value among prison officers. Although there are many men in the Prison Service who failed to be selected for police training and only 2·9 per cent of our sample had actually been policemen, prison officers as an occupational group have tended over the years to identify themselves with policemen, presumably because of the perceived power and status of the police officer in the community, and have based claims for pay and conditions of service on this comparison. At the same time, they have been hostile to the way in which, in these matters, the government equates them with postal workers. As one young senior officer put it:

'What we want is more recognition for the work we do. Also how can you compare a Prison Officer with a postman? The government does, every time our pay structure is discussed. We work among the most dangerous criminals in the country, but we get nothing for this. Yes—there are quite a few things about the service that are unfair.'

In fairness, it is necessary to point out that the prison where this officer worked contained, at the time of the research, the largest accumulation in the country of category A prisoners (i.e. those classified as representing such a threat to the community that their escape should be prevented at all costs).

There is thus a suggestion that the most important determinants of a decision to join the Prison Service include a concern with status and security. In their interviews with Pentonville officers, the Morrises[4] found that reluctance on the part of ex-servicemen to enter fully civilian occupations was the single most important determinant. A third (34·6 per cent) of their sample gave 'an extension of previous experience' as their primary reason for joining. In contrast, only 5 per cent of the respondents in this study made a similar choice. (This could of course be because of the end of national service—less experience (i.e. of a military kind) to 'extend'.) Rather, in the present study (as Table 7.11 shows), over half (56·4 per cent) of the prison officers chose 'security' as their primary reason (cf. 30·7 per cent of the Morrises' sample). Next in order of choice for the present sample was 'interest in people' but, by comparison, this vocational reason attracted relatively slight support (10 per cent). Beyond this, the most prominent reasons were also non-vocational and included the attractiveness of the pay and pension scheme and the opportunities which the job presented to make use of previous experience. The difference between these results and those reported in *Pentonville* may reflect the extent to which prison officers' military service backgrounds have changed over the years. The most important implication of these results, however, arises from the relative absence of vocational reasons. While it could be argued that, in present circumstances, with a predominantly working-class recruitment, this is to be expected, the lack of vocational motivation among entrants to the service poses problems for any change from custodial to treatment, training or rehabilitative objectives in prison.

Because the minimum age for joining the Prison Service is 21, most must have been in some other occupation before joining.

Table 7.11   *Reasons for joining*

Reasons	1st choice %	2nd choice %	3rd choice %	All choices combined %
Good pay and pension scheme	6·4	16·4	7·9	10·2
Good prospects for promotion	2·1	2·9	5·7	3·6
Security of employment	56·4	16·4	10·0	27·6
An extension of previous experience	5·0	10·7	15·0	10·2
Interest in people	10·0	15·0	15·7	13·6
Rentfree house	4·3	11·4	5·7	7·1
Unhappy in previous jobs	5·7	7·9	5·0	6·2
As a 'challenge'	1·4	5·7	10·7	6·0
Recommended by friends in the Prison Service	0·7	5·0	10·7	5·5
Special interest in prisons	—	—	2·9	1·0
Other	2·1	2·1	2·9	2·4
No response	5·7	6·4	7·9	6·7
Totals	99·8%	99·9%	100·1%	100·1%
N	140	140	140	420

However, as Table 7.12 shows, fewer than one in five (17·9 per cent) officers joined between the ages of 21 and 23. Recruitment, it would seem, does not often occur at the minimum joining age. Nearly half (45·7 per cent) of our sample joined between 27 and 35 years of age. This might have suggested that most prison officers joined the service with some experience of non-institutional life and an ordinary job, and therefore with more understanding and balanced attitudes, than those which might have resulted from early absorption into the prison world. How far this is so, however, depends upon the kind of previous experience gained. There are indications from this study that the older officers are on joining, the more likely it is that their backgrounds include military service engagements. Thus type 3 and type 4 officers, who have the highest average ages on joining (Table 6.2) also show much the largest proportions with previous military service. Type 2, with the lowest average age, show the lowest

Table 7.12   Age at which officers joined the prison service

Age joined	%
21-23	17·9
24-26	18·6
27-29	15·7
30-32	17·9
33-35	12·1
36-38	8·6
39-41	6·4
42-44	2·1
No response	0·7
Total	100%
N	140

proportion of military service. While, in Home Office circles, it seems often to be believed that such experience is an asset to the prison officer's work, it may be more appropriate to his traditional custodial role than to situations where there is less emphasis upon discipline (cf. self-discipline), security and custody. Later recruitment may not therefore ensure a broader previous experience.

The Prison Service experience of officers at each of the four prisons differed very little. Of the 140 men who completed the questionnaire, 25 were occupying their first post. Such men represented between 12 and 16 per cent of the staff in the medium-term closed and the medium- and long-term open prisons, but accounted for almost 40 per cent of all the staff in the short-term open prison, their presence in such high proportion in the latter revealing some of the problems faced by the Prison Department in staffing such relatively isolated, rural establishments. Most of the experience of the remainder (see Table 7.13) was in closed local or closed training prisons (68 per cent) followed by borstals, detention centres and remand centres which also would have been mainly closed institutions (25·2 per cent). While this is bound to be so in view of the fact that there are many more closed than open institutions, it is still worth drawing particular attention to the very limited amount of service in open prisons, only 6·2 per cent of the total previous experience of this group of officers. Excluding of course the 25 men who were in their first post, the average number of establishments

Table 7.13   Prison officers' previous experience of different
establishments*

Type of establishment	Periods of service	%
Closed local prisons	69	35·6
Closed training prisons	64	33·0
Open prisons	12	6·2
Borstals	28	14·4
Detention centres and remand centres	21	10·8
Totals	194	100%
N	115	—
No other establishments	25	—
Total	140	—

*It should be noted that the figures in this table refer to the number of postings
rather than the duration of postings to the various establishments. Although short
detachments and relief postings are more frequently undertaken in closed
institutions, these do not contribute significantly to the closed prison totals.
Therefore, there are no obvious reasons why the overall distribution would be
different if the proportionate durations of postings to each kind of establishment
were tabulated instead.

previously served in was 1·7 (Table 7.14). Generally speaking, men
with longer service had served in a greater number, although not
necessarily a greater variety of establishments.

Movement between establishments occurred in two ways. First,
there were permanent moves as a result of official transfer,
promotions, and requests by officers to change from their present
post. Second, there were temporary absences when officers were
obliged to undertake periods of detached duty in other establishments. The latter kind of movement was usually of short duration
and was normally prompted by staff shortages in closed local
prisons. Most of the movement between establishments occurred
without any consultation with the prison officer concerned; it is
expected that prison officers will change establishments during their
careers, although they may have mixed feelings about moving on. It
is not unknown for officers to turn down promotion in order to
remain in their present establishment. Because official reasons for
moving officers are not (except for promotion) divulged to them,
answers to the question about the reasons for movement within the
service are more likely to reflect individually rather than officially

Table 7.14   Number of previous establishments

Number	%
0	17·9
1	38·6
2	17·9
3	10·0
4	5·7
5	5·7
6	1·4
7	0·7
No response	2·1
Total	100%
N	140

initiated moves. For instance, it came to our notice that approximately one-quarter of the staff in one prison had been moved there as a disciplinary measure, but the questionnaire responses from this prison gave no indication of this or whether a similar state of affairs existed at any other prison in the study. The information presented in Table 7.15 must, therefore, be examined with this clarification in mind.

It seems possible that many officially prompted moves, especially centrally arranged transfers from one prison to another, are included

Table 7.15   Reasons for moving

Reason	% choice
No reason	19·4
Broadening your experience	14·3
Family reasons, e.g. living nearer home	16·0
Wished to find institution that suited you best	11·0
Moved by prison authorities (other than promotion)	12·7
Moved due to promotion	8·4
Other reasons	18·1
Total	99·9%
N*	95

*Excluded from these calculations were 25 men who were occupying their first post and a further 20 men who did not answer this question.

in the 'no reason' category. Officers' feelings over movement are quite mixed, although on balance 'moving around' is favoured (as the results in Table 7.16 indicate).

To judge from their additional comments (many officers made use of the opportunity provided in the questionnaire to comment more fully on some of the items), most officers consider that moves lead to

Table 7.16   The effect of movement on an officer's job performance

	%
The best officer is one who stays in one place	36·4
The best officer is one who moves around	49·3
No response	14·3
Total	100%
N	140

a broadening of experience, prevent stagnation and result in a better appreciation of both practical and administrative aspects of the job. Those who disagree maintain that staying in one place leads to a more informed understanding of inmate affairs and has a less disruptive effect on their family life. It is of note that officers who favoured movement did not refer to its effect on their domestic situation. Arguably the most perceptive comment on the topic of movement was made by a young basic grade officer at an open prison who wrote:

'I feel that by moving about, one prevents stagnation; sinking into routine can easily occur by staying in one place. A change say every 5 to 10 years is in my opinion, beneficial and helps to fight institutionalisation which I feel is a real danger in this job. You have to fight it especially living in quarters. You also get an overall picture of a service and its problems.'

Promotion, or rather the lack or comparative slowness of it, is an issue of central concern for many prison officers. Those who have obtained promotion feel that the process is fair. Older officers who have failed the necessary examinations feel that insufficient weight is given to 'experience'. Younger officers, facing the prospect of a fifteen-year wait, feel that it is too slow: that too much weight is given to 'seniority' and too little consideration is given to 'ability'. Respondents in this study were asked to indicate what, in their view, were the three main problems of promotion within the service. The results in Table 7.17 indicate clearly the broad range of criticisms of, and objections to, the promotion system. When given an opportunity

Table 7.17   Complaints about promotion

	%
It is too slow	13·6
The additional responsibility is not worth it	11·2
It often means a move from the present prison	18·1
It does not take experience into account	16·4
The face has to fit	12·4
Overtime is reduced	5·7
Not told enough about selection procedure	13·3
Others	5·5
No response	3·8
Total	100%
N	140

to clarify such criticisms—i.e. by writing at greater length on their questionnaire forms as well as in discussion with members of the research team—the officers suggested that a number of changes could be made to the promotion system. Many saw the Use of English examination as either threatening or irrelevant. Others thought that there should be much less emphasis on written examinations of any kind and more emphasis on proven experience and ability. There was also evidence of widespread suspicion that, because promotion boards were organised centrally and not locally within the prison, the system could work unfairly. Many officers felt that their prisons and, presumably, their interests were not fully represented on the existing boards. A small number of respondents complained that promotions were made without reference to the kind of establishment in which the promoted officer would serve, thus implying that a more purposeful promotion procedure is needed in which men would be selected on the grounds of their potential ability to fill particular vacancies. This is a point of great importance to which some reference will be made in the final chapter of this book. Finally, mixed opinions were expressed about the introduction, on the recommendation of the Mountbatten Report on escapes and prison security,[5] of the additional rank of senior officer. Discipline staff generally welcomed its introduction because it not only helped to ease the pressures caused by the number of men who had passed the promotion examination of principal officer grade and who still awaited promotion, but also because it offered a means of giving seniority to some officers with considerable service, but who had failed the principal officer examinations. Objections came primarily from engineer and trade assistant grades, who were among the more highly qualified personnel, but were not eligible for this rank.

Officers' family circumstances have a considerable bearing on their views on such aspects of their work as movement between prisons and promotion. Not unreasonably, wives are not always happy about moves that will take the family away from their relations, and for some officers their children's educational and occupational needs are given priority over their own personal advancement. Indeed, as Tables 7.18-7.20 reveal, prison officers are very family-centred. The great majority were married and apparently happily so, because the incidence of marital breakdown was extremely low. About two-thirds had two or more children and the vast majority at least one. This index of stability and respectability is reinforced by the fact that one in five lived as owner-occupiers in their own homes, despite the availability of free accommodation. However, three-quarters (74·3 per cent) lived in prison officers' quarters, which meant that their neighbours were also members of the Prison Service. This is bound to be institutionalising: even at home, they lived within the ambience of the prison. Although dissatisfaction with quarters did not rank high among problems listed by officers (see Table 8.7), they frequently expressed discontent with their accommodation in conversation, and it was listed as a problem more often by open prison men (Table 8.7). Thus there emerges a familiar picture which tends to add to the 'working class' image of the prison officer a definitely 'settled' aspect. This image is underlined by the information obtained about the social activities of prison officers and their choice of company for these activities.

Questions about social activities yielded the highest rates of non-response because many officers felt that what they did outside the prison was their own affair and beyond the scope and, indeed,

Table 7.18   Marital status of prison officers

Marital status	%
Married	92·9
Single	2·1
Separated	—
Divorced	1·4
Widowed	—
No response	3·6
Total	100%
N	140

Table 7.19   Number of children

Number of children	%
None	6·4
1	23·6
2	31·4
3	17·1
4	8·6
5+	5·0
No response	7·9
Total	100%
N	140

Table 7.20   Prison officers' accommodation

Type of accommodation	%
Officers' quarters	74·3
Own house	19·3
Rented accommodation	1·4
Other	0·7
No response	4·3
Total	100%
N	140

the relevance of this research. Of those who responded, the first choice of social activity for more than four-fifths (82·6 per cent) was home-centred, for instance relaxing at home or undertaking home maintenance tasks. Similarly, for 86·8 per cent, the company of their wives or girl friends was preferred to that of anybody else. The company of other relatives was infrequently sought, but prison officers spent more leisure time in the company of colleagues than might be thought usual. The neglect of relatives might be due to the frequency of movement, within the Prison Service, away from 'home' localities, although it is also only to be expected in view of the concentration on home and colleagues. And this latter concentration also is only natural in a group who are shut off together from most outside contacts, even at home where most of them live together in quarters—as already stated, still within the prison ambience. Such an effect may be particularly strong for officers serving in the relatively isolated, rural situations of open prisons. Thus, for instance, one officer felt constrained to qualify his questionnaire answers in the following manner: 'These answers apply only to —— Prison in view of the fact that it is an "inconvenience of locality" posting and one gets little or no chance to meet many friends outside of the Prison Service.' This kind of social insularity on the part of prison officers has an obvious bearing on the development of the prison officer culture referred to in the analysis of the CIES material.

Others were concerned about the general lack of amenities for staff in open prisons. A senior officer wrote:

'Lack of social life is in my own and my wife's opinion the major reason for discontent at —— Prison. At first we thought that this was our fault because being Irish we always found our social life among Irish groups in Birmingham, e.g. Irish dancing, singing, drama, music, even the pubs we frequented had Irish landlords. But it appears no other group had any better social life at prison. There is a prison officers' club in the process of being built for the past two years and it is no nearer completion. The Governor of the prison appears to lead the life of a recluse and not to need any social life and shows no interest in the social needs of his staff . . . . Prisoners at —— Prison have every facility for their leisure time, staff and more particularly children of staff are totally neglected in this respect; inmates are encouraged to do as they please, petty restrictions are placed on children from time to time. A sense of urgency to have club facilities available for the use of the camp alone would be appreciated. I feel that in posting officers with families to stations like —— Prison the Home Office should consider the age of the children and the employment prospects of children in a particular area when they leave school.'

One important consequence for officers of working long hours together, and being almost forced into one another's company during their rather limited opportunities for leisure, might be that of 'taking the prison home'.

As one put it:

'I feel the job has a bad effect on one's home life. Two-thirds of an officer's day is spent with a lot of morons. Unfortunately one tends to forget the better things in life because of this. Consequently when one arrives home, it is difficult to strike up a mutual conversation with the wife. So although I may not take my work home verbally, its effects mentally are always with me.'

A question to this effect was included in the questionnaire. The responses indicate (see Table 7.21) that, although for most the problem is not as serious as for the officer whose observations have been quoted, there are times for the vast majority when a prison officer's work clearly intrudes upon his private and domestic life.

Summary

This phase of our enquiry shows that our prison officers were in the middle age ranges, and entered the service at the age by which they

Table 7.21   *'Taking the prison home'*

	%
Usually	7·9
Sometimes	42·9
Rarely	30·7
Never	17·1
No response	1·4
Total	100%
N	140

could have had maturing experience of non-institutional life. But instead this period was filled for many by a stint of military service. Because the older men would have been required to undertake compulsory service during the national service period, it is difficult to ascertain whether there was any particular commitment on their part to the army, though this is suggested by the fact that most of them undertook engagements of over two years, and nearly two-thirds achieved promotion beyond their initial rank.

If one compares their first and last jobs, and also compares their last jobs with the main occupations of their fathers, there is some indication of at best a sideways, and sometimes a downward pattern of mobility. Their relatively low aspirations are confirmed also by the small number who see skilled jobs as possible alternatives to the Prison Service. A substantial proportion opted here for the police or saw no alternative to the Prison Service. Possible implications are that men who had found the highly organised life of the serviceman congenial were more attracted to the disciplined life of the police and the Prison Service than to the 'risky' life of the civilian worker; and also found this a way of obtaining a degree of security not usually available in the unskilled jobs to which they otherwise would have aspired.

They also showed only a basic level of educational attainment. There is no suggestion, of course, that they lacked ability. Especially among the older groups, educational opportunities would have been difficult to come by.

The one exception to all this was type 2 in our prison officer typology. Fewer of these had had previous military experience, and more of them had continued their education beyond the basic level. Occupationally, also, they were more ambitious in looking to skilled occupations as first job choices. As we have seen (Table 6.2) they were marginally the youngest group, also entering the Prison Service at the youngest age. These facts would seem to have some implications for Prison Service recruitment and training policy.

Reasons for joining the Prison Service seem rarely to be vocational in character but, as already pointed out, are concerned mainly with security of employment. This is very consistent with officers' family-centred life-style. Indeed their lives were very insular: they preferred to spend their leisure with their families, and failing that with Prison Service colleagues. As most of them lived in Prison Service quarters and some worked in prisons in rather isolated rural positions, the danger of institutionalisation is clear. It is therefore not surprising that so many of them found that they 'took the prison home with them'. The moves about the country which the Prison Service often demands of them seem less unpopular than might have been anticipated, some seeing it as a valuable 'broadening' experience. Where it was regretted it was on family grounds. Where they criticised the provision made for them by the prison it was also often the poor residential accommodation or the lack of amenities for families. But the promotion system also came in for its share of criticism.

8   Prison officers at work

We have, in the last chapter, looked at the factors in the backgrounds of our group of prison officers which might have affected their choice of the Prison Service as a career. It is only to be expected that social factors would also influence the way in which they saw the job, and therefore how they related to prisoners and to the organisation generally. A belief in the value of military discipline, an interest in becoming better educated, or the possession (or lack) of a vocational motivation for prison work, for instance, would all be likely to have their bearing on how the work was approached.

This chapter deals with the next stage, the training of staff after recruitment; and also with the eventual outcome in the shape of officers' attitudes to prison methods. We also examine aspects of the framework within which they do their work: how their services are deployed by the prison (studied with the aid of material collated from the prison officer's diary) and how much scope for the use of initiative and the exercise of discretion they feel they are permitted. Finally we examine some questionnaire data on punishments in prisons.

Training

The training of all prison officers includes at least one month at a prison, on probation, which is followed, for successful candidates, by a longer period at one of the two Officers' Training Schools where they receive basic instruction in all aspects of the prison officer's job. Successful completion of OTS training leads to a posting which may be in any Prison Department establishment. For the first few years of their service officers remain in a probationary status, after which training continues in a variety of ways. It is usual later on in their service for officers to attend refresher courses; while men required to undertake specialist duties such as security, staff training, catering and photographic work are provided with courses of instruction in these duties. Thus it would seem that staff training is accorded special attention by the Prison Department. However, as we have

177

pointed out, officers may differ with regard to their training potential. Officers entering from an industrial background may differ in the kind of duties in which they can best be trained from those with an armed forces background. For example, 'NCO skills', while appropriate to current custodial management practices, might be inappropriate to the non-custodial orientation called for by open prisons. How far those skills possessed at entry can be modified by training or how far entirely new and different skills are required are obviously important questions. Further consideration will now be given to the Prison Service training programme, and to officers' attitudes towards training and their evaluations of the training they have themselves received.

It is frequently contended by officers that, on arrival at the Officers' Training School, they are asked to forget all that they have learned during their first month in the prison and that, similarly, on taking up their first post they are told to forget the 'nonsense' taught at the training schools. We asked them in the questionnaire to evaluate both of these aspects of their training.

It is evident from Table 8.1 that fewer officers were satisfied with their initial training than were satisfied with the training given at the Officers' Training School. A recently trained officer distinguished neatly between the advantages and defects which he found in these two aspects of his own training. He wrote about his initial prison placement:

Table 8.1   Officers' opinions of the training received in their initial probationary placement and at the Officers' Training School

Opinion	Probationary placement %	OTS %
Very useful	33·6	44·3
Useful, but could be improved	35·7	47·1
Not very useful, needs a lot of improvement	22·1	6·4
Not at all useful	6·4	0·7
No response	2·1	1·4
Totals	99·9%	99·9%
N	140	140

'In this period we had an excellent training Principal Officer and the training given was generally fairly good. However, I do think we should have spent more time on the landings. Apart from that I have no complaint—I found most people helpful apart from the morons who saw us only as a threat to their overtime.'

And of the period spent at the Officers' Training School:

'Generally very useful apart from ridiculous marching routines. I did not want to join the army. Also the first-aid programme and the examination were farcical; otherwise the training course was excellent.'

The comments of other officers confirm these views. Where there was a conscientious training officer in post, that is an officer who had been detailed to superintend initial training activities, satisfaction was expressed or the training received was regarded as adequate. However, where this was not so, many officers complained about the absence of training, its 'trial and error' character or that it was impaired by staff shortages; and that other more experienced members of staff showed a complete lack of interest in the training exercise. The principal complaints about the course at the Officers' Training School were that it was too theoretical, too intensive or too short; that it contained unnecessary elements; or that its content was unrealistic. Finally, it is worth noting that respondents working in open prisons felt that the course was based on an assumption that there were no differences between open and closed, or adult and youth institutions, and therefore that special consideration was not given to ways in which their work might differ in these situations. As one young officer serving at an open prison observed:

'There is a considerable gulf between the role played by an officer in a closed prison and an officer working in an open prison which should positively be recognised, and the two types of staff, therefore, should consist of personnel selected and trained for either *open* or *closed* conditions, so that each individual is dedicated to the purpose of the type of establishment which he is working in.'

To summarise, the majority of officers felt that their training could be improved by making it more practical and by giving much more consideration to the variety to be found in the institutions in which they are later to be employed.

Application of the officer typology to the information about training affords some further clarifications (Table 8.2). There are few differences between the four types of officer in their evaluation of OTS training. There were proportionately more type 3 officers (older men who have been promoted) who considered the training school training could be improved a little. However, over 90 per cent

Table 8.2 Prison officer types' evaluation of probationary placement training

Evaluation	Type 1	Type 2	Type 3	Type 4
Very useful	25	18	40	37
Useful, but could be improved	29	49	36	41
Not very useful, needs much improvement	32	19	17	16
Not at all useful	14	14	7	3
No response	—	—	—	3
Totals	100%	100%	100%	100%
N	28	51	42	32

of all officers felt that this training was either very useful or required very little improvement. Evaluations of initial probationary placement training were more varied. The evidence here is that older officers (types 3 and 4) are much more likely than younger officers to consider such training to have been useful. On the other hand, of the younger officers, proportionately more type 1 (those with no further educational experience) expressed dissatisfaction with the training which they received at the beginning of their service.

Training, as we have indicated, continues well after the period at the Officers' Training School. As Table 8.3 shows, officers are exposed to a vast range of courses, although they are mainly of a technical rather than a vocational character. In all, 150 courses had been attended by the 140 officer respondents.

The majority of courses were clearly related to the need to train personnel to undertake specialist tasks; 81 per cent of the courses taken were of this kind. Vocational courses (19 per cent) were not only less frequently available, but were attended by only a few officers who had each completed several such courses. Similarly, certain older officers and promoted officers had taken several

Table 8.3   Courses attended by officers

Kind of course	Number attended
(i) *Technical courses*	
Refresher, Development and Promotion	34
Civil Defence	19
Projectionist/Photography and Fingerprints	13
Trade courses	11
Sports/PEI	10
Man-management	9
Principal Officer (Training)	8
Radio Instructor	8
Principal Officer (Security)	3
Medical courses	2
Parole	2
Observation and Classification	2
(ii) *Vocational courses*	
Probation and Social Work placements/ conferences on penal affairs	14
Social Studies courses	12
Group Counselling courses	3
Total	150
N	140

technical courses each. This means that some officers had attended no course at all. The nature of the imbalance is revealed by a typological comparison.

The information presented in Table 8.4 shows that in-service training courses have mainly been provided for men who were to be, or have been, promoted. Type 3 officers have, on average, attended three or four times as many such courses as any other group, and this includes type 4 officers who were similar in every way excepting that they had not been promoted during their career. It would seem that a substantial proportion of officers can spend a considerable period in the Prison Service without being exposed to the benefits which such further training might bring.

Our prison officers proved to be very critical consumers of these in-service training experiences. Their widespread dissatisfaction is perhaps most clearly expressed by reference to their own comments. The following were not at all atypical of comments made more

Table 8.4   The number of courses attended by each type of officer

Type of course attended	Type 1	Type 2	Type 3	Type 4
In-service training courses	10	23	82	25
Vocational courses	3	4	7	2
Totals	13	27	89	27
N	28	51	42	32
Average number of courses per man	0·5	0·5	2·1	0·8

generally and serve to illustrate many of the problems and short-comings in the courses offered to them as they are perceived by prison officers themselves.

(i)   'The probation attachment was not long enough. A fortnight would have been much better. You may have at least understood a few of the programmes.

The sports and games course has been of use to me personally but I have had no opportunity of passing that experience to inmates.'

(ii) 'A 10-week course at Wakefield, which included some aspects of sociology and the techniques of interviewing, by staff that did not seem interested in their job and did not really believe in the usefulness of sociology, casework, welfare work, in prisons or in progress of any kind.'

(iii) 'Laundry Instructors course. Training severely limited by work pressures on the Principal Officer instructor at Wandsworth Laundry. I found myself acting as an additional instructor, supervising prisoners for the major part of the course.'

(iv) 'Hospital Officers course. This course is totally inadequate for anyone who has no previous experience of nursing and needs a lot of improving to be of any real value.'

(v)   'A day release course (in Sociology) at Millbank College, Liverpool still exists today. Very useful if used in connection with the job, and fortified with appropriate reading. Used as a "day trip" in isolation, it is less than useless: could be dangerous. Some extramural activity in same subject at Liverpool University. Again rewarding for the open-minded officer who takes what he consumes with a little salt.'

(vi) 'The promotion course was given by various personnel, Chief Officers, Principal Officers, Staff College Principal, all very good, useful and very much appreciated. The refresher course was apparently aimed at getting the officers to discuss problems of their establishments. This in essence is a good idea, but in practice it seemed to encourage more shop talk rather than discussions.'

(vii) 'Staff course 1961; the main defects were:

(a) At that time officers selected for the staff course remained officers for the duration of the course whilst direct entrants held the rank of A.G.2 (i.e. Assistant Governor).

(b) We were subjected to much psychological pressure, e.g. being told at times not to worry, there was room for us all, whilst at other times it was strongly hinted that success was by no means certain.

(c) The whole thing was run on juvenile lines; with the benefit of hindsight I realised it was far more important to be a character than to be mature and hard working. I should have played touch rugby in the common room rather than working in my own room.

(d) This particular staff course included a number of Senior Officers. I now know that it was experimental. Someone had the idea that the Senior Officers and direct entrants would irritate and stimulate each other. This did not happen. Everyone involved saw through the ploy and all settled down to be the best of friends. The course as a result was rather stodgy. I feel that the experienced officers were blamed for this.

(e) I failed.'

Such a range of dissatisfactions with the training courses highlights some of the particular problems of staff training in the Prison Service. But do these dissatisfactions arise because such courses as are offered are unsuitable for prison officers, or because prison officers, by and large, are unsuited for the kind of training which is provided? If prison officers themselves are to be believed, it is the training which is inadequate: they seem to take the view that there is within the service a pool of ability which is not tapped by present methods for, if it were fully utilised, they argue, it would be unnecessary for one thing to have within prisons an independently staffed welfare service. They have reacted in the same way to the comparatively recent introduction into the prison system of professional industrial managers. The arrival of such personnel has been viewed by many officers as an unnecessary act of trespass and met by hostility and resentment. However, there is also a case to be made for the opposite point of view: that training fails because some prison officers are unable to benefit from the kinds of training provided or indeed, taking a broader view, the kinds of training needed if there is to be a successful breakaway from traditional patterns of prison organisation and management. Without wishing to absolve Home Office training policy from all blame (as will be seen later) we think that the evidence to be reviewed in this section lends some support to the latter view. This section will, therefore, be concluded by reviewing the evidence on the social characteristics and Prison Service careers of prison officers in the light of what seems to be its most important implications for staff training.

We have seen that differences between the staffs in the closed and open prisons in their social backgrounds, pre-Prison Service socialisation experience (pp. 153f.) and Prison Service careers (pp. 162f.) are small. In addition, and perhaps of greater significance, the training received by the staffs of the four prisons is similar: no special training is provided for open prison staff. Thus, the training received by open prison staff after Officers' Training School betrays a preoccupation with security which is more appropriate to the closed situations in which, admittedly, the majority of prison officers work. Missing are enough opportunities for learning what one might think were vital human relations skills. Nor even were there courses of a more general character in which the distinguishing features of open prisons could be explored. Officers seem to be expected, instead, to pick up the requisite special knowledge and skill as they go along. Whether or not this actually occurs or what happens if it does not would appear to be questions which have not yet greatly concerned prison administrators.

The absence of special training facilities for open prison staff could be taken to indicate a more general lack of awareness of the problems to be faced in creating correctional regimes which embody a departure from traditional custodial patterns. The literature indicates that if such ventures are to be successful, intensive training programmes are required, but that even where such courses are available, they are not wholly successful in encouraging staff to modify their custodial roles. Carl Jesness[1] has provided a good example in his evaluation of a programme to create purpose-built regimes in two Californian Youth Authority institutions—one a 'token economy' regime based upon operant conditioning theory, and the other organised in accordance with Berne's theory of transactional analysis. In both cases many difficulties were encountered over staff training. Intensive orientation courses proved to be inadequate and were followed up by numerous refresher courses, not all of which were judged to have been successful. For some of the correctional personnel involved, the acquisition of new roles proved to be impossible because they lacked the adaptability or educability needed to appreciate and practise the aims embodied in the training programmes.

The dearth of opportunities for special training could, alternatively, imply that the Prison Department has not yet come round to seeing most prison officers as suitable for it or even to any policy of selective training for the most suitable men. The trend, much to the resentment of prison officers, has been to recruit specialist personnel from outside the service. Thus the development of prison industries has resulted in the recruitment of a specialist grade of industrial managers; the expansion of prison welfare facilities has been made the responsibility of personnel from local probation departments; executive and clerical grade civil servants have been introduced into prisons in order to deal with the increasingly more complex administrative requirements. An illustration of the effect on prison officers of such developments is provided by Parker[2] in his account of a therapeutic regime in the psychiatric prison at Grendon Underwood. Apart from hospital officers, prison officers posted to Grendon appeared not to have received any special training. It is not surprising, therefore, that they reacted in varying ways to the appointment of a doctor as Governor and Medical Superintendent and the full-time presence within the prison of numerous other professional groups including psychiatrists, psychologists and welfare officers. While some officers (mainly on their own initiative) made very positive efforts to adapt to the requirements of the therapeutic regime, there were others who reacted against it. The presence of the latter was undoubtedly a hindrance to the development of the regime, and a hindrance which might have been avoided had more attention been paid to staff selection and training.

Some of our respondents, as we have seen, showed awareness of the role which could be played by the adoption of more purposeful selection and training procedures with particular tasks in mind. Although each officer brings his own individual skills and experience to the job, questions have, on our evidence, rarely been asked about who is most suitable for doing or being trained to do what. Obviously many improvements could be made, but at various points in this study there is more than a hint that more thought should be given to the question of how to select suitable men for specific tasks or, alternatively, how effectively to train men with varying experiences and abilities to function differently in different kinds of establishment.

The Grendon experience does indicate that there were prison officers who possessed sufficient adaptability and educability to have responded to the requirements of the unusual new regime; who saw the advantage of working with the professionals who had been appointed; and who acquired, mainly on their own initiative, the requisite skills. However, it may well be the case that, owing to the nature of and the publicity given to this particular experiment, Grendon attracted more than its share of such officers, and did so even in the absence of purposeful selection and training procedures. While a similar state of affairs may have prevailed with regard to open prisons when they were first introduced, the evidence here, given the overall similarities between staffs in open and closed prisons, is that it no longer seems to be so.

The other problem, ignorance of how to create correctional regimes, also seems to be important, however. Except in the long-term open prison there seems to be little clear idea within the Prison Service of what an open prison regime should be like. Until the Prison Department has at least decided what staff are going to be expected to do in open institutions, for instance, it is not possible to select or train them specifically for that purpose.

Three related features of Prison Service selection and training procedures have an important bearing on the situation described above. First, all recruitment and initial training is undertaken in closed prisons and it is, therefore, most probable that an applicant's suitability for the work is measured largely with regard to their staffing requirements. Although we have no positive information on this score from our research this may also influence the kinds of persons who offer themselves for appointment or who leave during their probationary period. Reference has been made earlier (p. 179) to officers in this study who, for instance, found the attitude of existing staff towards trainee officers to be, if not overtly hostile, at least perplexing. Second, as has been shown, training appears to proceed without recognition that there may be different requirements for staff of open prisons or of closed prisons, local or training prisons, or of Prison Department facilities for younger offenders. Third, the evidence from this study shows that staff are posted to open prisons on an apparently random basis, presumably in the expectation that they will nevertheless respond adequately to the demands of such an unfamiliar situation. Given that officers in open prisons have arrived with experience gained mainly in closed prisons, it would be surprising if there were no problems of adjustment for them or if some officers, failing to adjust to open conditions, simply carried on as before. (During the research period an officer who had been involved to the point of serious personal injury in the Parkhurst prison disturbances of 1969 was posted to one of the open prisons. He found conditions there so lax and personally intolerable that he immediately requested a transfer to another closed prison.)

The Grendon experience in particular supports our view that even with training, not all prison officers would be able or would want to operate within an open prison framework. This is not to call into question the relevance of the social skills, experience or previous training of some, for work in primarily custodial institutions where security, good order and discipline, and inmate conformity to Prison Rules are the most important things. But the success of open prisons would be heavily dependent upon the willingness and ability of prison officers to acquire social skills which are rather different. In what follows, therefore, attention will be focused on the evidence from this study about staff potential for open prison work, and on the bearing of this on existing selection and training procedures. Thus, while what we have to say may have general implications for selection and training generally in the Prison Service, only those aspects which have a bearing on the staffing of open prisons will be developed at this point.

There is depressingly little evidence from this study that many prison officers, including those currently employed in open prisons, joined the service because they were interested in people or for similar 'vocational' reasons. Similarly, there are comparatively few indications that, during their Prison Service careers, officers become interested enough in this aspect of their work to pursue appropriate studies, for instance courses in groupwork or social studies. Their motivation in joining the Prison Service was more likely to have been to obtain the status and security of a respectable job. Their main concern was with the security, pay, pension and accommodation provided. For many also, the Prison Service represented a congenial billet after prolonged engagements in the armed forces, as compared with civilian life. In other words, the vast majority of prison officers did not join the service with the ambition of acquiring more effective skills to be employed in the treatment and training of prison inmates.

The accumulating evidence on the *suitability* of some officers for this sort of training holds equally gloomy implications. The initial downward mobility or sideways movement into 'dead end' occupations noted in many prison officers' careers before joining the Prison Service may have its relevance according to the reasons for it. For instance, there may have been an economic reason: a preference for occupations which were immediately rewarding to the school-leaver as opposed to much less well paid apprenticeships. Or there may have been a psychological reason: apprenticeships were not taken because the individuals concerned were not prepared to accept the continuation of a 'school' role in the way implied in an apprenticeship. On the other hand, it is possible that the choice of skilled craft occupations was low because some of these men were personally or educationally more suited to the kinds of work they had chosen. While none of these explanations can be ruled out entirely, there is some evidence from this study which suggest that the latter was probably the most influential of these factors.

Examination of the educational histories of prison officers in the four prisons revealed that, for the group as a whole, there was limited trace of formal educational interest and attainment. Moreover, the typological comparison showed that such evidence as there was, was concentrated within one group. So if there is, as prison officers themselves claim, an untapped pool of ability within the Prison Service, it seems mainly to be represented by this group of officers—type 2 officers: younger men with some further educational experience. However, there is an important *caveat* to be considered: lack of formal educational attainment for a working class group, in particular for a group which left school between 1935 and 1950, is not necessarily proof of lack of ability. This apart, there are indications from this study which suggest a positive association between proof of educational attainment and the training potential of our officer respondents.

In the first place, evidence in a man's career of further educational experience does suggest that he may be both willing and able to undertake the training needed in order to operate effectively in therapeutic roles. Also the achievement of jobs in skilled crafts by type 2 officers meant that any overall trend of downward mobility did not apply to this group. There is less evidence also for this group of the exodus from civilian occupations into professional military service which is characteristic of the other types of officer.

The effect of military service introduces another possibility which cuts across the suggested relationship between the educational attainments and the training potential of different types of prison officers. Although it seems from the make-up of our 'types' that the educational experiences of officers who entered professional military service differ from those who did not, the experience of military service itself may itself help to blunt the training potential of Prison Service entrants from that source. Looking at the Prison Service as a whole, what evidence there is suggests that the most prevalent social skills possessed by prison officers are similar to, and sometimes derive from, those utilised by the non-commissioned officer in the armed forces. Indeed, the majority of officers in this study for whom information is available did, at some stage, occupy such ranks (Table 7.8).

More generally, the relevance of a military model for interpersonal relations in prisons is evident in the paramilitary structure of the service and in the kinds of relationship maintained between staff at all levels within the formal hierarchy. These may be appropriate to the disciplinary requirements of the closed custodially oriented institutions in which officers are recruited and trained, and tend to spend the largest part, if not all, of their Prison Service careers; but not to other settings, including open prison. They seem to require different approaches especially in the handling of interpersonal relations both between staff members themselves and between staff and inmates. As we have seen, there was an absence of such differences between the staff of open and closed prisons in this study, with obvious implications for the way in which officers perceive and perform their work in open prisons. In other words, the predominance of residual NCO social skills in open prisons is an indication of inappropriate selections or training or both. In fact, there is evidence of 'trained incapacity'.

Robert Merton[3] defined 'trained incapacity' as:

> that state of affairs in which one's abilities function as in-
> adequacies or blind spots. Actions based upon training and
> skills which have been successfully applied in the past may
> result in inappropriate responses *under changed conditions*. An
> inadequate flexibility in the application of skills, will, in a
> changing milieu, result in more or less serious maladjustments

. . . . In general, one adopts measures in keeping with one's past training and, under new conditions which are not recognised as *significantly* different, the very soundness of this training may lead to the adoption of the wrong procedures . . . training may become an incapacity. (italics in original)[4]

Thus, while bureaucratic structures exert constant pressures on participating individuals to be 'methodical, prudent and disciplined', displacement of goals (in which adherence to the rules, instead of being a means, becomes an end in itself) may occur. An effect of this, possessing an immediate relevance for prison personnel, is as Merton puts it, that:

Discipline, readily interpreted as conformance with regulations, whatever the situation, is seen not as a measure designed for specific purposes but becomes an immediate value in the life-organization of the bureaucrat. This emphasis, resulting from the displacement of original goals, develops into rigidities and an inability to adjust readily. Formalism, even ritualism, ensues with an unchallenged insistence upon punctilious adherence to formalized procedures.[5]

In the case of open prisons, such 'trained incapacity' among staff probably originates from their previous experience as professional servicemen. It will be recalled that similar proportions of staff working in open and closed prisons had shared such experiences. If it did not mature at that juncture of their careers, its development was almost certainly encouraged by their initial experience of work in closed institutions, nurtured by the paramilitary structure of the Prison Service itself and buttressed throughout by the kinds of training received. It will also be recalled that there is some evidence for a staff culture which clearly reflects the past experiences of the majority of prison officers and the kinds of training which they have received. This culture also fosters the development of behaviours and attitudes which may not be relevant to the requirements of open prisons. In these circumstances, it would be most surprising if an examination of the pattern of work undertaken by prison officers in open prisons and their attitudes and opinions about their work revealed substantial departures from what happens in closed prisons.

A more purposeful training programme for open prison staff which would root out some of the worst effects of 'trained incapacity' is obviously called for. There is also a further possibility that not all entrants to the Prison Service are equally suitable for such training, particularly with regard to their educational abilities or, more generally, their adaptability. It may, therefore, also be necessary to implement more refined recruitment and selection procedures for the staffing of open prisons.

Staff deployment

A comparative picture of the kinds of work undertaken by prison officers in each prison and the proportionate amount of time spent by them on the performance of various duties is provided by the prison officer's diary. The results are presented in Table 8.5.

Generally, the differences between prisons were very slight, though there were differences in the average number of hours worked. Officers in the medium-term closed prison (and those in the long- and short-term closed prisons which have been excluded from this analysis) on average worked a longer day than those in the open prisons. Beyond this, there was a definite pattern in the variation in the number of hours worked in different open prisons which holds for uniformed staff of all ranks. As found in the analysis of the CIES data, the short-term open prison was most similar to the closed prisons, and the medium- and long-term open prisons progressively more different. A second overall difference between open and closed prisons was that in closed prisons, staff above the rank of senior officer worked a longer day than basic grade staff, while the reverse was the case in open prisons. It may be of interest that there is, within the Prison Service, a fairly widely held opinion that the long service of certain senior officers is informally rewarded by their being 'put out to grass' in open prisons. It would appear that a few did make use of this opportunity to 'graze'.

Examination of the proportions of time allocated overall to various duties (see Table 8.5) reveals only slight differences in the kinds of work undertaken and in the priority given to particular tasks. In both open and closed prisons inmate supervision, security functions and administration accounted for the bulk of staff activities. In contrast, comparatively little time was spent on rehabilitation, staff discussion and staff training, although there was slightly more emphasis on these in the medium-term and long-term open prisons. Staff in each prison above the rank of senior officer had greater variety in their work than basic grade officers, a difference to be expected in view of the special responsibilities which go with seniority.

Table 8.5   Prison officer's Diary: percentage of working day spent on listed activities

Job category*	Medium-term closed			Short-term open		
	ASO	BG	All ranks	ASO	BG	All ranks
A Supervision	14·7	58·2	43·3	31·6	71·2	65·9
B Security	8·1	28·9	21·8	1·7	17·4	15·3
C Staff supervision	51·1	0·4	17·8	15·4	—	2·1
D Observation	—	—	—	—	—	—
E Court duty	—	—	—	—	—	—
F Rehabilitation	0·4	—	0·1	—	—	—
G Staff discussion	1·7	—	0·6	—	—	—
H Staff training	—	—	—	—	—	—
I Administration	19·9	9·3	12·9	7·7	11·4	11·0
J Other duties	4·1	3·2	3·5	43·6	—	5·8
Total %	100%	100%	100%	100%	100%	100·1%
Average number of hours worked	10·1	9·9	9·9	8·4	9·3	9·1

Job category*	Medium-term open			Long-term open		
	ASO	BG	All ranks	ASO	BG	All ranks
A Supervision	11·4	39·2	33·8	34·2	52·7	48·2
B Security	0·8	18·7	15·2	3·1	13·5	11·0
C Staff supervision	24·3	0·3	5·0	12·1	—	2·9
D Observation	3·0	—	0·6	—	—	—
E Court duty	—	6·8	5·5	—	7·2	5·4
F Rehabilitation	8·2	9·8	9·5	7·1	3·3	4·2
G Staff discussion	3·0	0·3	0·8	3·7	—	0·9
H Staff training	18·0	1·2	4·4	3·7	—	0·9
I Administration	27·8	16·7	18·8	32·6	6·2	12·6
J Other duties	3·5	7·1	6·4	3·4	17·1	13·8
Total %	100%	100·1%	100%	99·9%	100%	99·9%
Average number of hours worked	7·7	8·7	8·5	6·2	7·8	7·5

ASO = Uniformed staff of senior officer rank and above.
BG = Basic grade uniformed staff.
*Job categories are defined in Appendix 3.

An approximate measure of the degree of similarity between the four prisons in the allocation of priority to particular tasks was obtained by ranking the various duties in order of the proportion of time spent on them by the staff of each prison and computing Kendall's rank correlation coefficient (tau) for each constituent pair of prisons. The results of this analysis (Table 8.6) indicate an overall similarity in the patterning of staff activity. Such differences as exist parallel those already noted for the number of hours worked—and also those found in the CIES material. The medium-term closed and the short-term open prisons are very similar—the highest degree of concordance is found between these two. There is

Table 8.6 Within-groups correlation matrix (tau) for the proportionate distribution of time spent on each staff activity in each prison

	Short-term open	Medium-term open	Long-term open
Medium-term closed	0·88	0·57	0·48
Short-term open	—	0·68	0·59
Medium-term open	—	—	0·71

progressively less similarity in the patterning of staff activity as one compares these two prisons with first, the medium-term open prison and then the long-term open. Finally, as may be expected, there is some resemblance between work patterns in the medium- and long-term open prisons. These data also support the familiar continuum in which the shorter the period for which open prisons hold inmates, the closer the patterning of staff activity within them becomes to that found in the closed prison. The medium- and long-term open prisons appear as slightly different from the medium-term closed and short-term open prisons because there is less emphasis on duties connected with inmate regulation and security and a little more on such aspects as rehabilitation, staff discussion and staff training. However, these differences are marginal and can in no way be said to measure up to the expectations of those who favoured, and campaigned for, the introduction of open prisons. Even allowing for the ambiguity of such categories as supervision and administration, the total amount of time devoted to duties connected with inmate control and security must be greatly in excess of such expectations and point out the extent to which 'closed prison' definitions of staff duties and responsibilities seem to have been transplanted to open prisons.

In all prisons, proportionately more time was spent on the supervision of inmates than on any other activity. This itself is not wholly surprising because the rubric 'supervision' does cover such a wide range of more or less necessary activities including the oversight of association and exercise; the provision of escorts for inmates using educational, recreational, welfare and medical facilities; the control of work parties and workshop supervision; visits and adjudications. There were some local differences in circumstances which suggest amendment of the general picture presented in Table 8.5. For instance, although a smaller proportion of the working day was spent on supervision in the medium-term open prison, this is partly accounted for by the presence within the prison of a large number of civilian instructor officers who took away from uniformed staff a substantial part of the burden of workshop control. Similarly, it is likely that this category of activity in other prisons was relatively increased by demands made for the supervision of outside working parties. Such qualifications apart, any expectations which there may have been that there would be less need for inmate supervision in open prisons are not matched by this information on staff deployment. Inmates seem to be even more closely supervised in open than they are in closed prisons—a confirmation of our earlier conclusion that this appears to be expected as a *quid pro quo* for any relaxation which openness brings with it.

There was, on the other hand, a real difference in both the actual and proportional allocation of time to security duties, more time being spent on these in the closed prison. Although all open prisons were differentiated from the medium-term closed in this respect, there were differences also between the long-term open prisons and the other two opens. These might be accounted for by the kinds of inmate held. Inmates of the long-term open were selected by the Governor, who took into account not only their chances of responding constructively to the regime, but also looked for a low security risk. The inmates of the other open prisons were regarded as marginally more likely to escape and, thus, perhaps the greater concern with security at these prisons. This was evident in the physical presence of boundaries such as chain-link fencing and in the number of parades, roll calls and other checks on inmate activities conducted daily in the short-term and medium-term open prisons. The overt persistence of the containment motive is obvious enough; the supervision figures examined above reflect a less transparent approach to security. If formal bars to escaping are fewer, the supervision of prisoners takes up the strain instead. This is obvious enough in the high figures for supervision in the long-term open. In the short-term open, with less commitment to 'openness', nearly two-thirds of officers' time is devoted to prisoner surveillance, but without the long-term open's countervailing slightly lower figures for security.

A second aim of the diary was to determine the extent to which staff in open prisons were encouraged to take a more active role in running the prison and in the rehabilitation of inmates. The first of these aspects was covered by entries under 'staff supervision' and 'administration' and the second under 'rehabilitation'.

Staff supervision was largely the preserve of officers above the rank of senior officer. Most of this activity was routine and there seemed to be very few opportunities for more imaginative involvement in the day-to-day-management of the prisons. Even where such opportunities did exist, as was the case at the medium-term closed prison, their practical effects (for reasons discussed earlier—see pp. 39f.) were negligible. The proportion of time devoted to staff supervision was highest in that prison (17.8 per cent). Although time spent on staff supervision in all open prisons was by comparison low, twice as long was devoted to it at the medium-term open prison as compared with the other two. There was a widely held belief among basic grade staff at this prison that it had 'too many chiefs and not enough Indians'. Another way of looking at staff supervision, however, is as a way of supporting and guiding basic grade staff, who do have to bear most of the heat and burden of the day in prisons. Seen from this viewpoint basic grade staff in open prisons are not very well supported. Having lost the formal back-up of the closed regime, they do seem, in the light of the low percentages for staff supervision, to be thrown a good deal on to their own resources. In a situation in which open prison objectives are unclear, such a lack of support seems bound to lead to uncertainty, and an undue reliance on the kind of support from each other, which adherence to a staff culture would bring with it. This may be one of the consequences of the inactivity of those senior staff who have been (as it was alleged) 'put out to grass' in open prisons.

The amount of time spent on administration is equally revealing. It was expected that those prisons accommodating men with shorter sentences would be involved in more administration because of the work involved in processing the frequent population movements. This, in fact, was not so. It seems that home leaves, parole, etc., take their toll in the time which has to be devoted to administrative work. In all cases senior officers were more involved in these administrative duties and a substantial proportion of their working day was occupied in carrying them out. The evidence of high levels of bureaucratisation in prisons, however, may in other ways be felt to have disturbing implications. It suggests, for instance, that paperwork is receiving greater priority than the treatment or training of inmates. Only in the medium-term open prison where some officers were attached permanently to a parole and pre-release unit and, to a lesser extent, the long-term open prison, did the time given to duties connected with the rehabilitation of inmates rise above a derisory level. Where they were attended to, they appeared to be undertaken more frequently by senior staff.

The third aim in administering the diary was to discover to what extent time was set aside in open prisons to enable staff to equip themselves for the performance of their rehabilitative role. It will be recalled that very little provision was made for such requirements in Prison Department training courses. Consequently one might have anticipated that there would be such opportunities for staff training and staff discussion in the open prisons themselves, in compensation. Such expectations were in no way realised—as might have been expected in view of the small amount of time devoted to rehabilitation itself. While there was some evidence of greater concentration on these activities in the medium-term and long-term open prisons, the overall level was so low that the differences found do not count for much. It cannot be said that staff discussion and staff training were regular features in any of the prisons surveyed, open or closed. Even such marginally hopeful signs as can be discovered in Table 8.5 are less comforting when looked at more closely. The 18 per cent devoted to training in the medium-term open prison, for example, reflects mainly the activities of senior officers who have special responsibilities for in-service training, or the occasional officer on day-release studies, representing overall a good deal of preparation but very little actual training. It is worth noting that even in this prison, little of the working time of basic grade staff was allocated for training them, yet they represent the ostensible targets for all this senior staff activity. Yet another instance of the poor utilisation of the more favourable senior to basic grade staff ratios in open prisons is thus revealed.

It seems that just as there has been no provision for the special training requirements of open prisons in centrally sponsored courses, so also there has been very little provision made for such training in open prisons themselves. This is partly because the need for a special kind of training is not recognised, but also results from a feeling that men could not be spared. In other words, inmate supervision, security duties and administration are clearly defined as having higher priority than training, even in open prisons. Given careful and elaborate screening of inmates before they are selected for open prison conditions, this hardly seems a satisfactory state of affairs.

Very little time was spent in any prison on observation and classification duties or on legal aid work. Although these duties are usually undertaken earlier, in local prisons, this category was included in order to establish how far legal aid facilities were available and utilised in open prisons. With the exception of the medium-term open prison where this activity was restricted to the work of one officer, it would seem that there were few facilities of this nature.

Court duties were carried out exclusively by basic grade staff. It is noticeable that these escort duties were undertaken only by officers from the medium-term and long-term open prisons where there were the more favourable staff-inmate ratios. They would seem also to be providing relief officers for other prisons. If this is so then it has serious implications, because if prisons with high staff-inmate ratios are seen as having a pool of staff available for duties in other prisons, the point of having them seems to be lost, to the detriment of both staff and inmates.

To summarise, the evidence from the prison officer's diary reveals an overall similarity in the kinds of work carried out in open and closed prisons. However, although differences between prisons are not great, there is a distinctive patterning in these differences. Both with regard to the length of the working day and with regard to the allocation of priority to particular tasks, the closed prison and the short-term open prison are most similar. Beyond this, there is progressively less similarity between these and the medium-term and long-term open prisons, the latter being least like the closed prison. The assessment and comparison of prison regimes in earlier chapters revealed the same kind of pattern, bringing out the relationship between staff activities and regimes. Although there was evidence of a greater emphasis on security in closed prisons, there was a parallel emphasis on inmate supervision in the open prisons which seems, in a less formal way, to serve the same purpose. Little time seems to have been devoted anywhere to staff training and no recognition at all given to the different training needs of open prison staff. Everywhere administration looms quite large. Finally, there is the deficiency in staff supervision by senior staff of the open prisons: a lack of support for basic grade staff in a situation which is already likely to seem confused and threatening because of the lack of clarity about aims and methods.

Attitudes to the job

In their Pentonville study, the Morrises found that staff discontent with their job occurred mainly as a result of staff shortages, overcrowding, poor residential and working facilities for staff, and staff conflict and lack of teamwork. There is no reason to believe that any improvement has occurred in such aspects of local closed prisons like Pentonville during the ten years since the Morrises' work. Indeed, given the rapid increase in the prison population and the generally poor level of staff recruitment during this period, it is possible that such problems may have intensified. This is certainly suggested by Richard Sparks's[6] more recently published study. The situation could, however, be different in both closed training prisons and open prisons. Both have been sheltered to some extent from the immediate effects of overcrowding. In order to explore these questions, prison officers were asked to list in order of priority the three main problems which tended to render their work more difficult (see Table 8.7).

Whereas a typological analysis shows that there were no major differences between types of officer respondent with regard to their selection of problems, there were considerable differences between staffs in open and closed prisons. Staff in the medium-term closed prison, as well as those in the prisons excluded from the statistical analysis, i.e. the short-term and long-term closed, identified high working hours (a reflection of staff shortages), overcrowding and poor working conditions (for instance, the old buildings), as their main problems. Low pay was high on the lists of staff in both open and closed prisons, and the frequency of its inclusion may reflect a general concern within the Prison Service about this matter. However, given that staff in open prisons worked fewer hours on average, and therefore presumably earned less overtime, there is perhaps greater justification for the inclusion of low pay in the responses from them. Apart from this aspect it may be concluded that, as far as closed prisons are concerned, officers' perceptions of the main problems associated with their work differ very little from the picture revealed by the Pentonville study.

Table 8.7   The three main problems in prison officers' work

Problem	Medium-term closed	Short-term open	Medium-term open	Long-term open
1 Low pay	17	9	30	19
2 Conflicting instructions	8	18	34	10
3 Poor conditions of work	20	9	15	18
4 Overcrowding in prisons	20	6	11	11
5 High working hours	26	8	7	3
6 Lack of teamwork among officers	6	6	11	12
7 Lack of co-operation from prisoners	4	2	6	8
8 Inadequate staff quarters	1	6	1	10
9 Increased 'paperwork'	2	4	9	3
10 Lack of amenities for prisoners	1	0	0	1
11 Others	4	1	8	4
12 No response	5	0	3	3
Total	114	69	135	102
N	38	23	45	34

Chi-squared (items 1-6), 15 d.f., $= 55\cdot990$, $p < 0\cdot001$.

Responses from open prisons revealed some differences. In addition to references to low pay, the principal complaints about work in open prisons concerned conflicting instructions, lack of teamwork among the staff and, to a lesser extent, the inadequacy of staff quarters. Concern with the first two of these three issues would seem to reveal a degree of uncertainty among administrators and senior staff about the ways in which open prisons should operate. This, like evidence from the observational chapter of this study as well as the CIES and the Staff Diary, point to the same ambiguity between containment and openness, which may represent the main problem in developing distinctive and effective open regimes. It is worth noting that the staff of the long-term open, in which the Governor was clearer about his aims, made fewer complaints about conflicting instructions—only marginally more than in the closed prisons. This does not mean, as we have seen, that this Governor had no staff opposition to meet: there were some expressions of hostility, both overt and covert, towards his policy. These were, however, more of a minority view, especially among staff who had had longer periods in service in the prison.

The concern with the quality and condition of their quarters expressed by prison officers in open prisons may in the first place actually reflect the poor quality of the accommodation made available to them. This was almost certainly so at the short-term open prison, where many of the staff lived in prefabricated housing very close to the main prison. However, there were as many complaints at the long-term open prison, where there was a purpose-built estate of recent and sound construction. It is possible, therefore, that complaints were not exclusively about the quality of accommodation, but referred also to such inconveniences as the lack of shopping amenities, and of recreational, educational and employment opportunities for staff and their families in isolated rural postings. The likelihood of this second reason being true is increased by the evidence from the third, the medium-term open prison, where there was also a modern estate for staff but where the incidence of complaints about quarters was low. Staff of this prison are much less isolated. The prison is situated near important urban centres, giving easy access to facilities of every description.

When asked to evaluate changes that had occurred in prisons since they had joined the service, prison officers showed a good deal of agreement (see Table 8.8). The majority (71·4 per cent) thought that there was less discipline, and disapproved of this. A similar proportion approved of the increase in prison security and a much larger proportion still (85 per cent) thought that the implementation of Mountbatten Report recommendations had been generally good for prisons. All of which embodied the familiar containment viewpoint. Somewhat at variance with this were the views expressed about welfare provisions for prisoners, informal staff contact with them, and rehabilitation and training facilities for them. In each case, a substantial majority of officers approved the increase in such activities. Although there were dissenting minority groups, real disagreement in staff opinions occurred only over the extent to which the status of officers had changed, and concerning evaluations of the perceived increase in Home Office control.

It would appear that, contrary to the view usually expressed about the attitude of staff to custody and treatment in prison management, prison officers are not conscious of their ambivalence in supporting, on the one hand, custodial measures designed to increase prison discipline and security and, on the other, therapeutic measures

Table 8.8 Prison officers' perceptions of changes in the Prison Service

	An increase approved	No change approved	A decrease approved	An increase disapproved	No change disapproved	A decrease disapproved	No response	N
Prison discipline	2	9	19	—	3	100	7	140
Prison security	86	19	1	7	5	11	11	140
Welfare provisions for prisoners	86	12	—	26	2	—	14	140
Informal staff contact with prisoners	98	17	1	9	2	5	8	140
Rehabilitation and training facilities for prisoners	83	22	1	5	11	8	10	140
Status of officers	28	15	—	—	32	56	9	140
Home Office control	35	35	4	31	14	3	18	140

aimed at the improvement of prison welfare, rehabilitation and training and better staff-inmate communication and interaction. How far does the strength of this ambivalence differ in different prisons? Table 8.9 gives figures separately for each of the four prisons. If one adds the first three responses, as generally containment-oriented, and compares them with the last three as therapy-

Table '8.9   *The percentage of staff in each prison subscribing to selected perceptions and evaluations of changes in the Prison Service*

	Medium-term closed (%)	Short-term open (%)	Medium-term open (%)	Long-term open (%)
Prison discipline (less disapprove)	71	73	78	56
Prison security (more approve)	58	74	64	53
Mountbatten Report (generally good for prisons)	89	87	84	79
Welfare provisions for prisoners (more approve)	58	48	60	76
Informal staff contact with prisoners (more approve)	66	48	69	91
Rehabilitation and training facilities for prisoners (more approve)	50	52	56	79
N	38	23	45	34

oriented the following ratios are obtained: medium-term closed 1·26; short-term open 1·58; medium-term open 1·22; long-term open 0·76. The most obvious feature of these figures is the usual distinctive position of the long-term open, which once again shows the lowest level of conflict between the two ostensible objectives of the prison, a conflict which is bound to be particularly characteristic of the open prison, but in the light of Rule 1 of the Prison Rules exists in closed institutions also. (Rule 1 states: 'The purpose of the training and treatment of convicted prisoners shall be to encourage and assist them to lead a good and useful life.') The particular force of this paradox in the open prisons is shown by these figures. The short-term open displays it in even more acute form than does the closed prison and even the medium-term open is hardly less ambivalent than the latter.

In calling attention to the contradictory objectives of open prisons, one may be identifying a major conflict in all modern, theoretically rehabilitative penal institutions. It seems that this conflict may not be consciously recognised by prison staffs. There is, however, an alternative possibility. It may be that compatibility between custodial and treatment or training objectives in prison management is still possible because, while approving of changes involving, for instance, the provision of more or better rehabilitation and training facilities, prison officers are prepared to concede their introduction only within the context of secure and disciplined regimes. The level of support within the Prison Service and the Prison Officers' Association at the present time for the introduction of such improvements in prisons with high perimeter security would tend to support this interpretation. In addition, there is the evidence from the prison officer's diary showing the extent to which, even in open prisons, staff were deployed on supervisory and security duties at the expense of treatment or training tasks, and the massive approval expressed in all kinds of prison for the increased security measures advocated by the Mountbatten Report (see Table 8.8).

The dilemma in which the staff of open prisons then find themselves is clear, for they can find no comfort in formal safeguards of this kind, which would be impossible to institute under open conditions. There seems to be no alternative to a redefinition of containment as an aim for open prisons, unless their 'open' character is to continue to be vitiated by informal security practices of the sort referred to in the discussion of the diary material. As long as officers feel that escape from an open prison is considered officially to be such a serious matter, they will feel pressured by the system to subvert 'openness'—as sheer self-defence—and that irrespective of any more appropriate selection or training process with its possible effect of employing in open prisons staff who are well disposed towards freer regimes. It is, of course, the need for a clarification of the question: What is an open prison? which is involved here.

That such clarification could help is shown by the experience gained in the long-term open prison. This prison shows that staff attitudes and behaviour are not necessarily shaped completely by the prison staff culture referred to above, but may also be influenced by a particular prison regime. Such effects have been demonstrated in material reviewed so far, and are seen also in data shortly to be analysed, setting out officers' opinions about the initiative and discretion allowed them in their work, and also their attitudes towards the punishment of inmates.

The application of our officer typology to this material gave little further clarification. The only statistically significant difference was in perception of changes in officer status (Table 8.10). Beyond this, there was only the rather obvious conclusion that older, longer serving officers would be more likely to have perceived changes during their service, especially in respect of changes in inmate welfare provision, the increase in informal staff contact with prisoners, and rehabilitation and training facilities. This may be taken as indicating the extent and recency of such changes. On the status question it was to be expected that type 3 officers (older men who had been promoted) were more likely to consider that the status of officers had improved, and to approve of this change. At the same time, type 4 officers (older men who had not been promoted) were much less likely to perceive such improvement and more likely to view this state of affairs with disapproval. These apart then, it may be concluded that there was some evidence of similarity among the four types of prison officer in their perception and evaluation of changes in the service. This finding indicates that differences in attitudes found between the staff groups in the four prisons (Table 8.9) would be the result of the kind of prison in which they worked rather than the social background characteristics of the officers themselves.

Initiative and discretion

Recruitment advertising for the Prison Service often gives prominence to the scope within the service for the exercise of initiative. After joining, however, many officers find that there is less opportunity for this than they had expected, and others come to regard what scope there is as burdensome. In their Pentonville study, the Morrises found that, although the majority of officers considered that initiative had to be exercised in order for their work to be done, the absence of clear directives from their seniors on issues not covered by Prison Rules or Standing Orders left them vulnerable as regards their personal accountability for any decisions they might make. Consequently, although some officers disagreed, the majority

Table 8.10 Prison officer types' perception of changes in the status of officers

	Type 1	Type 2	Type 3	Type 4
Same or more approve	8	12	19	5
Same or less disapprove	17	35	22	25
N	25	47	41	30

Chi-squared (Yates' correction applied), 3 d.f., $= 7 \cdot 284$, $p < 0 \cdot 05$.

of Pentonville staff preferred 'a simple system of clear and un-ambiguous objectives' and were prepared to tolerate changes from this position only with the greatest reluctance.[7] Although such an attitude often seems to be justified (see observations on the short-term and medium-term open prisons on pp. 78, 88-9) it hardly makes for success in the development of truly open regimes. How far prison officers in open prisons felt that there were increased opportunities to act on their own initiative and what they thought about utilising such opportunities were questions which obviously required asking. The results are set out in Table 8.11.

Staff at the medium-term closed and long-term open prisons appear to be encouraged to use initiative more frequently than their colleagues in the short-term and medium-term open prisons, a result which appears to be partly at odds with the general expectation that it would be most encouraged in open situations. There is, of course, the question of whether in an open prison, appetite for the exercise

Table 8.11 Staffs' opinions about initiative held by the staff at each prison

	Medium-term closed	Short-term open	Medium-term open	Long-term open
Initiative is encouraged	24 (63·2%)	5 (22·7%)	18 (42·9%)	27 (81·8%)
Initiative is not encouraged	14	17	26	6
N	38	22	44	33

Chi-squared, 3 d.f., $= 23 \cdot 261$, $p < 0 \cdot 001$.

of initiative may 'grow by what it feeds upon', so that there is dissatisfaction with a level of initiative which would be considered high in a closed prison. Also physical conditions may make all the difference, for example the problems for prison-wide communications presented by the medieval architecture of the medium-term closed prison, thus enforcing the exercise of local initiative by officers. Nevertheless, the high score for the encouragement of initiative in the long-term open and the very low level in the short-term open are what might have been expected in the light of earlier results for these prisons. There is also support for the familiar gradient, declining initiative with a decline in length of sentence, which fits in with the broader generalisation that the shorter the sentence length the more custodial and 'clockwork' the regime. The high levels of initiative in the medium-term closed are understandable in a prison with such barriers to communication; presumably staff on the spot have to be allowed to get on with the job.

A typological comparison shows some statistically significant differences (Table 8.12). Only 37 per cent of type 2 officers (younger men with further education) felt that initiative was encouraged, whereas 63 per cent of type 1 (younger men with no further educational experience), 65 per cent of type 4 (older men who had not been promoted) and 76 per cent of type 3 (older men who had been promoted) felt that, in their cases, it was. While it might be anticipated that officers of senior rank would have more responsibility and greater freedom in which to act on their own initiative, the same cannot be said about the differences between the three basic grade types. Such differences are more likely to indicate differing perceptions of opportunities for acting with initiative rather than

Table 8.12 Opinions about initiative held by each type of prison officer

	Type 1	Type 2	Type 3	Type 4
Initiative is encouraged	17 (63%)	19 (37·3%)	31 (75·6%)	20 (64·5%)
Initiative is not encouraged	10	32	10	11
N	27	51	41	31

Chi-squared, 3 d.f., = 15·042, *p* <0·01.

real differences in actual opportunities for doing so; of course, the similar 'mix' of these various types in the different prisons would tend to cancel out such 'type differences' in perception, in comparing one prison with another, giving a degree of objective validity to inter-prison differences at least. However, the qualification that not all officers in the same regime have similar perceptions of such opportunities merits some emphasis. Any increase in the number of type 2 staff recruited might result in still more staff dissatisfaction with the amount of initiative permitted by existing (even open) prison regimes.

Even now, when asked whether more opportunities to use initiative would be desirable, four out of every five officers agreed that they would. Although there was not a statistically significant difference between prisons in this respect, the proportion expressing a desire for more initiative was slightly lower in the closed prison (74 per cent) as compared with the three open prisons (86, 89 and 85 per cent). This overall 80+ per cent trend is in strong contradistinction to that described in the Pentonville study ten years previously and is worth recording for this reason. While much would seem to depend upon how initiative is subjectively perceived and defined in contrasting regimes and between different types of officer, there may now be a greater preparedness among prison officers to accept a different approach to their work, which could provide a base from which to try to counteract the more general effects of the staff culture.

As regards opportunities for the use of discretion, also, our results differed from those (cited earlier) in the Pentonville study. Only eight among the 140 officer respondents in our four prisons felt that they had more than enough discretion (defined as 'being able to make decisions in the course of their work without reference to a higher authority'). Clearly there is no evidence here of a widespread yearning for increased bureaucratic safeguards. This might be distinguished from the 'support' gained from supervision by helpful senior officers. Rather over half of the rest (54·6 per cent) were content with the discretion available to them, so there is no desire for more discretion comparable with that for more initiative. There were, however, differences between the four prisons and these were along similar lines to those found for the questions about initiative (see Table 8.13). Dissatisfaction is high in the short-term and lowest in the long-term open, though as with initiative, the results from the medium-term open are slightly anomalous (more dissatisfaction

Table 8.13   Opinions about discretion held by the staff at each prison

	Medium-term closed	Short-term open	Medium-term open	Long-term open	Total
Enough or more than enough discretion	26 (72·3%)	7 (30·4%)	20 (45·5%)	26 (81·3%)	79
Not enough discretion	11	16	24	8	59
N	37	23	44	34	138*

Chi-squared, 3 d.f., = 16·953, $p < 0·01$.
*Two non-responses.

than the short-term open). The length-of-sentence gradient is once more maintained, with high figures again displayed by the medium-term closed.

Additional clarification of this pattern was forthcoming from another question, asking officers about the kinds of decision which they were allowed to make (see Table 8.14). Although there was an overall similarity between responses at all prisons, those from the

Table 8.14   Kinds of decision made by the staff at each prison

	Medium-term closed %	Short-term open %	Medium-term open %	Long-term open %
About routine matters only	42·1	56·5	46·7	41·2
Non-routine but with reference to a superior	21·1	30·4	31·1	35·3
Non-routine without reference to a superior	23·7	4·4	20·0	17·7
Those concerning major policy in the running of the prison	2·6	4·4	2·2	5·9
No response	10·5	4·4	0	0
Totals	100%	100·1%	100%	100·1%
N	38	23	45	34

short-term open prison were most distinct. Proportionately more officers at this prison made routine decisions only, and only a minimal proportion made non-routine decisions without reference to a superior. The highest rate of non-routine decisions without consultation with superiors occurred in the medium-term closed prison, and this is probably another consequence of the physical structure of the prison, already referred to. Possibly the most important feature of this information on discretion is its similarity with that on initiative, supporting once again, in very broad terms, the 'length of sentence' hypothesis.

A typological comparison (Tables 8.15 and 8.16) gave similar results to those on initiative. Type 3 officers (older men who had been promoted) felt that they had sufficient discretion, a fact which is borne out by the amount of their autonomous non-routine decision-making (Table 8.16). Type 4 officers (older men who had not been promoted), on the other hand, while almost as satisfied with the degree of discretion allowed them, made more 'routine only' decisions, and type 1 officers (younger men without further educational experience) exhibited a similar pattern. In contrast, type 2 officers (younger men with further educational experience) felt that they had insufficient discretion while, at the same time, being involved in non-routine decisions with reference to a superior far more frequently than the other groups. This affords some confirmation, not only that respondents' judgments were made from differing perceptual standpoints, but also that, as with initiative, untapped potentialities for the exercise of more discretion do exist among type 2 men.

To summarise, the research information on officers' perceptions and opinions on initiative and discretion shows that there are

Table 8.15 Opinions about discretion held by different types of prison officer

	Type 1	Type 2	Type 3	Type 4
Enough or more than enough discretion	16 (57·1%)	22 (43·1%)	34 (82·9%)	21 (65·6%)
Not enough discretion	12	29	7	11
N	28	51	41	32

Chil-squared, 3 d.f., = 15·613, *p* <0·01.

Table 8.16   Kinds of decision made by different types of prison officer

	Type 1	Type 2	Type 3	Type 4
Routine matters only	16	28	10	20
Non-routine but with reference to a superior	4	14	11	6
Non-routine without reference to a superior	6	6	17	6
N	26	48	38	32

Chi-squared (Yates' correction applied), 6 d.f., $= 18\cdot151$, $p < 0\cdot01$.

statistically significant differences both between prison and between types of prison officer. Three main conclusions seem to follow from these results. First, because the staff at each prison perceive different opportunities for using initiative and discretion, there is hope that the prison staff culture need not be wholly enveloping and that prison regimes can have some effect on how officers perceive and perform their work. This is borne out by the distinctive results from the long-term open, notwithstanding the physical features favouring initiative and discretion in the medium-term open. Also there is evidence here for what has become a recurring pattern in such differences between regimes—the shorter-term open prisons being most like closed prisons and the longer-term open prisons being least like closed prisons.

The second conclusion derives from the typological comparison, which suggests that there is a strongly subjective element in perceptions of initiative and discretion. Put another way, this means that officers with similar scope to act with initiative and discretion in their work perceive such opportunities differently: some are more satisfied than others with the same amount.

The third conclusion also concerns the typological comparison, reaffirming the separate character of type 2 officers (younger men with further educational experience) who have in other ways been shown to differ in experience and outlook from the rest. It will be recalled that this was the group for whom there was positive proof of educational interest and attainment and no evidence of downward occupational mobility, lateral movement into dead-end occupations or election for professional military service—the last point also suggesting that this group was least likely to have suffered the effects of trained incapacity. It is this group which now shows the most dissatisfaction with the amount of initiative and discretion allowed to them, demonstrating a readiness to assume more responsibility and to work without the supportive but restrictive backing of the customary paramilitary and bureaucratic framework. It is difficult to escape the conclusion that it is from this group that the open prison staffs of the future must be recruited if open institutions are to emerge with any real identity of their own.

Punishment

The disciplining and punishment of inmates was the last aspect of staff activity examined in this study. This contentious topic is not one which is readily opened out and explored, not least because of the closed and secretive way in which it is handled by prison administrators and personnel. There are, of course, strong pressures in the form of the 'custodial compromise' towards alleviating the natural conflict situation of the prison and thus making life together workable for both parties. One of our closed-prison officers described his strategy very well:

'The average officer in this establishment only brings a man before the Governor as a last resort. The majority of cases are dealt with by the officer. A sharp word, or a quiet talking-to often produces an apology and the desired effect. No personal satisfaction is experienced by placing men on report and their being punished perhaps many times per year. . . . I consider time, place, environment, individual personal problems, normal behaviour, before taking this step; and of course there are times when the officer has no option but to report i.e. wilful disobedience, violence, escapists, etc. This is really a question of the officer's experience, age and maturity.'

Formal charges and disciplinary proceedings are, therefore, usually a last resort, although the Prison Rules are a reminder that they are there, as a kind of 'cane in the cupboard'. Unofficial punishment, when it occurs, must be seen in a similar light. Thus, in the main, prison officers are not sadistic thugs who delight in inflicting injuries on their 'defenceless charges': it tends often to be forgotten that prison is 'a man's world' which is not always one-sided. Staff and inmates share a common cultural heritage in which ideals of manliness and toughness are among the most pre-eminent. Horseplay, and physical jockeying and rivalry are deeply rooted elements of the behaviour of both staff and inmates. Problems arise only when this pattern of background activity gets out of hand, and it is on such occasions that Prison Rules are 'remembered' or called upon.

While such coercive elements are certainly present in closed prisons, it might have been expected that circumstances in open prisons would be different. Those who wrote, perhaps with un-realisably high hopes, about open prisons in the early days, anticipated that new methods and new opportunities for interacting with inmates would be available to staff in open institutions and that, accordingly, prison officers would develop different kinds of authority relationships with inmates. We set out to try to determine whether anything like this had taken place in the open prisons which we studied. With this in mind, officers were asked two questions about punishment. First, they were asked to state how many men they had placed on report in the previous six months, to permit comparison to be made of rates of punishment in open and closed establishments. Second, in order to see how far reports for disciplinary offences resulted in punishment and, therefore, staff were encouraged, as it were, in resorting to this rather than more informal methods in the various prisons, officers were asked: Are the prisoners you put on report usually punished? They were also free to make such additional comments as they wished.

As the results in Table 8.17 show, there were statistically significant divergences between prisons in the rates at which officers reported inmates for breaches of discipline. Such reporting was most frequent in the medium-term closed prison. Next in order were the short-term and medium-term open prisons, while the long-term open prison, on this count as on so many others, was most different from the rest. Put in proportional terms, whereas 75 per cent of the long-term open prison staff had placed no one on report in the previous six months and only 12·5 per cent had placed three or more inmates on report, comparative figures for the medium-term open, short-term open and medium-term closed prisons were, respectively, 50 and 18 per cent; 39 and 30 per cent; and 29 and 44 per cent. Clear open-closed differences, and the special position of the long-term open emerge here, as also in respect of the average number of reports per officer respondent in each prison (Table 8.18). The Prison Department's annual statistics showing the average number

Table 8.17 Frequency of reports in each prison during a six-month period before the research

	Medium-term closed	Short-term open	Medium-term open	Long-term open
No reports	10	9	22	24
1 or 2	9	7	14	4
3 or more	15	7	8	4
N	34	23	44	32

Chi-squared (Yates' correction applied), 6 d.f., $= 18 \cdot 760$, $p < 0 \cdot 01$.

of offences per head of average daily population (Table 8.19) show moreover that such differences in the number of punishments actually imposed have been consistent over several years. There is an echo of the length-of-sentence hypothesis; but this is marred by the reversal of the customary positions of the short-term and medium-term open prisons. This reversal is so consistent as to suggest that it is meaningful. Perhaps punishment is likely to be less pronounced in a short-term institution, where prisoners have so little time to find their feet, and where the day is more full anyway of necessary routine. Open prison advocates would no doubt find all this very heartening, particularly the results from the more fully 'open'

Table 8.18 Average number of reports per officer respondent in each prison

	Medium-term closed	Short-term open	Medium-term open	Long-term open
Total no. of respondents	38	23	45	34
No. not answering this question	4	0	1	2
No. of returns	34	23	44	32
No. of reports for all respondents	91	34	69	17
Average no. of reports per officer respondent	2·7	1·5	1·6	0·5

Table 8.19 Average annual number of offences per head of average daily population in each prison, 1965-1970

Year	Medium-term closed	Short-term open	Medium-term open	Long-term open
1965	1·2	0·5	0·9	0·5
1966	1·5	0·7	0·7	0·5
1967	1·2	0·7	0·5	0·3
1968	1·3	0·6	0·6	0·4
1969	1·3	0·3	0·5	0·2
1970	1·1	0·3	0·4	0·2

Source: Annual Reports of the Work of the Prison Department (1966-71).

regime of the long-term open prison. This prison shows a low rate of punishment not only in comparison with the other *open* prisons in this study but also in comparison with all our other prisons, both open and closed.

This tendency for open prison staffs to place fewer men on report is countered to some extent by the fact that more of them believe that their Governors follow up by imposing actual punishments on the men reported than do the staff of our closed prison (Table 8.20). Taken together these two facts suggest that this particular discretion is being exercised by the officers themselves, rather than by the Governor. This is an interesting possibility which seems directly in line with what may be the essence of the officer's role in the open prison situation—his ability to deal with ongoing interpersonal

Table 8.20 Answers in each prison to the question 'Are the prisoners you put on report usually punished?'

	Medium-term closed	Short-term open	Medium-term open	Long-term open
Sometimes	36·8	13·0	31·1	32·4
Usually	47·4	43·5	31·1	29·4
Always	15·8	43·5	33·3	35·3
No response	0	0	4·4	2·9
Totals	100%	100%	99·9%	100%
N	38	23	45	34

situations without continual dependence on formal rules and the formal authority structure of the prison.

Although favouring the open prisons, the level of Governor-support perceived by prison officers is not high. The exception is the short-term open; apart from this, the proportion who believe that they were supported by the Governor 'usually' or even more often than that, does not reach two-thirds in any of our prisons. In spite of the figures cited above, this so-called 'lack of support', no doubt reinforced by the closed-prison oriented staff culture, remains a stick with which to beat the open prisons. One officer in his thirties and with a few years' experience behind him made the following comment about the open prison in which he was employed:

'A great many of the staff have become disillusioned particularly with the Governor's award at adjudications. It is well known among the inmates that the cost of disobeying an order, "slagging" an officer or refusing labour is either a caution or a 6d. fine. But God help you if you are caught with a couple of tomatoes. Awards vary from 3 to 7 days' remission, It appears that staff are a low priority, here. This leads to an attitude of "laissez faire" amongst the staff and can only be bad for training as well as discipline. Rules should be at the absolute minimum but what few there are should be enforced.'

Many other officers at this prison and at the long-term open prison made similar comments. The Governor at the latter, the most 'open' of those we examined, was widely regarded among his staff as 'a con's Governor'. Although he had their respect and support in other ways, such divisiveness was bound to affect badly his efforts to communicate with some of his staff and to create workable open conditions. On the other hand, the short-term open prison Governor who, as we have seen from a variety of perspectives, managed a regime which was closest to that obtaining in the closed prison, commanded wide and genuine respect from his staff for doing so. It is worth noting in this connection that officers returning from open to closed prisons seem to experience none of the 'problems' of adjustment which officers moving from closed to open prisons claim!

Our observational data (chapter 3) gives us reason to believe that the overriding staff culture is active in resisting any moves towards real 'openness' in open prisons—even in the long-term open. The approbation given to discipline, security and the Mountbatten Report in all the open prisons (Table 8.9) provides further support for this view, as do these data on punishment. It cannot be over-looked in any attempt either to evaluate open prisons, or to make more of a reality of their pretensions.

Summary

A general criticism of staff-training programmes in the Prison Service has been their deficiencies from the point of view of practicality and specificity. In particular there is a feeling that experts should not be imported from outside, but trained by means of specialist courses from within the service. Training for work in open prisons is seen as lacking in the same way, because of the 'containment-oriented' nature of the training and experience provided for all officers. The more or less random distribution of staff between prisons means also that staff of open prisons (or any other particular kind of prison) are not selected specially, either. Yet data already reviewed on type 2 prison officers, referring to their educational aptitudes, career patterns and limited military experience, indicate that they may be more suitable for specialist training for open prison work; as well as more suited to the work itself by virtue of their possible ability to operate without the support of a strong structure of authority. This latter conclusion is strengthened by the pressure from type 2 officers for more initiative and more opportunities for the exercise of discretion.

This enquiry on discretion and initiative also gives results in accordance with the length-of-sentence gradient: i.e. the longer the sentence, the more discretion and initiative the staff see themselves as enjoying. It also confirms the special position of the long-term open.

Among the most revealing conclusions to be drawn from our study of officers' attitudes to the job is their apparent inconsistency: regretting a perceived decline in security and discipline, while welcoming more welfare, rehabilitation, and informal relationships with prisoners. This ambivalence has been noted before, in our observational work and the CIES results, and as so often before, declines with increases in the length of sentence, the long-term open standing out in this respect. The staff of the open prisons are also more concerned than those of the closed prisons with 'conflicting instructions' and 'lack of teamwork', though again not the long-term open—perhaps a result, for the other opens, of having neither the firm structure of the closed prison nor the clear objectives of the long-term open. Beyond these, the officers' major concerns are predictable (though not therefore unimportant): low pay in all prisons; and long hours, overcrowding and poor working conditions in the closed institutions.

In the Diary material, the low level of staff supervision in the opens appears to leave staff, already confused by lack of clear objectives, with too little support and guidance from their seniors. This may be partly explained by shorter senior staff hours in the opens; hours of work are generally longer in the closed prison but senior staff hours are relatively longer still. More generally, staff hours of work, and duty priorities follow the length-of-sentence gradient. The main duty priorities are security in the closed prison, and inmate supervision in the opens. The latter may reveal the ambivalence referred to above in a new form: replacing the physical restraint of the closed prison by closer personal surveillance of inmates.

An analysis of the frequency of officers' reports shows less punishment in the opens and a pattern of results generally in accordance with the gradient. However, this is countered by more punctilious support by open prison Governors when officers do report inmates—especially in the long-term open. In other words, this particular discretion has been placed, in the opens, more in the hands of officers, indicating the kinds of quality they are expected to display. But even in these prisons, there is general belief that Governors favoured the inmates.

9   Policy implications

We set ourselves the task in this study of comparing open and closed prisons, with the idea of determining how far open institutions realised the expectations of those who have advocated them over the past half-century. Among the many justifications offered on their behalf, it has been argued, first of all, that they provide a more realistic social setting within which to learn law-abiding behaviour; as well as the need to assume responsibility for one's behaviour instead of becoming dependent on the routines of the institution. In this way, it was believed, the institutionalising effect of the traditional prison would be averted. Attention has been directed secondly to their ability actually to reverse the process of criminalisation which has been found to be a major consequence of incarceration in a maximum security institution. This is said to be achieved by the weakening of the corrupting inmate culture, with a consequent strengthening of staff-inmate interaction; and a greater degree of inmate identification with the rehabilitative aims of the institution.

Many threads from our research have to be drawn together in order to be in a position to attempt such judgments. These include the complex skein issuing from the observational accounts in chapters 2 and 3, as well as the more focused quantitative data of subsequent chapters. As is not uncommon in the study of social situations, the results are sometimes ambiguous and vague, and this tendency has been exacerbated by the limited response of the staff of some of our closed prisons, making some of our staff comparisons less telling than we should have liked. Nevertheless there is a weight of very varied evidence pointing in certain directions.

It has not demonstrated any clear distinction between open and closed regimes, at least as these are represented in our research prisons, but 'serendipity'[1] has played its part in our research, as in so many others in the past. So other kinds of comparison have emerged as important. These will now be outlined, together with the bearing of these results on prison policy.

First of all then, the original *raison d'être* of this research, the comparison of open and closed prisons as such, proved to be less

218

fruitful than had been anticipated. Open-closed differences are slight. Thus in the results from the Correctional Institutions Environment Scale, significant subscale differences emerge only for three: Involvement, and Order and organisation for inmates and Autonomy for staff. The reciprocal nature of the last two, dependent as they are on the differing perspectives of prisoners and officers, is clear enough. Although there is in addition some evidence in the CIES scores for more Clarity in the opens, the questionnaire indicates the contrary: more concern among open prison staff about conflicting instructions and lack of teamwork. The CIES also suggests a wider range of both staff and inmate perceptions of the regimes within which they live, than are found among the closed prisons. Some differences are also found in the results obtained from the diary. They show lower figures for staff supervision in the open prisons, and also a difference in the priorities for the deployment of staff time—security ranking highest in closed prisons, and inmate supervision in the opens. Also from the questionnaire comes evidence that the staffs of the open prisons record fewer punishment reports on inmates than their closed counterparts—though open prison Governors tend to back up their staff more often when they do report inmates in this way.

There are a number of features of these results which cast doubt on the progressive image of the open prison. First of all there is the ambivalent attitude represented by the emphasis on both Involvement, and Order and organisation. And although, as we have seen, security received more emphasis in the closed institution, it does look as though such formal restraints are replaced by closer inmate surveillance in the open prisons. These differences, at any rate, seem paradoxically enough to serve only to underline the identity between both kinds of institution.

We get some clue in the rest of the data as to why this may be. Although the high figures for Clarity in the opens represent a discordant note, the evidence from the questionnaire is that the staff do feel themselves in an anomic situation, seeing orders from their superiors as conflicting with one another. This is borne out also by the perplexity observed among basic grade staff in our short-term and medium-term open prisons; the exception both for the quantitative and the observational data is the long-term open, about which more will have to be said shortly. The relatively small amount of time devoted by senior staff to staff supervision in the opens suggests basic-grade staff received little support in dealing with this situation.

It is not surprising, in view of the inchoateness of the opens, that they do manifest more varied perceptions than the closed prisons. The evidence on punishment indicates at least one of the pressures which they are expected to sustain without much senior staff support.

As will now be evident, the data from the long-term open prison do not fall into the same pattern as from the other two opens. It is distinct from them in a whole range of CIES subscales, indicating that it has managed to distinguish itself effectively from the closed prisons. The observational material does show that although a significant proportion of the staff at this institution disagree with the Governor's policy, he has managed to communicate that policy to the majority, and to carry them along with him on it. This is supported also by the prison's high Clarity score and low staff-inmate disagreement on this subscale of the CIES, as well as low scores on 'conflicting instructions' and 'lack of teamwork' in the questionnaire. There is also evidence from the CIES multivariate analysis of more staff-inmate overlap in perceptions than in any of our other prisons. A significant aspect of this is the degree of staff-inmate overlap in perceptions of Clarity. Both elements in the prison community are agreed in feeling they 'know where they're going'. This open prison concept apparently so effectively communicated by the Governor seems, according to the questionnaire results, to include the exercise of more discretion and initiative by the staff, and less ambivalence between rehabilitation and security, i.e. a more straight-forward acceptance of rehabilitative norms than in any of the other prisons.

To sum up, the long-term open seems to have acquired a more clearly open identity, partly because of the success of the Governor in developing and communicating his idea of what an open prison should be. But the evidence is that there may be two other factors operating in the situation. Probably most important is the length-of-sentence gradient: the longer-term the institution, the more liberal it is perceived to be. This operates both for closed and open prisons, though it is less marked in the closed prisons because differences between them are fewer in any case. Similar results emerge in the data from the questionnaire. Thus ambivalence between rehabilitative and security norms tends to be less with length of sentence as do (broadly speaking) punishment reports, while discretion and initiative by the staff tend to show a parallel increase.

The reasons for this have been discussed in the text. They are probably partly organisational, in that the shorter-term the institution the less time can be spared from discipline and security for informal relationships and training. Obviously the longer-term the institution, the less large such structural constraints are likely to loom, and the more likely it is that prisoners will have settled down to 'do bird' and will have become familiar and manageable to the staff. There was also a real feeling in our prisons that men serving longer sentences should receive special consideration—an attitude which seems to be widespread within the Prison system, being reflected, among other things, in better staffing ratios in longer-sentence establishments.

This length-of-sentence gradient was bound to operate in such a way as to reinforce the 'open' trends in the long-term open prison. Another result of it was that our short-term open tended to resemble the closed prisons rather more than its open fellows. It bore a particular resemblance to the short-term closed, in some cases being more similar to that prison than were the other closed institutions. This does seem to underline the power of the 'length of sentence' factor as compared with other regime-forming elements.

There is, however, some suggestion from our data that there is still another influence at work: the varying characteristics of the inmate populations of the different prisons. Unlike staff, who seem to have been allocated to their institutions largely on a random basis, inmates are distributed systematically and, as we have seen, vary considerably in such characteristics as age, seriousness of offence, social class, and the nature and extent of previous criminality. Thus the young but institutionally experienced population at the medium-term closed prison contrasted with the older but institutionally inexperienced population at the long-term open. We called attention in chapter 2 to the possible importance of a generation gap in contributing to the strongly 'closed' orientation of the first of these prisons. The social skills of the middle-class element in the latter were also strongly in evidence. Our CIES Validation Study (see appendix 5) also provided support for the importance of inmate characteristics. Based on inmate CIES results, it gave a person-setting ratio of 60 : 40 ($\pm$ 5 per cent). In other words six out of ten differences in perception could be attributed to the personalities of respondents, and the remaining four to the regime.

If one compares staff CIES responses with those of inmates the staff turn out, rather surprisingly, to display a greater degree of consensus than the inmates. This has been interpreted in the text as implying that there is a prison-staff culture that is even more powerful than the more commonly recognised inmate culture of prisons. Such a supposition is strongly supported also by the observational material reviewed in chapters 2 and 3. There are nevertheless rifts in the lute. The observational material shows divisions among the staff, as between, for example, specialist staff and the rest; and between those with a strong security orientation, with traditional attitudes towards long-term prisoners, say, or homosexuals, and others with more interest either in training or in the individualisation of treatment. But the widest rift undoubtedly occurred between the basic grade officers and those above them. This is revealed also in a comparison of CIES responses for the two groups; basic grade officers are seen throughout as giving responses nearer to those of the inmates. One way of interpreting this would be to say that unlike their seniors the officer on the wing, having to contend with prisoners at first hand, is bound to be more vulnerable to the 'custodial compromise'.

In general, the staff CIES responses gave higher scores than those for inmates—and that irrespective of whether the subscales in question reflected attitudes favourable to training and rehabilitation, or to security and discipline. The one, rather significant exception to this was the subscale for Staff control, in which staff responses were actually lower than those for inmates. Staff disciplinary activities obviously loom larger in the minds of the prisoners than they do in those of the officers concerned.

The general picture presented by the preceding, however, is of some ambivalence in the minds of prison officers as between training and security, and this is borne out by data of other kinds. For instance, the questionnaire responses show that at one and the same time, officers value welfare, rehabilitation, and informal relationships with inmates, and also security and discipline. The data collected from the open prisons are particularly revealing. On the one hand they have a formal remit to training, while on the other hand observational work shows there is constant preoccupation with security. This is borne out by the prominence given, in the CIES results for these prisons, to both Involvement and Order and organisation; and by the evidence in the diary analysis that the lack of formal safeguards for security seems to be compensated for by an increased amount of inmate surveillance. In other words the staff culture referred to does not seem to be undilutedly security-minded, but this element in it is strong enough to infiltrate into the open prisons in the absence of any strong concept of 'openness'. In this connection it is interesting to note that ambivalence is very much less marked in the long-term open where, as we have seen, there is just such a clear concept. Incidentally there is some evidence of a 'length of sentence' effect in respect of ambivalence also.

There is further, more indirect support for the overall ambivalent nature of the staff culture. The main subscales showing differences between inmate and staff responses to the CIES are for Support, Autonomy, Clarity (with the exception of the long-term open), and Personal problem orientation; at the same time the subscales on which staff show the highest degree of agreement are those concerned with system maintenance, i.e. Order and Organisation, and Clarity— the latter seeming to have both its control and its rehabilitation aspect.

It is not surprising that security and discipline should play such a prominent part in the prison-staff culture having regard to the antecedents of many of the staff. They came into the Prison Service at a fairly mature age, after what seems, for a number of them, to have been a chosen period of military service. Having rather limited educational attainments behind them, there is also evidence of downwards or at the best sideways occupational mobility. In this situation the Prison Service often seems to have represented a haven which provided a secure job and a disciplined and quasi-military context within which to work. All the evidence is that for the majority, the main attraction of the Prison Service is the job security which it supplies rather than any vocational interest in rehabilitating anti-social men. Such a preoccupation with security is wholly consistent with the officers' family-centred life-style. Their main leisure companions would either be their wives or girl friends or, ominously for the development of the staff culture, other prison officers. Their main gripes similarly were concerned with pay, longer hours, or working conditions.

It is only when one carries out a typological analysis of the staff responses that any break in this general picture can be discerned. It then becomes apparent that there is a group, referred to in this study as type 2 officers, who have more often acquired an education beyond the most elementary level, have less frequently undertaken extended military service commitments, and instead of displaying the sideways or downwards mobility pattern already referred to, give evidence of having previously held jobs in skilled occupations. If one sees, as a further requirement for effective work in open prisons, the ability to make decisions off one's own bat, and to take initiatives, then the type 2 officers seem again to possess advantages over the rest; the questionnaire items on discretion and initiative show that they do tend to be more dissatisfied than the rest with the amount of discretion and initiative which is allowed to them in their prisons.

The training of prison officers, however, does not take account of such special abilities or potentialities. Overwhelmingly our prison officers were trained and gained their experience in closed prisons. They also received a single-minded basic training for the Prison Service, which is primarily directed to the skills which are assumed to be required in a kind of standard closed prison. What our research shows, of course, is that even in closed prisons circumstances vary very greatly, calling for a variety of special abilities.

For instance, there are the characteristics of inmate populations, which we have shown to be very varied. It is surely important, for example, to ensure that officers working in the medium-term closed should be good at communicating and working with younger men. Then there is the large size of the long-term closed institution. Its unity would be difficult to sustain in any case, but the way in which it was run led to a high degree of wing insularity. Obviously this could have been avoided by some other style of central management, in which case the operational task for prison officers would have been different. But this is very much a result of the particular policy adopted by the Governor. In the medium-term closed, he had fewer options open to him. The very peculiar architectural characteristics of this institution almost enforced a pattern of local autonomy on both officers and prisoners. As we have seen from the questionnaire, officers in this prison did see themselves as exercising high levels of discretion and initiative, but they were without the training to equip them to use these opportunities in a positive way. Containment-oriented as they were, they opted for the 'custodial compromise', leaving the dormitory groups to their own (possibly nefarious) devices. They might, if they had been appropriately trained, have developed in these dormitories some form of groupwork, rooted in the daily life of the institution—something approaching the pattern of a therapeutic or (perhaps to use a more appropriate term) correctional community.

The staff of the short-term closed, for their part, like that of the short-term open prison, faced the problem of a rapid inmate turnover. The problem is essentially twofold: how to avoid becoming so busy with the organisational tasks thus presented that there was no time for anything else, and how to develop a 'something else' which might make progress (rehabilitative, educational, vocational, etc.) with prisoners in a very short time. The danger of becoming over-preoccupied with routine was increased in the short-term closed prison because of the rigorous factory-type work programme developed there. Unless the rehabilitative aim of the prison were to be seen simply as inculcating certain habits in the men, steps would have to be taken to enable the programme to escape from the dead hand of routine. This would not be easy for men who had been trained to aim at 'peace and quiet' and at going 'by the book'.

Special features are no less apparent among the open prisons. References have already been made to the shared problems of the two short-term open prisons; and the 'factory system' of the short-term closed has its mate in the medium-term open. In fact, rigidity is not a feature of either of these two open prisons. Our observational data show that in the short-term open the main characteristic of staff behaviour is the lack of any unified policy from the top downwards, leading to *ad hoc* solutions, while in the medium-term open it is an unwillingness to make decisions at all, because of the failure of senior staff to take proper responsibility for the acts of those who are under their orders. Which neatly sums up the major problem of open prisons: as we have so often pointed out before, these particular problems arise because they have, as open prisons, no clear sense of direction.

But if they had they would still need men who could operate within such regimes. The staff tensions of the long-term open show that because a consistent open prison model has been devised, unity does not magically establish itself. Special training does seem to be indicated for work in various special prison situations—like for example, those of our fourteenth-century castle or of short-term institutions. But above all it is needed for work in open prisons. A number of our officers recognised this unsatisfied need for 'more practicality and specificity' in training, especially for the staff of open prisons.

There also seem to be differences between officers in their suitability for work in different kinds of situation. While many officers seem more suited to closed prison work, our type 2 officers appear to be better adapted to the less structured, less supportive open situations. Not only do their previous experience and education provide such an indication, but the questionnaire results on Initiative and Discretion show that they would prefer freer, if more hazardous situations, where they could use their own judgment more. This ability to operate without powerful bureaucratic and disciplinary supports is surely a *sine qua non* for effective work in any real open prison.

Two broad policy requirements emerge from all this.

(1) a recognition that prisons do differ in ways which are significant for their operation, and that it is necessary to clarify the nature of such differences. While most of these differences may be contained within the general concept of the closed prison, those between open and closed institutions are more radical, calling for a more explicit definition of what constitutes an open prison.

(2) A recognition that staff will need to be specially selected and trained for open prison work.

The first main policy implication of this research, then, is that more thought should be given to the special characteristics of particular kinds of prison. Sometimes these special characteristics are forced on the prison authorities by circumstances: for example, the peculiar architectural features of the medium-term closed prison. In such cases, appropriate policies can only be developed *post hoc*, and within the limitations already present in the situation. In other cases the special characteristics are a result of Prison Department policy, but usually without full consideration of the effect of such a policy on the regime as a whole. Such a case, among our prisons, arises once again in the medium-term closed, where the high proportion of younger prisoners seems to have led to a 'generation gap'. The formulation of a policy according to length of sentence also seems indicated. How to increase the spontaneity and rehabilitative tempo of short-term prisons, and to ensure that the tolerant climate of the long-term institution does not simply become an institutionalising 'indulgency pattern', seem to be the important questions. But from our point of view, the failure to develop a clear and adequate concept of the open prison seems the most important shortcoming.

One ought not to underestimate the difficulty of defining penal objectives and the means by which they could be achieved with this degree of definiteness. It has not been customary to do this kind of thing in Britain. The solitary exception has been the procedures developed for the maintenance of security; as one would expect, the Home Office Standing Orders, under which our prisons operate, do spell out in considerable detail the measures which are considered necessary for the effective performance of the containment function. What we are now talking about is giving equally detailed consideration to the role of open prisons—a role which, by definition, is antithetic to containment.

For a variety of reasons discussed in the first chapter of this book, the open prison is supposed to reduce the pressure of containment. If the field staff of these institutions are going to co-operate in producing a more 'open' climate, then those above them in the hierarchy have to be prepared to accept the responsibility for the consequences which are likely to ensue. Only too often in the past, officers have complained that they have been instructed to carry some penal innovation into effect, while being warned that if anything went wrong as a result, they would be held responsible.

This has been a longstanding complaint within the service. Years ago, when new prison visiting arrangements were being introduced into one of our large London prisons, officers claimed that they were told (in effect): 'We want to produce a more informal setting for visits by the family or friends of prisoners, so you must avoid being too obtrusive. But at the same time you must see that no visitor passes on contraband to a prisoner.' If prison officers (whether justified or not) believe that they are going to have to pay the price for penal reform, they are going to protect themselves, even if this means effectively preventing the reform in question from being implemented. And who could blame them?

In case it should be thought that this kind of thing did not happen nowadays, one should look again at the observational material from our medium-term open prison. Where senior officers do not take proper responsibility for making decisions, or for the consequences of those decisions when made, everybody else starts to play 'safety first', so that activity becomes, as we have seen, almost 'imperceptible'.

There remains the danger that if a genuine minimum security regime did emerge, the essential nature of the prison as a 'lock-up' would then reassert itself through the tightening up of criteria for admission to open prisons. The criterion would continue to be, as at present, whether the individual was likely to escape or not, but even the low levels of risk which are acceptable at present would have presumably to be curtailed further. The outcome would then be that while we might at last have real open prisons, very few prisoners would be found suitable for them. The effect of parole, and other changes affecting mainly low-risk offenders, in simply reducing the populations available for open prisons, rather than making it possible to transfer more people from closed institutions (see chapter

1), shows how difficult we find it to relax our traditional and rather timid standards in this respect. This does not mean that no limits need to be set. As our research shows, the composition of a prison's population is of great importance. Some kinds of prisoner would probably have to be excluded because of the risk to the public. Thus there are some powerful and dangerous men who would soon make an open prison unworkable, and most psychopathic criminals would also probably have to be excluded. Some regard also has to be had for the general balance of the population of the institution, and the general character which it is intended that it should acquire. The main criterion must nevertheless remain rehabilitative-suitability for an open regime, rather than security-risk categories, of doubtful validity even for such a narrow purpose.

But though the claims of containment may be reduced in the open prison they cannot be entirely eliminated. This would, in any case, be an unrealistic aim at present, having regard to the ambivalence of staff (even in the long-term open) between security and rehabilitation. Changes proposed below in the methods used for the recruitment and training of open prison staff should make this consideration less important in the future, but what the public expects from prisons will remain a factor in the situation.

The long-term open has shown that containment can nevertheless recede into the background if *preventing* escapes is not a constantly recurring preoccupation. Instead of removing responsibility from people in this way, the aim should be to free them to make choices— with the proviso that they must suffer the consequences of those choices afterwards. Whether this means that absconders should be removed to a closed prison immediately on recapture would depend on the individual case, but it would certainly mean this in many cases. Some short-term risk for the public would clearly be involved in a programme of this kind, but ought to be compensated for by the more humane penology involved, as well as by hoped-for better success-rates.

What we are, of course, constantly encountering here is the paradox of trying to develop open institutions as places for rehabilitation, through social experience and the assumption of responsibility for oneself, while at the same time calling them prisons, and trying to domesticate them within a prison system. And yet there is no acceptable alternative to the coexistence of open and closed prisons. Open prisons are intended for real criminals, who would in the absence of open establishments find themselves in closed prisons. They represent also a means by which release from a closed prison may be graduated, and therefore be made easier to sustain for an inadequate or institutionalised prisoner. And above all, the juxtaposition of the two types of institution enables the open prisons to constitute a liberalising force. They will be able to show that more could be achieved with prisoners than closed prisons were perhaps willing to attempt; and also to represent a standing reproach to unnecessarily close incarceration, offering an ever-present alternative for the disposition of whatever proved, at any particular time, to be the marginal group among prisoners. But here we come full-circle, for such a strain towards a wider use of open prisons could come only from an open prison sector and staff who knew what they were doing, and were convinced of its worthwhileness. In other words, where the open prison task was fully understood.

It would be premature to attempt to provide a detailed blueprint of the kind of regime which might then be envisaged, but it should include many opportunities for assuming responsibility and for learning by experience of daily life, both in prison and outside. This would seem to be of the essence of what the open prison has to offer. But it is idle to pretend that simply being free to interact, and to gain experience in this way, will necessarily serve any useful rehabilitative purpose. Indeed both experience and theory indicate otherwise. Thus there is plenty of evidence for the view that prisoners can be seriously corrupted by the people they meet in prison.[2] Something must be attributed to the fact that relationships between prisoners in a closed prison take place in the context of the inmate culture. As a kind of contra-culture, this is the anti-social mirror image of the law-abiding, surface society of the prison, and is said to be created as a defensive response to the 'pains of imprisonment' in a closed institution.[3] On such an assumption, the contaminating effects of imprisonment would be less in an open prison where the inmate culture should be weaker because (presumably) the 'pains of imprisonment' are less. There is some slight support for such a conclusion from this research: the higher inmate score for Involvement, for example, in the opens; and the higher percentage of 'staff-like' responses among inmates of the more typically 'open' long-term open prison (Table 5.12). However, the other explanation of that same culture is that it gives expression to the shared attitudes of criminals, who have brought their anti-social norms into prison with them.[4] In that case, as Leslie Wilkins has pointed out,[5] mutual interaction between them could only serve to confirm and reinforce their criminality.

The truth is probably somewhere between the two. Although one must expect a community of criminals to display criminal tendencies, these would be strengthened in an institution in which deprivation, and a demand for surface behaviour of an unrealistically conformist kind alienate them from the staff and the institution, and from the conformist values which the latter represent.[6] The key is the 'custodial compromise', the unspoken formula for which (from the staff side) is: 'Behave yourself and we will leave you (and your inmate culture) alone.' So, facilitating freer interaction, as in an open prison, will certainly free criminals for criminal behaviour and mutual corruption, but it will also remove some of the pressures tending to divide the institutional community and therefore to worsen those undesirable tendencies.

But there are other limitations on the value of simply emancipating men from the structural constraints of a closed prison. While this would make it possible for them to 'learn by experience', it would not ensure that they did. And in the past they do not seem to have learned from experience the kind of lessons which a rehabilitative penal system would like to teach, i.e. how to be well-adjusted and law-abiding citizens. In other words they need not only to suffer the consequences of their own mistakes, but also to find themselves in a social situation in which they are constrained to recognise how those consequences have been brought about, and how by changing their behaviour they can avoid them in future. In terms of community life, this means participating in a group-learning situation in which they are under pressure to examine their common problems, and arrive by a rational process of discussion at workable solutions to them. Shared responsibility for institutional decision-making[7] is one way of achieving this, though one could see an active programme of group[8] and individual counselling serving some of the same purposes.

The experience available for sifting in this way must of course be rich enough to teach the necessary lessons. All of our open prisons were deficient in this respect. As we have seen, their educational programmes were largely of a hobby character, plus some not very well-attended courses for remedying personal educational inadequacies. There is no gainsaying the importance of both of these, but there is more to education than they can provide. The most obvious practical shortcomings are on the vocational side, and this ties in (or rather does not tie in) in the short-term and long-term opens with a limited and socially unrealistic work programme. The experience to be gained must be relevant to a prisoner's life outside, teaching him lessons about himself, about others, about society, about work, and about leisure, which will stand him in good stead when he is discharged—and in this respect it must be sharply distinguished from experience gained in a closed prison, which teaches institutionalising lessons relevant only to a better adjustment 'inside'.

The work programme of the medium-term open may at first sight seem to meet all the requirements for such work experience. Modern methods of labour deployment, industrial training and production are certainly used, but the general effect is to so hedge the prisoners around with workshop imperatives as to give them little or no latitude for experience and learning. Thus prison officers often regretted their inability under this system to reward effort as distinct from achievement. And for the prisoners themselves, attaining their work targets so as to maximise their pay, came to dominate their thinking to such an extent as to limit their interests (and therefore their experience) very greatly. Even work itself as a learning experience seems to have been impoverished by this kind of tunnel-vision. But of course the opportunities for social learning need not be confined to education and work but could extend over the whole pattern of life in the institution. Maxwell Jones has shown[9] that this kind of regime can be workable with individuals who are much more socially maladjusted than those envisaged here in open prisons.

Within such a framework there is scope for regimes embodying either radical experimentation or cautious reform. In either case the principles, deriving from the concept of openness itself, remain the same.

It would be fatal, however, if this became just another and more subtle way of managing prisoners—of keeping them quiet, and in this way satisfying one of the requirements for effective containment.

Too much of the programme of the prisons which we studied, both open and closed, seemed to be directed towards tension reduction. The aim of the open prison must not be to enable prisoners and staff to 'do bird' amicably together. Experience both in casework and in therapeutic groups has shown that learning can take place only where there is stress and conflict.[10] Instead of making prisoners content, therefore, one should perhaps be arousing in them discontent—with their predicament as prisoners, with their ideas, their way of life and also their probable future. If that makes them a little more difficult to manage, it is a price which has to be paid if we are to have any chance of changing them. The alternative is to put their difficulties in social adjustment into cold storage for the duration of their sentences.

A system like this is going to make very great demands on the staff of an institution, to which the appropriate response is often seen to be that of providing them with more and better training. If we have meanwhile acquired a clearer concept of the open prison, we have put ourselves in a better position to know what such training should include. There remains nevertheless the further preliminary question of the personal suitability of particular entrants into the Prison Service, both for the kind of work they would have to do in open prisons, and for the kind of training which it entails. What must be recognised is that in the open prison any change in prison attitudes or behaviour is not going to be brought about against the 'stationary friction' generated by a massive and highly bureaucratised organisation, but by a fluid relational pattern. This calls for staff who are personally flexible, and sufficiently confident to be able to take action and make decisions on day-to-day matters on their own responsibility, i.e. without a need for institutional back-up all the time. Although our prison officer typology does not, without further research, provide an adequate guide as to where one might look for staff with these qualities, it does give us some indications. There appears to be, in our type 2, a group of officers who do not (as do many of their colleagues) display a particular preference for a military occupational style, but do positively welcome opportunities for the exercise of initiative and discretion.

Their educational and work histories support this view of them as amenable to training for new kinds of prison role. They have mostly undertaken further education beyond the basic level, which could imply more intellectual ability than is found among the generality of prison officers, but this is not necessarily the case. Educational opportunities have greatly expanded in recent years, as well as working-class interest in further education for their children—and type 2 officers are among the younger men. Probably at least as important as ability, therefore, is motivation: type 2 officers display such a drive to improve themselves in their early preference for skilled jobs as well as in their better educational background. Most of the other officers joined the service later in their lives, with security in mind and a strong preference for settled family life. What they probably value most is a peaceful, safe existence, more likely to be found in closed than open prisons, and to which training for new and unfamiliar roles would appear irrelevant.

A word is necessary about the significance of such distinctions between prison officers. There is no implication that type 2 officers are, as prison officers, any better in general than the rest. Just as they seem better suited for open prison work than others, so it seems likely that they may be less well suited than those others to work in closed institutions. Their discontent with the amount of discretion and initiative permitted to them in the orthodox penal institution would appear to have that kind of implication. Of course, many will come to accept the inevitable as closed prison officers, and become effective cogs in the containment machine, but some with their kinds of characteristics may well be part of the not inconsiderable wastage which occurs during training and early service. It is worth recalling the research of Isabel Menzies on the nursing profession, which showed that the ethical and behavioural restraints imposed by that profession upon the behaviour of nurses had the effect of driving out nursing recruits whose personal make-up was more attuned to individual autonomy and the establishment of emotionally toned relationships with patients.[11]

Much has been made above of the need for open prison staff to be able to work without strong background support. This in no way reduces the importance of the role of management, or implies that there is no need for the exercise of authority. Management could be as vital in the open prisons of the future as it is in existing institutions, though its aims could be different. Its role would be directed towards maintaining the policy of the institutions, and that would mean in part the restraining of behaviour by either staff or inmates which threatened it. But it would also have its positive side: encouraging, supporting, guiding and advising junior staff in the performance of their proper function. And as we have seen in discussing the observational material collected at the short-term and medium-term opens, staff do need to feel, if they are to work with confidence, that they will receive backing from their seniors if they act in good faith—even if things do go wrong. There is nothing more immobilising than to have to keep one eye on the prisoners and the other on your superiors. And it is important that senior staff should be prepared to take responsibility for any decisions which they themselves have made. All of which has implications for the selection and training of staff, no less than for the development of an open prison model.

It has particular relevance for the selection of both intermediate and top managerial staff. The qualities called for—'enabling' ability, a readiness to accept responsibility for the actions of others, non-authoritarian attitudes, and a sympathetic understanding of how an open regime must operate—probably imply that managers at all levels will usually (though not necessarily always) be recruited from open prison staffs.

But native qualities by themselves will not be enough. They will need to be developed and informed by a type of training which is very different in character from that provided at present. The need for specialised training for open prison work was frequently referred to by our officer respondents. Less attention would be given in such training, of course, to containment, and more to the making of relationships and the changing of attitudes. In particular the emphasis on fairly rigid procedures for the maintenance of society would have to change. As an example one might contrast, as ways of maintaining order in the institution, the use of the rules, authority, and the lock-up with the skilful use of personal relationships and of group decision-making.[12]

It will be necessary also to extend the interpersonal confidence of the staff, by enabling them to confront difficult relational situations and discover that they can cope with them. Although in developing such skills they will need support and guidance, and the opportunity of discussing their work with those who have more experience, there really is no substitute for personal experience. What is being sought is skills which run, as it were, to the end of the fingers, rather than remaining chastely immured in the intellect. Lectures and even personal tutorials ultimately can only lead to progress when they have been tried out: when the officer concerned has had to try to find solutions to immediate practical situations, in which he stands alone, face to face with his charges. It is a kind of virtuoso function. He has to rely entirely on himself, with the aid of only such skill and resolution as he can personally muster.

All of which may make the task sound impossibly difficult. Changing people is difficult, but may not be impossible. And the alternative to attempting it may be to give up the struggle and admit that Professor Rupert Cross[13] was right when he argued that all prisons could hope to do was to contain offenders under conditions in which they do not suffer rapid personal and social deterioration. Fortunately to attempt such a task does not call for a university education, or an IQ of 140 plus; it calls instead for personal traits which our typology study gives us some hope of finding in sufficient numbers among prison staffs. If such a role were available within the Prison Service, moreover, it would undoubtedly change the public image of prison work, and possibly attract into the service more type 2 candidates otherwise repelled by traditional prison methods.

Training is not, however, confined to formally organised lectures and classes; it takes place also in a more informal way through early experience within the Prison Service, in which officers adapt themselves to group and organisational pressures within the institution—learning not only what is practicable, but also what staff 'public opinion' will put up with. It is at this stage that the staff culture, referred to frequently in previous chapters, comes into its own. Often of course the formal training and these informal pressures operate in the same direction, but where they clash it is the staff culture which appears to win out. 'A chief officer of long experience, referring to the predicament of the new recruit to the service put it to the writer like this. . . . Everyone says the prison must advance with the times, but what do they say when they are left to talk among themselves? What trend does the gatehouse chaff take? "Treatment or training?—I'd hang the . . . . lot of them".'[14] The problem is how to break a vicious circle in which each new generation of prison officers is socialised into containment attitudes by the staff already in post. This is clearly not going to be done by continuing the present practice in which open prison staffs gain most of their previous experience in closed prisons. Instead, potential open prison staffs will have to be selected for that kind of work at the very outset of their careers, so that they can begin to acquire more suitable experience, presumably in open prisons, from the very beginning. The further development of our typology may provide a basis for selecting them.

It would be wrong to conclude this discussion about penal policy without referring to the view, often expressed nowadays, that because prisons are so much more likely to damage than to improve the social adjustment of those committed to them, reformers should concentrate on trying to find alternatives to imprisonment, rather than trying to patch it up. There would be more to be said for such a view if there was no viable alternative to the traditional closed institution—though even here one must accept that for a long time to come people are going to demand containment-oriented institutions to protect them (as they see it) from dangerous men. So whether we go along with Professor Cross's pessimism and hope for no more than to reduce the damage they do to prisoners, or see possibilities of reforming them to fulfil a more positive role, we shall need to continue the debate about how they should be run. But what is being proposed here, in the form of open prisons which live up to their name, is a more radical departure, far removed from the institutions which have led to these sombre conclusions.

If instead we concentrate all our efforts on keeping people out of prison, the net result may not be all that we hoped for. Recent experience shows that if existing penal attitudes remain unchanged, a reduction in the number of persons in prison, as a result of the provision of more alternative forms of disposition outside, will result in the closing of open rather than closed institutions. A better understanding of the need for and the role of open prisons will do something to moderate closed prison attitudes, as well as providing living proof that there is a viable alternative.

Appendix 1
The Moos Correctional
Institutions Environment
Scale: instrumentation

(a) Advance notice to inmates
(b) Introduction to the Moos for inmates
(c) The Correctional Institutions Environment Scale (CIES) Form C
(d) Subscale descriptions and scoring key
(e) Staff scoring sheet

Appendix 1 a

University College, Cardiff
Department of Social Administration

The Open Prisons Research Project

To all inmates

As you will probably know, a research project is being undertaken at (name of the prison) along with five other prisons under the direction of Professor Howard Jones of Cardiff University, for which I am the researcher.

The research is concerned with studying the effectiveness of open and closed prisons. In this stage of the research we wish to collect information about the way in which this prison operates and the feelings of people here about it.

One of the devices that we are using for the above purpose is the Social Climate Scale which is not in any way a 'psychological' test but a scale to determine the social atmosphere of (name of the prison). There are no 'right' or 'wrong' answers to the test and you will not be asked to account for the replies that you give either to me or the prison staff.

I have picked 100 inmates at random from the population of (name of the prison) and will be seeing them on (date) in the (testing centre) in groups for just under 45 minutes.

PLEASE BE ON TIME FOR YOUR GROUP

If you do have any queries about the test or would at any time like to talk to me about (name of the prison), please see me or leave a note at the (room in which researcher was accommodated).

(signed) Research Fellow

Appendix 1 b

Introduction to the Moos for inmates

First of all the numbers attending were checked by means of a roll call and if any individuals were missing, the researcher usually asked about their whereabouts. The introduction went as follows:

'My name is Richard Stockford from Cardiff University, and I am working with Professor Howard Jones on a project to compare the effectiveness of open and closed prisons. The exercise that I want you to do is concerned with this. We hope to assess through this test the social atmosphere of the prison, so that the prisons in our research projects can be compared and we can find out something about your feelings concerning these prisons. The test is very easy, all I want you to do is listen to the statements that will be read over the tape-recorder and to decide if you think they are true or false. It is important that you should know that I am nothing to do with the Home Office, and that nothing you write down will be seen by anyone other than the research team. We intend to use all the replies on a grouped basis so that they will all be added up and an average for each prison obtained. Finally, a report on this part of the research will be coming out in October of 1971 and if you want a copy all you have to do is write to me at this address . . . .'

(Then use blackboard)

'Before we can start on the test, I would like you to fill in the top line on your scoring sheet with me, because it is a little complicated. Please don't fill in any of the sections until I tell you to.'

(The procedure is then explained on the blackboard, and inmates fill in the top row step by step.)

'Finally, to explain the exercise, you will hear a statement about the prison read out, the staff and the inmates or the unit (the unit in this case stands for the landing you are at present located on)—I want you to decide if you think the statement is generally true or generally false.

'If you think it is generally true, circle the "T", if you think it is generally false, circle the "F". Remember, "unit equals landing" (this was also written on the top of the blackboard). Are there any questions. . . . If there are any difficulties with a statement during the test, they can be repeated when we finish, if necessary, so please don't shout out while the test is going on.'

Appendix 1 c

Given to all staff

The Correctional Institutions Environment Scale (CIES)

Introduction

This scale is being used in this and five other training prisons within the scope of the research as part of an international collaborative project. [An international project had been planned at the time by the National Council on Crime and Delinquency, Davis, California, USA.]

The scale is intended to indicate, on various levels, the social 'atmosphere' of the prisons concerned and should be invaluable as a comparative measure of the different prisons within the compass of the research. The results, which will be treated in strict confidence, will be used solely as part of the body of information gathered for the research project.

Method of completion

You are provided with a booklet (affixed) containing 140 statements [This was CIES Form B, from which data were transferred after collection to Form C (see below Appendix 1 d).] pertaining to the unit and prison to which you are attached and a scoring sheet (affixed) with four rows of squares printed on it.

The top row on the SCORING SHEET asks for a certain amount of information relating to the individual officer; below are detailed instructions for its completion. This information is necessary merely to hold certain variables constant and not in order to identify any individual member of staff. The research is not in any way concerned with the opinions of individuals as such, but in overall totals.

Instructions for completing the TOP ROW of the SCORING SHEET

N.B. There should be only ONE letter or number in each box.

Rank
3

Enter here the code number of your rank as given in this table e.g. if you are a Senior Officer (S/O) enter '3' in the box (as shown)

RANK CODE NOS.	
0	Governor Grade
1	C/O
2	P/O (incl. H/P/O)
3	S/O (incl. H/S/O, S/O Instr.)
4	Instr.
5	T/A
6	Officer (incl. H/O)
7	C & B, Caterer, P.E.I.
X	Other

12

PRISON

Enter here prison name

14

UNIT	
A	4

Enter here the number of the landing or ward to which you are attached (n.b. if not attached to any unit leave blank). e.g. Landing A4.

18

DATE	
Day	Month
1	4	0	7

Enter here date of completing test. e.g. 14th July.

20

Age	
2	9

N.B. One column for tens and one for units.

26

Time on this Unit		
Years	Months	Weeks
0	0	0	3		2

Enter here the time you have been attached to your landing or ward.

32

Time in this Prison		
Years	Months	Weeks
0	4	1	0		1

Enter here length of service in this prison, e.g. 4 years 10 months 1 week.

Instructions for completing the 2nd, 3rd and 4th rows on the SCORING SHEET

The remaining 3 rows of squares (numbered 1-140) are for the test and are completed in conjunction with the booklet. For each statement in the booklet you are asked to decide if the statement is generally TRUE or FALSE of the unit (i.e. landing or ward) to which you are attached at present.

If generally TRUE, circle the T.
If generally FALSE, circle the F.

If errors do occur cross out boldly and circle the appropriate letter.
Finally, please be sure to answer every statement.

Thank you for your co-operation.

Appendix 1 d

Correctional Institutions Environment Scale (CIES) Form C

Subscale Descriptions and Scoring Key

The following list is the scoring key for the Correctional Institutions Environment Scale, Form C. An item listed as 'true' is scored 1 point if marked 'true' by the individual taking the scale, and an item listed as false is scored 1 point if marked false. The total subscale score is simply the number of items answered in the scored direction.

1. INVOLVEMENT: measures how active and energetic prisoners are in the day-to-day functioning of the programme, i.e. interacting socially with other prisoners, doing things on their own initiative, and developing pride and group spirit in the programme.

 6+ Prisoners put a lot of energy into what they do around here.
 37— The prison has very few social activities.
 39+ The prisoners are proud of this unit.
 49— Very few things around here ever get people excited.
 58+ There are pretty interesting discussions on this unit.
 63+ This is a friendly unit.
 65— Prisoners don't do anything around here unless the staff ask them to.
 74+ Prisoners here really try to improve.
 81+ Prisoners on this unit understand each other.
 83— There is very little community spirit in this unit.

2. SUPPORT: measures the extent to which prisoners are encouraged to be helpful and supportive towards other prisoners, and how supportive the staff is towards prisoners.

 2— Staff have very little time to encourage prisoners.
 11+ Staff go out of their way to help prisoners.
 18— Prisoners seldom help each other.
 21+ Staff are involved in prisoners' activities.
 25+ Staff are interested in how prisoners are going to get on once they leave.
 27+ The staff help new prisoners to get to know each other.
 35— Welfare officers have very little time to encourage prisoners.
 45+ The more capable prisoners on this unit help take care of the less capable ones.
 46+ The staff encourage group activities among prisoners.
 79+ The staff understand what the prisoners want.

3. EXPRESSIVENESS: measures the extent to which the programme encourages the open expression of feelings (including angry feelings) by prisoners and staff.

 1+ Prisoners say anything they want to the welfare officers.
 10— Prisoners are careful about what they say when staff are around.
 24— When prisoners disagree with each other, they keep it to themselves.
 34+ Prisoners are encouraged to show their feelings.
 44— It is hard to tell how prisoners are feeling on this unit.
 53+ Staff and prisoners say how they feel about each other.

66+ On this unit staff think it is a healthy thing to argue.
70+ People say what they really think around here.
78— Prisoners tend to hide their feelings from the staff.

4. AUTONOMY: assesses the extent to which prisoners are encouraged to take initiative in planning activities and take leadership in the prison.

9— The staff discourages criticism.
17+ The staff take notice of prisoners' suggestions.
33+ Prisoners are expected to organise their own activities.
52+ Prisoners here are encouraged to be independent.
60— The staff give prisoners very little responsibility.
61— Staff seldom give in to prisoners' pressure.
69+ Staff encourage prisoners to start their own activities.
77— There is no prisoner self-government in this prison.
86+ Prisoners have a say about what goes on here.

5. PRACTICAL ORIENTATION: assesses the extent to which the prisoner's environment orients him towards preparing himself for release from the programme. Such things as training for new kinds of jobs, looking to the future, and setting and working towards goals are considered.

3+ This prison emphasises job training.
12— Staff care more about what prisoners feel than about their practical problems.
19+ Prisoners here are expected to work towards their goals.
26— There is very little emphasis on making plans for release from the prison.
36+ Prisoners are encouraged to plan for the future.
41+ New training approaches are often tried in this prison.
55+ Prisoners must make plans before leaving the prison.
62— There is very little emphasis on what prisoners will be doing after they leave the prison.
71+ Prisoners are encouraged to learn new ways of doing things.
80— There is very little emphasis on making prisoners more practical.

6. PERSONAL PROBLEM ORIENTATION: measures the extent to which prisoners are encouraged to be concerned with their personal problems and feelings and to seek to understand them.

5— Prisoners are seldom asked about personal problems by the staff.
14+ Prisoners are expected to discuss their personal problems with each other.
20— Prisoners seldom talk about their personal problems with other prisoners.
29+ Staff are very interested in learning about prisoners' feelings.
48+ Personal problems are openly talked about.
57— The staff discourage talking about sex.
64+ Staff try to help prisoners understand their problems.
73— Prisoners hardly ever discuss their sexual lives with each other.
72+ Group discussion in this prison emphasises the understanding of personal problems.

7. ORDER AND ORGANISATION: measures how important order and organisation is in the programme in terms of prisoners (how they look), staff (what they do to encourage order) and the prison itself (how well it is kept).

4+ The staff make sure that the unit is always neat and tidy.
7— Things are sometimes very disorganised around here.

13— The association room is often untidy.
28— Many prisoners look untidy.
38+ Prisoners' activities are carefully planned.
47— The unit usually looks a little untidy.
54— Welfare officers sometimes don't keep their appointments with prisoners.
56+ The staff set an example for tidiness and orderliness.
72+ This is a very well organised unit.
85+ Prisoners are seldom kept waiting when they have appointments with any of the staff.

8. CLARITY: measures the extent to which the prisoner knows what to expect in the day-to-day routine of his programme and how explicit the programme rules and procedures are.

15+ Staff tell prisoners when they're improving.
22— Staff are always changing their minds.
30— Staff sometimes argue with each other.
31+ If a prisoner's routine is changed, someone on the staff always tells him why.
42— Prisoners never know when they will have a call-up from a welfare officer.
50+ If a prisoner breaks a rule, he knows what the punishment will be.
59— Prisoners never know when they will be moved to another unit.
67+ The prisoners know when welfare officers will be available.
75— Staff are always changing their minds here.
84+ When prisoners first arrive on the unit someone shows them around and explains how the unit operates.

9. STAFF CONTROL: assesses the extent to which the staff use measures to keep prisoners under necessary controls, i.e. in the formulation of rules, the scheduling of activities, and in the relationships between prisoners and staff.

8+ Once a routine is arranged for a prisoner, he must follow it.
16— Prisoners are rarely punished by being deprived of their privileges.
23+ Prisoners will be transferred to another unit if they don't obey the rules.
32— Staff don't order the prisoners around.
40+ If one prisoner argues with another, he will get into trouble with the staff.
43+ All decisions about the prison are made by the staff and not by the prisoners.
51— Prisoners may criticise staff members to their faces.
68— Prisoners may call staff by their first names.
76+ The staff regularly check up on the prisoners.

Appendix 1 e

SCS Staff scoring sheet

		12	14		18	20			26				32
	Prison		Unit	Date		Age	Time on this unit			Time in this prison			
				Day	Month		Years	Mths	Weeks	Years	Mths	Week
S													

1									10										20					
1	2	3	4	5	6	7	8	9	10	11	12	13	14	15	16	17	18	19	20	21	22	23	24	25
T	T	T	T	T	T	T	T	T	T	T	T	T	T	T	T	T	T	T	T	T	T	T	T	T
F	F	F	F	F	F	F	F	F	F	F	F	F	F	F	F	F	F	F	F	F	F	F	F	F

1									10										20					
51	52	53	54	55	56	57	58	59	60	61	62	63	64	65	66	67	68	69	70	71	72	73	74	75
T	T	T	T	T	T	T	T	T	T	T	T	T	T	T	T	T	T	T	T	T	T	T	T	T
F	F	F	F	F	F	F	F	F	F	F	F	F	F	F	F	F	F	F	F	F	F	F	F	F

1									10										20	
101	102	103	104	105	106	107	108	109	110	111	112	113	114	115	116	117	118	119	120	12
T	T	T	T	T	T	T	T	T	T	T	T	T	T	T	T	T	T	T	T	T
F	F	F	F	F	F	F	F	F	F	F	F	F	F	F	F	F	F	F	F	F

71	72	73	74	75	76	77	78	79

				30										40										50
26	27	28	29	30	31	32	33	34	35	36	37	38	39	40	41	42	43	44	45	46	47	48	49	50
T	T	T	T	T	T	T	T	T	T	T	T	T	T	T	T	T	T	T	T	T	T	T	T	T
F	F	F	F	F	F	F	F	F	F	F	F	F	F	F	F	F	F	F	F	F	F	F	F	F

				30										40										50
76	77	78	79	80	81	82	83	84	85	86	87	88	89	90	91	92	93	94	95	96	97	98	99	100
T	T	T	T	T	T	T	T	T	T	T	T	T	T	T	T	T	T	T	T	T	T	T	T	T
F	F	F	F	F	F	F	F	F	F	F	F	F	F	F	F	F	F	F	F	F	F	F	F	F

							30											40
22	123	124	125	126	127	128	129	130	131	132	133	134	135	136	137	138	139	140
T	T	T	T	T	T	T	T	T	T	T	T	T	T	T	T	T	T	T
F	F	F	F	F	F	F	F	F	F	F	F	F	F	F	F	F	F	F

Appendix 2
The prison officer's questionnaire

University College, Cardiff

Open and closed prison study

Prison Staff Questionnaire

Prison .... Questionnaire No. ....

Age ....

At the end of most of the following questions you will find a space for other comment: if, after marking the relevant boxes you feel that the answers you have given are not quite adequate, it would be of great help to us if you would fill in this end-section as fully as possible.

If you find that there is insufficient space for your comments after each question, please continue on the back of the relevant page.

The individual replies to this survey will be treated in strict confidence and will be revealed to no one—least of all prisoners, other officers or the prison authorities.

1. (a) *Reasons for joining*
   Which 3 reasons in the list below (or any other ones you might like to add) do you think *most* influenced your choice of the Prison Service as a career? Order these reasons 1, 2 and 3 (1 being the most important) by entering the appropriate number in the box next to the reason.

   Good pay and pension scheme
   Good prospects for promotion
   Security of employment
   An extension of previous experience
      (e.g. military/police service)
   Interest in people
   Rent-free house
   Unhappy in previous jobs
   As a 'challenge'
   Recommended by friends already in the service
   Special interest in prisons, e.g. security aspects
   Others please specify
   ....
   ....
   ....

246

(b) Could you give your age when you joined the service

(c) Did you choose the prison service as a career after considering another occupation? If so, what was the alternative?

....

2. *Changes in the Prison Service*
   (a) Do you think any of the aspects of prison life listed below have changed since you joined the service, and do you approve or disapprove of these changes?

EXAMPLE
Prison discipline: if you think there is more prison discipline now than when you joined the service and you disapprove of this change, tick the boxes in this way.

Prison discipline

More	Same	Less	Approve	Disapprove
✓				✓

and so on for each category stating whether you think there has been any change and whether you approve or disapprove. You can add any other categories you want to mention, in the space provided at the end of the list.

	More	Same	Less	Approve	Disapprove
Prison discipline					
Prison security					
Welfare provisions for prisoners					
Informal staff contact with prisoners					
Rehabilitation and training facilities for prisoners					
Status of officers in Prison Service					
Home Office control					
Others (please specify)					
....					
....					
....					

(b) What are your views of the security aspects of the Mountbatten Report? (Tick *one* box only)

They have been generally good for the prisons
They have been generally bad for the prisons
They have not made any difference to the prisons

Have you any other opinions on the Mountbatten Report? If so, please write them below, giving, if you would, reasons for your views.

3. (a) *Problems of the prison officer*
What aspects of the Prison Service do most to make your task more difficult?
(*Please number in order of priority* (1-3)). For example: if you find lack of
teamwork the major problem, put 1 in the box next to it: if you find low pay comes
next, put 2 in the box next to it, and so on down to the third.

Low pay

High working hours

Poor conditions of work (e.g. old buildings)

Inadequate quarters

Lack of teamwork among officers

Conflicting instructions from superiors

Overcrowding of prisons

Lack of co-operation from prisoners

Lack of amenities for prisoners

Increase in 'paperwork'

Others (please specify)

....

....

....

(b) Do you find yourself 'taking the prison home' with you?
(Underline the one that applies to you)

Usually   Sometimes   Rarely   Never

4. (a) *Promotion*
Which problems do you feel most strongly about in the system of promotion?
(*Number in order of priority 1-3*)

It is too slow

The additional responsibility is not worth it

It often means a move from the present prison

It does not take experience into account

The face has to fit

Overtime reduced

Not told enough about selection procedure

Other (please specify)

....

....

(b) Could you state briefly the grounds on which you think promotion should be
decided?

5. *Training of officers*
   What was your opinion of the training given to you:

   (a) *in your probationary period* at your first prison?
   (Please tick one box only)

   Very useful
   Useful, but could be improved upon
   Not very useful, needs a lot of improvement
   Not at all useful

   Could you list any particular advantages or defects that you found during this period of training?

   (b) *at the Officers' Training School?*
   (Please tick one box only)

   Very useful
   Useful, but could be improved upon
   Not very useful, needs a lot of improvement
   Not at all useful

   Could you list any particular advantages or defects that you found during this period of training?

   (c) Other courses? Give details of any you have taken below
   (If none, write NONE............................)

Type of course	Length	Very useful	Useful, but could be improved on	Not very useful, needs a lot of improvement	Not at all useful

   Could you list any particular advantages or defects that you found during these training courses on the back of this sheet?

   (d) *Education.* (Tick the boxes that apply)
   Secondary Modern/Elementary
   Grammar
   Training College/Polytechnic/University
   Evening School or Evening College
   Technical College

   (e) At what age did you finish full-time education?   ....yrs.

(f) Give details of any qualifications, either academic, trade, or professional obtained at school, during work, or in the services.

Qualification	Where obtained

Initiative and Discretion

Initiative is used here to mean taking the lead or being enterprising.

Discretion is used here to mean being able to make decisions in the course of your work without reference to a higher authority.

6. (a) *Discretion*
   Do you feel that in this prison you are given:
   (tick one box only)

   enough discretion in your actions?
   not enough discretion in your actions?
   more than enough discretion in your actions?

   (b) What sort of 'on the job' decisions are you allowed to make?
   (tick one box only)
   Those concerning routine matters only
   Those concerning non-routine matters, as they occur usually with reference to a superior
   Those concerning non-routine matters, as they occur usually without reference to a superior
   Those concerning major policy in the running of the prison

   (c) Are prisoners you put on report punished?

   Sometimes [ ]   Usually [ ]   Always [ ]

   (d) How many prisoners have you put on report in the last six months?
   (If none, write NIL)

7. *Initiative*
   i. Do you think individual initiative is encouraged in this Prison?   YES/NO

   ii. Do you want more initiative?   YES/NO
   If yes, why and if no, why not?

8. *Career and family*
   (a) Which other prisons, borstals, remand or detention centres have you worked in and for how long?
   If none, write NONE and move to part (c)

Type of institution	Name of institution	Month and year of appointment

(b) If you have moved through a number of institutions what have been your motives for changing from one institution to another? e.g. if you left your first post mainly due to family reasons, tick the first column against 'Family reasons'. Similarly tick your main motives for leaving each of the institutions in which you have been employed.

	Moves from institutions						
	1st	2nd	3rd	4th	5th	6th	7th
Broadening you experience							
Family reasons, e.g. living nearer home							
Wished to find the institution that suited you best							
Moved due to promotion							
Other							
....							

(c) Whether you have moved or not, what man do you think makes the best prison officer, one who moves around or one who stays in the same place for a reasonable time?

Stays in one place [ ]

Moves around [ ]

Could you state briefly why you feel this is so?

(d) Did you belong to the ATC, the ACF, or the Sea Cadets at school?   YES/NO

(e) Please list your first job after finishing your full-time education and the last two you had before entering the service.

	Occupation	Date of leaving and entering
First job		
Last two before join-ing the service		

(f) Were you, at any time, in the armed forces?   YES/NO

If YES   (i) What rank did you obtain? ....

            (ii) What was your length of service? .... yrs.

(g) What kind of experience, qualifications and personality best suit a man to become a Governor?

(h) Are you: married

                single

                separated

                divorced

                widowed

(i) If married, how many children do you have?.....................................

(j) Do you live in: Officers' quarters

                        Your own house

                        Rented accommodation

                        Other (please specify)

            ....

(k) What was/is your father's main job? (Please be as detailed as possible)

....

....

9. *Social life*
(a) When you have a night off duty what do you usually do?
(Please number the first three in order of preference—e.g. if you most prefer to go to the cinema, put 1 in the box, if your second preference is home maintenance, put 2 in the box and so on down to 3).

Relax at home

Go to the cinema or theatre

Go to a pub or club

Visit friends

Home maintenance

Others ....

....

....

(b) When you go out in company who do you usually go along with?
(Please number in order of frequency 1-3)

Wife/girl friend
Other prison officers
Other prison officers and their families
Relatives
Friends outside the Prison Service
Other (please specify)

If there are any further comments that you would like to make, please note them below or call in to see me at your convenience.

Thank you for your co-operation

Appendix 3
The prison officer's diary

Introduction

This diary is being used in the research to build up an accurate picture of the function and routine of a prison officer's job in the institutions within the scope of the research. It is in no way intended or designed to measure personal performance, but to give us, if possible, an overall view of the prison officer's activities during his working day.

As you will realise, the accuracy of the final product depends very much on you, the individual officer. Any extra work the diary might cause ought to be minimised by the coding on the following pages.

Please take care of this diary, its contents will probably be irreplaceable. However, if you should lose it, please see me and a new one will be issued.

Finally, the contents of the completed diaries will be treated as totally private and confidential; no individual officer's name will be divulged in any circumstances.

Thank you for your co-operation

Instructions

1. Familiarise yourself with the contents of the diary and coding method. It is intended to run the survey over three days in a three week period, and you will be notified as to which days these will be.
2. In the interests of accuracy DO NOT wait until the end of the day to fill in the table: it is quite possible that inaccuracies could become very large if this is done. Instead, enter the code letter pertaining to your job *when you reach the end of the half-hour period.*
3. When you have completed the diary section please complete the two questions on page vi, the 'job satisfaction' question on page vi and, if necessary, the comment sheet on page vii.
4. There will be a completed 'specimen' diary on the gate (or staff notice board) for scrutiny by any member of the prison staff.
5. The completed diary should be placed in the envelope supplied, which should be sealed and handed to me.

Coding instructions

The job-code letter should be entered against the appropriate half-hour division.

Job-code Letters   A. SUPERVISION
B. SECURITY
C. STAFF SUPERVISION
D. OCAL
E. COURT DUTY
F. REHABILITATION

254

G.   STAFF DISCUSSION
H.   STAFF TRAINING
I.   ADMINISTRATION
J.   OTHER DUTIES
O/D.   OFF DUTY AND MEAL BREAKS

The jobs in the various categories (A to O/D above) are broken down in the pages following. Thus, for example: If, from 14.30 to 15.00 you were handling visits, then the job-code letter 'A' would be written against the time 15.00.

Job-code letters

A. SUPERVISION—including: association, educational, exercise, feeding, recreation, religious services (all), MO/Psychiatrist/Psychologist (inmates with, to and from).
Party control: inside, outside working party workshops.
Visits: inmates (relatives, etc., police/solicitors) tradespeople, workmen, any other visitors.
Adjudications: Governor's reports, VC reports.
Special supervision: outside (hospital, home visits), punishment block, Rule 43.

B. SECURITY—including: examining prison (cell examination, etc.), fire prevention, locking up, roll check, unlocking.
Searching: inmates, prison, remands (food, etc.), vehicles.
Patrols.
Gate and key control.
Security control: e.g. TV security control.

C. STAFF SUPERVISION

D. OCAL—including: observation and classification unit.
Legal aid: legal aid and appeal.

E. COURT DUTY—including: escorts and productions.

F. REHABILITATION—including: attendance at boards, group counselling, hostel/outworkers, individual counselling, progress reports, any other.

G. STAFF DISCUSSION—including: formal, informal.

H. STAFF TRAINING—including: instructing in technical, instructing in in-service, receiving technical, receiving in-service.

I. ADMINISTRATION—including: all written reports, documentation and routine administration not included in other categories.

J. OTHER DUTIES—including: bank escort, canteen/earnings, driver, information centre, mess caterer, messenger, photographer, projectionist, records clerk, relief to specialist grade.

O/D. OFF DUTY AND MEAL BREAKS

N.B. Please fill in all off-duty hours with the code-letters 'O/D'.

Job code		
A.	SUPERVISION	
B.	SECURITY	
C.	STAFF SUPERVISION	
D.	OCAL	
E.	COURT DUTY	
F.	REHABILITATION	
G.	STAFF DISCUSSION	
H.	STAFF TRAINING	
I.	ADMINISTRATION	
J.	OTHER DUTIES	
O/D.	OFF DUTY AND MEAL BREAKS	

(Please see preceding page for sub-divisions.)

DATE: 13 January 1971

Time	Job code	Time	Job code	Time	Job code
00.00		08.00		16.00	
00.30		08.30		16.30	
01.00		09.00		17.00	
01.30		09.30		17.30	
02.00		10.00		18.00	
02.30		10.30		18.30	
03.00		11.00		19.00	
03.30		11.30		19.30	
04.00		12.00		20.00	
04.30		12.30		20.30	
05.00		13.00		21.00	
05.30		13.30		21.30	
06.00		14.00		22.00	
06.30		14.30		22.30	
07.00		15.00		23.00	
07.30		15.30		23.30	

Job code	A.	SUPERVISION
	B.	SECURITY
	C.	STAFF SUPERVISION
	D.	OCAL
	E.	COURT DUTY
	F.	REHABILITATION
	G.	STAFF DISCUSSION
	H.	STAFF TRAINING
	I.	ADMINISTRATION
	J.	OTHER DUTIES
	O/D.	OFF DUTY AND MEAL BREAKS

(Please see preceding page for sub-divisions.)

DATE: 14 January 1971

	Job code		Job code		Job code
00.00		08.00		16.00	
00.30		08.30		16.30	
01.00		09.00		17.00	
01.30		09.30		17.30	
02.00		10.00		18.00	
02.30		10.30		18.30	
03.00		11.00		19.00	
03.30		11.30		19.30	
04.00		12.00		20.00	
04.30		12.30		20.30	
05.00		13.00		21.00	
05.30		13.30		21.30	
06.00		14.00		22.00	
06.30		14.30		22.30	
07.00		15.00		23.00	
07.30		15.30		23.30	

Job code

A. SUPERVISION
B. SECURITY
C. STAFF SUPERVISION
D. OCAL
E. COURT DUTY
F. REHABILITATION
G. STAFF DISCUSSION
H. STAFF TRAINING
I. ADMINISTRATION
J. OTHER DUTIES
O/D. OFF DUTY AND MEAL BREAKS

DATE: 15 January 1971

	Job code		Job code		Job code
00.00		08.00		16.00	
00.30		08.30		16.30	
01.00		09.00		17.00	
01.30		09.30		17.30	
02.00		10.00		18.00	
02.30		10.30		18.30	
03.00		11.00		19.00	
03.30		11.30		19.30	
04.00		12.00		20.00	
04.30		12.30		20.30	
05.00		13.00		21.00	
05.30		13.30		21.30	
06.00		14.00		22.00	
06.30		14.30		22.30	
07.00		15.00		23.00	
07.30		15.30		23.30	

Could you please enter here:

(i) Your rank:

PLEASE TICK ONE ONLY

Govnr. Grade	
C/O	
P/O (incl. H/P/O)	
S/O (incl. H/S/O, S/O Instr.)	
Instr.	
T/A	
Officer (incl. H/O)	
C & B, Caterer, P.E.I.	
Other	

(ii) Your fixed post (if any)

PLEASE TICK ONE ONLY

Classn. Unit	
Censor	
Gate	
Reception	
Training	
Security/Security Control	
Catering	
PE	
Regl. Office	
Legal aid	
Rehabilitation	
Other	

Job satisfaction

Could you please list below, in order of priority (1-3) the names of the jobs that give you the most satisfaction (even if you have not been doing these jobs during the survey)?

1	
2	
3	

Comment sheet

If there are any comments or observations concerning the job of the prison officer that you would like to mention, please write them below:

Appendix 4
Prison officers' typology matrix

Age	Under 39	Under 39	Under 39	Under 39	Under 39	Under 39	Under 39	Under 39	Over 40	Over 40	Over 40	Over 40	Over 40	Over 40	Over 40	Over 40	Misc.
Length of service	Under 7	Under 7	Under 7	Under 7	Over 8	Over 8	Over 8	Over 8	Under 7	Under 7	Under 7	Under 7	Over 8	Over 8	Over 8	Over 8	
Education	SM	SM	Fur.	Fur.	SM	SM	Fur.	Fur.	SM	SM	Fur.	Fur.	SM	SM	Fur.	Fur.	
Rank	abg	bg	abg	bg	abg	bg	abg	bg	abg	bg	abg	bg	abg	bg	abg	bg	
ltc A(53)	—	8	—	7	2	5	2	1	—	1	—	1	9	5	8	4	—
mtc B(38)	—	2	—	12	—	1	2	2	—	3	—	2	6	4	2	2	—
stc C(36)	—	3	—	4	—	—	1	3	—	1	—	2	9	8	4	1	—
lto D(34)	—	2	—	8	—	1	—	4	—	1	—	—	9	7	—	2	—
mto E(44)	—	7	—	11	—	1	—	2	—	4	—	2	6	5	2	2	2
sto F(23)	—	6	—	9	—	—	—	—	—	—	—	1	3	3	—	1	—
228	—	28	—	51	2	8	5	12	—	10	—	8	42	32	16	12	2
A + B + C (127)	—	13	—	23	2	6	5	6	—	5	—	5	24	17	14	7	—
D + E + F (101)	—	15	—	28	—	2	—	6	—	5	—	3	18	15	2	5	2

Key to abbreviations:

SM = Secondary Modern   ltc = long-term closed   lto = long-term open
Fur. = Further   mtc = medium-term closed   mto = medium-term open
abg = above basic grade   stc = short-term closed   sto = short-term open
bg = basic grade

Appendix 5
A tentative evaluation of the Moos CIES

When the adaptation of the Moos CIES for use in British prisons was discussed (see pp. 91-4), the need for fresh assessments of the test's validity and reliability was acknowledged. This section contains an account of the work carried out on this. The operations reported here were all undertaken with the longer Form B version of the test; it will be recalled that our test data, although collected on the Form B version, were converted to Form C for presentation in Chapter 5.

(i) The assessment of validity: the person/setting ratio study

The census taken of the inmate population in each prison showed that the populations in the prisons studied were not exactly comparable. In each paired situation, open prisons had a higher proportion of older inmates and there were, in addition, differences in the degree of criminality as reflected in the variable 'number of previous court appearances'. Further differences between prisons emerged when the offence characteristics of inmates were compared, the most distinctive feature being that open prisons contained inmates only of a particular security category, that is, they were regarded by the Prison Department as presenting the least public danger if they escaped from custody. Closed prisons contained few such inmates. It was, therefore, possible that differences in the CIES scores between prisons were attributable to such demographic variables and that the CIES was assessing differences in 'personality' rather than differences in 'regime'. It will be recalled that the CIES was originally developed to assess 'person/setting interactions'. The following procedures were undertaken in order to test the degree to which the CIES was making an assessment of either or both of these aspects.

It was hypothesised that:

(1) If groups of inmates with similar personality/biographical features could be identified as 'identical' components of the prison populations to be compared then it would be possible to test for differences in the CIES scale scores of these individuals.

(2) The extent to which statistically significant differences in CIES scores between the 'identical' groups paralleled those between the various prisons from which the various group members came, would provide an indication of the extent to which the CIES scores reflected differences in regime rather than differences in the personality structure of prison populations.

(3) In this way it would be possible to compute an approximate person/setting ratio for the test.

The first problem encountered in the experimental programme undertaken to make such an assessment of the validity of the CIES was caused by the lack of an independent assessment of the personality of CIES respondents. However, it was revealed that there was sufficient theoretical and empirical support for the assumption that biographical and criminal career variables are systematically related to differences in the personality of offenders. (See, for example, Clarence Schrag, 'Some Foundations for a Theory of Correction', pp. 309-57 in D. R. Cressey (ed.), *The Prison: Studies in Institutional Organization and Change*, New York: Holt, Rinehart & Winston, 1961. L. E. Hewitt and R. L. Jenkins, *Fundamental Patterns of Maladjustment: the*

Table Appendix 5.1   Results of the person/setting ratio study

Matrix group	Prisons	Number in groups	Number of significantly different scales	Number of significantly different comparisons
1. Murder, etc. all ages, 0-2 precons	LTC LTO	14	10	5
2. Breaking and entering (B + E) 24-36 years, 6+ precons	MTC MTO	8 12	8	4
3. B + E 24-36 years, 6+ precons	LTC MTO	8 12	8	3
4. B + E 24-36 years, 6+ precons	STC MTO	8 12	6	4
5. B + E 19-28 years, 6+ precons	MTC MTC	9 17	8	3
6. B + E 19-28 years, 6+ precons	MTC STC	17 10	4	0
7. B + E 19-28 years, 6+ precons	MTO STC	9 10	6	2
8. Theft 29+ years, 0-5 precons	LTO MTO	9 13	10	5
9. Theft 29+ years, 0-5 precons	LTO STO	9 12	11	6
10. Theft 29+ years, 0-5 precons	MTO STO	13 12	7	0
11. False pretences 29+ years, 0-5 precons	MTO LTO	9 14	10	6
Totals			88	38

		Long-term	Medium-term	Short-term
Prisons:	Closed	LTC	MTC	STC
	Open	LTO	MTO	STO

Dynamics of their Origin, Michigan: Illinois Child Guidance Institute, 1946.) On this assumption a three-dimensional matrix was computed on data from every inmate in every prison in the study (i.e. 2,488 cases). This matrix was based on the semi-interquartile range distributions of the variables 'age' and 'number of previous court appearances'. The third dimension was created by the development of a classification of offences based on data available for the most recent conviction. This classification included the following offence categories: murder, attempted murder and man-slaughter; other offences of violence against the person; robbery; other crimes against property with violence (e.g. all breaking and entering offences and taking and driving away); offences against property without violence, I (principally theft and receiving); offences against property without violence, II (principally fraud, forgery and em-bezzlement) and malicious damage to property (e.g. arson). There was also a miscellaneous category. The distribution of matrix-derived types differed enormously from prison to prison. Once the matrix was developed, the CIES respondents in each prison were identified and allocated matrix locations.

When the matrix allocation for CIES respondents was completed, it was possible to identify 'identical groups'. Not all matrix categories were represented in more than one prison. The concentration of sexual offenders at the long-term closed prison, for instance, prevented a comparison of this matrix category. A number of comparable groups, however, did emerge and it was possible to embark on the planned programme of statistical testing (the Mann-Whitney u test was used). The results of this programme are shown in Table Appendix 5.1.

The incidence of statistical significance in this analysis (38/88 cases) at 43 per cent is far too high for it to be attributable to chance. Given that the operation of chance in a programme of this kind is likely to produce at $p = 0.5$ five significant results in every hundred cases, it is almost certain that this estimate has a probable error of ± 5 per cent. It may be concluded from this analysis that the approximate person/setting interaction ratio for the CIES in this data is 60 : 40. The claim that the CIES scores reflect the impingement of regimes upon behaviour may be regarded as valid within such limits as these.

(ii) The assessment of reliability

Split-half reliability coefficients were calculated for both the staff and inmate data. As this is a measure of internal consistency for each individual, response data for the staff at the long-term and short-term closed prisons were included. The reliability coefficients reported in Table Appendix 5.2 are corrected estimates based on the Spearman-Brown formula.

Table Appendix 5.2   Moos CIES: split-half reliability coefficients

	N	Spo.	Sup.	Pra.	Aff.	Ord.	Ins.	Inv.	Agg.	Var.	Cla.	Sub.	Aut.
Inmates	539	0·36	0·60	0·57	0·59	0·70	0·47	0·62	0·63	0·41	0·48	0·63	0·52
Staff	200	0·51	0·58	0·62	0·71	0·76	0·67	0·73	0·73	0·41	0·57	0·47	0·64

Note: for 100 d.f. and beyond a correlation coefficient of 0·32 is significant at the 0·001 level.

(iii) **Other work on the test**

Scale intercorrelation was measured. The results of this analysis, which was based on the same data used in the split-half reliability assessment, are reported in Tables Appendix 5.3 and 5.4. The degree of intercorrelation between subscales shown in these tables is higher than that reported in early work on the social climate scale. The difference is accentuated by the much larger number of cases in the data reported here. These high correlations between subscales cast doubt on the independence of the scales. The subscales are treated as independent because they were independently derived from what was essentially a sorting, ordering and judging process. Consequently, the development and formal application of the Correctional Institutions version of the test proceeded without any preceding test of the original methods of test construction. Dr Moos has himself subjected the results of CIES administration to factor analysis, but has concluded that the intercorrelations were not high enough to justify a collapsing of the subscales.[1] The same conclusion may not be justified in the light of Tables Appendix 5.3 or 5.4. A factor analysis of each sample intercorrelation matrix (separate matrices have been derived for each staff and inmate sample and show much variation) might constitute an extremely useful way of descriptively summarising CIES data. Whatever the case, however, it must be tentatively concluded that there is some doubt concerning the independence of CIES subscales. Similarly it must be concluded that there are grounds for doubting the assumptions implicit in the test that the subscales assessments are of equal 'weight' and of equal relevance to the assessment of prison social climates.

The criticisms reveal a basic fault in the construction and rationale of the CIES, that the subscales were derived from the application of procedures which had very little reliance upon objective statistical techniques of appraisal. For instance, a cluster analysis of the original pooled CIES items might have produced evidence concerning the independence of subscales, thus allowing some appraisal to be made of their relative weighting.

The evidence from this project suggests that in its present form the CIES is capable of discriminating between different prison regimes. However, there is also evidence from an item-by-item statistical comparison of the results that the test still contains a large number of items which fail to discriminate between prison regimes, and that the discriminatory potential of the test (even in its Form C version) is blunted by such inbuilt redundancy. Though a very useful aid in the assessment of prison regimes, this does not mean that it is not capable of further refinement or that the possibility of doing this should be overlooked. Indeed, we are pursuing such possibilities at the present time, by developing a new, empirically derived item pool, built up within the correctional setting.

No assessment was made of test-retest reliability. Estimates of this coefficient for the original social climate scale were high. However, it was possible to test for differences between the two halves of each inmate sample. Samples were split by including alternate cases in each of the two groups. There were six samples and twelve subscales. A 1/3 sample testing between the two halves of each sample over all subscales produced no statistically significant differences. A similar programme has not been undertaken with the staff data.

Table Appendix 5.3 Moos CIES combined correlation matrices—inmate samples

	Supp. C	Supp. O	Exp. C	Exp. O	Aut. C	Aut. O	P.O. C	P.O. O	P.P.O. C	P.P.O. O	O. & O. C	O. & O. O	Clr. C	Clr. O	S.C. C	S.C. O	
L	0·56	0·45	0·11	0·17	0·29	0·34	0·15	0·39	0·32	0·31	0·42	0·58	0·46	0·40	—0·11	—0·02	Inv.
M	0·28	0·49	0·09	0·27	0·30	0·33	0·29	0·51	0·21	0·30	0·29	0·56	0·21	0·36	—0·06	—0·02	
S	0·53	0·24	0·24	0·05	0·29	0·22	0·55	0·23	0·42	0·32	0·32	0·32	0·15	0·30	—0·35	—0·26	
L			0·31	0·28	0·37	0·50	0·33	0·49	0·57	0·25	0·43	0·36	0·55	0·48	—0·34	—0·26	Supp.
M			0·37	0·34	0·52	0·47	0·70	0·47	0·14	0·38	0·58	0·48	0·44	0·39	—0·08	—0·10	
S			0·22	0·27	0·38	0·36	0·65	0·52	0·43	0·09	0·27	0·43	0·35	0·43	—0·34	—0·10	
L			L		0·34	0·39	0·11	0·18	0·33	0·15	0·17	0·06	0·30	0·03	—0·36	—0·32	Exp.
M			M		0·39	0·45	0·50	0·31	0·13	0·36	0·36	0·31	0·44	0·28	—0·25	—0·02	
S			S		0·30	0·32	0·27	0·28	0·30	0·07	—0·06	0·16	0·03	0·30	—0·33	—0·05	
L					L		0·35	0·32	0·36	0·33	0·22	0·20	0·17	0·29	—0·52	—0·43	Aut.
M					M		0·53	0·42	0·33	0·27	0·50	0·34	0·33	0·39	—0·19	—0·08	
S					S		0·38	0·51	0·36	0·10	0·25	0·18	0·21	0·23	—0·23	—0·27	
L							L		0·21	0·39	0·12	0·47	0·34	0·42	—0·21	—0·0	P.O.
M							M		0·22	0·28	0·60	0·46	0·51	0·27	—0·09	—0·08	
S							S		0·32	0·06	0·30	0·33	0·36	0·35	—0·23	—0·2	
L									L		0·23	0·34	0·34	0·31	—0·35	—0·01	P.P.O.
M									M		0·16	0·29	0·08	0·21	—0·15	—0·17	
S									S		0·13	0·08	0·11	0·15	—0·32	—0·09	
L											L		0·47	0·56	—0·24	—0·03	O. & O.
M											M		0·61	0·38	—0·06	—0·06	
S											S		0·30	0·53	0·00	0·19	
L													L		—0·10	—0·15	Clr.
M													M		—0·02	—0·28	
S													S		—0·06	—0·04	

L Long-term
M Medium-term
S Short-term
C Closed
O Open

Table Appendix 5.4 *Moos CIES combined correlation matrices—staff samples*

Row	Term	Supp. C	Supp. O	Exp. C	Exp. O	Aut. C	Aut. O	P.O. C	P.O. O	P.P.O. C	P.P.O. O	O. & O. C	O. & O. O	Clr. C	Clr. O	S.C. C	S.C. O
Inv.	L		0·71		0·29		0·23		0·62		0·40		0·71		0·48		0·28
	M	0·49	0·48	0·42	0·37	0·47	0·25	0·37	0·10	−0·02	0·19	0·15	0·51	0·18	0·45	−0·10	0·07
	S		0·81		0·43		0·80		0·67		0·64		0·39		0·16		0·06
Supp.	L				0·47		0·35		0·72		0·38		0·61		0·45		0·25
	M			0·38	0·37	0·26	0·23	0·44	0·36	0·03	0·30	0·22	0·44	0·33	0·44	0·03	−0·01
	S				0·45		0·60		0·68		0·68		0·50		0·38		0·08
Exp.	L						0·28		0·50		0·42		0·25		0·32		−0·02
	M					0·43	0·44	0·14	0·09	0·41	−0·03	−0·12	0·29	−0·05	0·33	0·01	−0·35
	S						0·32		0·36		0·30		0·22		0·08		−0·07
Aut.	L								0·62		0·25		0·15		0·31		−0·27
	M							0·12	0·05	0·34	0·05	−0·27	0·39	0·07	0·26	−0·36	−0·20
	S								0·70		0·63		0·37		0·05		0·11
P.O.	L										0·44		0·44		0·47		0·18
	M									0·22	0·13	0·31	0·43	0·49	0·38	0·02	0·08
	S										0·44		0·26		0·31		0·26
P.P.O.	L												−0·01		0·22		−0·15
	M											−0·07	−0·05	0·05	0·09	0·05	−0·29
	S												−0·20		0·16		0·18
O. & O.	L														0·41		0·27
	M													0·44	0·53	0·27	0·18
	S														0·61		0·19
Clr.	L																0·08
	M															0·17	0·08
	S																0·03

L Long-term
M Medium-term
S Short-term
C Closed
O Open

Notes

Chapter 1　Open prisons: their origins and aims

1 Cesare Beccaria, *Essay on Crime and Punishment*, 1967. See E. Monachesi, 'Cesare Beccaria', in H. Mannheim (ed.), *Pioneers in Criminology*, New Jersey: Paterson Smith, 1972, pp. 36 ff.

2 John Howard, *The State of the Prisons*, 1777. See D. L. Howard. *John Howard: Prison Reformer*, London: Christopher Johnson, 1958.

3 Howard Jones, *Crime and the Penal System*, London: University Tutorial Press, 1968, p. 148.

4 Howard Jones, 'Punishment and Social Values', in T. Grygier *et al.* (eds), *Criminology in Transition*, London: Tavistock, 1965, pp. 15 ff. Howard Jones, 'The Approved School: a Theoretical Model', in P. Halmos (ed.), *Sociological Review Monograph No. 9*, 1965.

5 Ibid.

6 Home Office, *Report of the Inquiry into Prison Escapes and Security* (The Mountbatten Report), HMSO, CMND 3175, 1966.

7 M. Ancel *et al.*, *Modern Methods of Penal Treatment*, International Penal and Penitentiary Foundation, 1955, p. 77.

8 W. H. Commons, T. Yakhub, E. Powers and C. R. Doering, *The Development of Penological Treatment at Norfolk Colony in Massachusetts*, Stanford University Press, 1940.

9 H. E. Barnes and N. K. Teeters, *New Horizons in Criminology*, Englewood Cliffs: Prentice-Hall, 1959, pp. 354-9.

10 Lionel Fox, *English Prison and Borstal Systems*, London: Routledge & Kegan Paul, 1952, p. 152.

11 Barnes and Teeters, *op. cit.* (1945 edition), p. 799.

12 D. Clemmer, *The Prison Community*, New York: Rinehart, 1958.

13 M. H. Cooper and R. D. King, 'Social and Economic Consequences of Prisoners' Work', especially p. 47, in Halmos, op. cit.

14 E. Goffman, 'The Characteristics of Total Institutions', in *Asylums*, Harmondsworth: Penguin, 1968.

15 Gresham M. Sykes, *The Society of Captives*, New York: Atheneum, 1968, pp. 40 ff.

16 Howard Jones, *Crime in a Changing Society*, Harmondsworth: Penguin, 1971, pp. 108-10.

17 Leslie T. Wilkins, *Social Deviance*, London: Tavistock, 1964, pp. 88 ff.

18 Sykes, op. cit.

19 H. F. Cline and S. Wheeler, 'The Determinants of Normative Patterns in Correctional Institutions', in Nils Christie (ed.), *Aspects of Social Control in Welfare States*, London: Tavistock 1968, pp. 173 ff.

20 G. H. Mead, *Mind, Self and Society,* University of Chicago Press, 1934. H. S. Becker, *Outsiders: Studies in the Sociology of Deviance,* New York: Free Press, 1963.
21 *Modern Methods of Penal Treatment,* p. 78.
22 Fox, op cit., p. 136
23 Gresham M. Sykes and David Matza, 'Techniques of Neutralisation: a Theory of Delinquency', in M. E. Wolfgang *et al.* (eds), *The Sociology of Crime and Delinquency,* New York: Wiley, 1962, pp. 249 ff.
24 Zvi Hermon, 'The Advantages of Detaining Short-term Prisoners in Open Institutions', *British Journal of Criminology.* vol. 3, 1963, pp. 83-4.
25 W. H. A. Jonkers *et al., Open Gesticht en Recidive,* Nijmegen: Catholic University, 1969 (English summary available).
26 Paavo Uusitalo, 'Recidivism after Release from Closed and Open Penal Institutions', unpublished paper prepared for the 7th World Congress of Sociology, Varna, Bulgaria, 14-19 September 1970.
27 Anthony Heckstall Smith, *Eighteen Months,* London: Allan Wingate, 1954, pp. 226 ff.
28 Madeline Kerr, *The People of Ship Street,* London: Routledge & Kegan Paul, 1958.
29 Bernard B. Berk, 'Organisational Goals and Inmate Organisation', *American Journal of Sociology,* vol. 71, 1965-6, pp. 522-34.
30 Rudolf Moos, *Systems for the Assessment and Classification of Human Environments: an Overview,* Social Ecology Laboratory, Stanford University.
31 Keith Hope, *Methods of Multivariate Analysis,* University of London Press, 1968.

Chapter 2   The closed prisons

1 Howard Jones, 'Approved Schools and Attitude Change', *British Journal of Criminology,* vol. 13, 1973, pp. 148-56.

Chapter 3   The open prisons

1 Alvin W. Goulner, *Patterns of Industrial Bureaucracy,* London: Routledge & Kegan Paul, 1955.
2 M. H. Cooper and R. D. King, 'Social and Economic Problems of Prisoners' Work' in P. Halmos (ed.), *Sociological Review Monograph No. 9,* 1965, pp. 145-72.

Chapter 4   The measurement of prison regimes

1 Henry Murray *et al., Explorations in Personality,* New York: Oxford University Press, 1938.
2 For an account of this work see Rudolf Moos and Peter Houts, 'Assessment of the Social Atmospheres of Psychiatric Wards', *Journal of Abnormal Psychology,* vol. 73, no. 6, 1968, pp. 595-604; and Moos

and Houts, 'Differential Effects of the Social Atmosphere of Psychiatric Wards', *Human Relations,* vol. 23, no. 1, 1969, pp. 47-60.
3 Rudolf Moos, 'The Assessment of the Social Climates of Correctional Institutions', *Journal of Research in Crime and Delinquency,* vol. 5, 1968, pp. 174-87.
4 Rudolf Moos, *The Community-Oriented Programs of Environment Scales (COPES): Technical Report,* Dept of Psychiatry, Social Ecology Laboratory, Stanford University, 1971. A similar technical report on the CIES has yet to be produced. We have, however, been supplied with basic normative data which will ultimately be incorporated into such a report on the CIES.
5 See, e.g. C. A. Moser and G. Kalton, *Survey Methods in Social Investigation,* 2nd ed., London: Heinemann, 1971; and A. N. Oppenheim, *Questionnaire Design and Attitude Measurement,* London: Heinemann, 1966.
6 Thomas A. Ryan, 'Multiple Comparisons in Psychological Research', *Psychological Bulletin,* vol. 56, 1959, pp. 26-47.
7 Keith Hope, *Methods of Multivariate Analysis,* University of London Press, 1968.

Chapter 5   How the regimes are perceived

1 Rudolf Moos, 'The Assessment of the Social Climate of Correctional Institutions', *J. Res. in Crime and Delinquency,* vol. 5, 1968, pp. 174-87.
2 Ibid.
3 Gresham M. Sykes, *The Society of Captives,* New York: Atheneum, 1968.
4 T. and P. Morris, *Pentonville: Sociological Study of an English Prison,* London: Routledge & Kegan Paul, 1963.
5 Howard Jones, *Crime and the Penal System,* London: University Tutorial Press, 1968, pp. 242-4. Howard Jones, 'The Approved School: Theoretical Model', in P. Halmos (ed.), *Sociological Review Monograph No. 9,* 1965, pp. 110-11.

Chapter 6   Studying prison staffs

1 Erving Goffman, *Asylums: Essays on the Social Situation of Mental Patients and Other Inmates,* Harmondsworth: Penguin Books, 1968 (originally published in New York by Doubleday in 1960).
2 Gresham M. Sykes, *The Society of Captives,* Princeton University Press, 1958; New York: Atheneum, 1968.
3 See, e.g. Richard McCleery, 'Communication Patterns as Bases of Systems of Authority and Power' in *Theoretical Studies in Social Organization of the Prison,* New York: Social Science Research Council, 1960. Sykes (1958), op. cit.; David Street *et al., Organisation for Treatment,* New York: Free Press, 1966. J. E. Thomas, *The English Prison Officer Since 1850: A Study in Conflict,* London: Routledge & Kegan Paul, 1972. European Committee on Crime

Problems, *The Status, Selection and Training of Basic Grade
Custodial Prison Staff,* Strasbourg: Council of Europe, 1967. The
Howard League for Penal Reform Memorandum submitted to the
Departmental Committee on Conditions of Service of Prison Staff
(undated). Prison Officers' Association: 'The Role of the Modern
Prison Officer', an updated version of a document presented to the
Annual Conference of the Prison Officers' Association, 1963. D.
Long, 'The Swansea Experiment', *Prison Service Journal,* vol. VIII,
1969, pp. 34-9. D. W. Mannering, 'Future Role of the Prison Officer',
Prison Service Journal, vol. 1 (New Series), 1971, 19-20. John J.
Galvin and Loren Karacki, *Manpower and Training in Correctional
Institutions,* Staff Report of the Joint Commission on Correctional
Manpower and Training, Washington, D.C., 1969. Peter Timms,
'Prison Officer: Thoughts on the Modern Role', unpublished paper
(undated).

4 See, e.g. T. and P. Morris, *Pentonville: Sociological Study of an
English Prison,* London: Routledge & Kegan Paul, 1963. B. Marcus,
'Dimensions of Prison Officer Attitudes', London: Home Office,
Office of the Chief Psychologist C.P. Report Number 36, 1970.

5 See, e.g. L. W. Merrow Smith, *Prison Screw,* London: Herbert
Jenkins, 1962. Harley Cronin, *The Screw Turns,* London: John Long,
1967.

6 Thomas Mathiesen, 'The Sociology of Prisons: problems for future
research', *Brit. J. Sociol.,* vol. 17, 1966, pp. 360-79.

7 See, e.g. Donald Clemmer, *The Prison Community,* New York: Holt,
Rinehart & Winston, 1958 (originally published in 1940). Gresham
Sykes and Sheldon Messinger, 'The Inmate Social System' in
Theoretical Studies in Social Organization of the Prison, New York:
Social Science Research Council, 1960.

8 Gresham Sykes's phrase. See Sykes, *The Society of Captives.* See also
Erving Goffman (1960), op. cit.

9 See, e.g. Thomas Mathiesen, *Defences of the Weak,* London:
Tavistock, 1965. David Street *et al.* (1966), op. cit. Bernard B. Berk,
'Organizational Goals and Inmate Organization', *Amer. J. Sociol.*
vol. 71, 1965-6, pp. 522-34. Thomas Wilson, 'Patterns of Management
and Adaptations to Organizational Roles: a study of prison inmates',
Amer. J. Sociol., vol. 74, 1968-9, pp. 146-57.

10 The reference here is to a vast and widely ranging theoretical and
empirical literature. The main points, however, are covered by the
following references. John Irwin and Donald Cressey, 'Thieves,
Convicts and the Inmate Culture', reprinted from *Social Problems* in
Howard Becker (ed.), *The Other Side,* New York: Free Press, 1964.
Stanton Wheeler, 'Socialization in Correctional Institutions', in D.
Goslin (ed.), *Handbook of Socialization Theory and Research,*
Chicago: Rand McNally, 1969, pp. 1005-23. Thomas Mathiesen,
Across the Boundaries of Organizations, Berkeley: The Glendessary
Press, 1971. Thomas Mathiesen *et al., Aspects of the Prison
Community,* Report for the European Committee on Crime Problems,
Strasbourg: Council of Europe, 1973.

11 McCleary, op. cit. D. Cressey, 'Prison Organisation', in J. G. March, *Handbook of Organisations;* Chicago: Rand McNally, 1965; D. Cressey, 'Limitations on the Organisation of Treatment in the Modern Prison', in *Theoretical Studies in the Organisation of the Prison,* New York: Social Science Research Council, 1960; J. Galtung, 'Prison: the Organisation of Dilemmas', in D. Cressey (ed.), *The Prison: Studies in Institutional Organisation and Change,* New York: Holt, Rinehart & Winston, 1960; Gresham Sykes (1958), op. cit., etc.

12 See, e.g. W. H. A. Jonkers *et al., Open Gesticht en Recidive,* Nijmegen: Catholic University, 1969. Paavo Uusitalo, 'Recidivism after Release from Closed and Open Penal Institutions', unpublished paper prepared for the 7th World Congress of Sociology held in Varna, Bulgaria, 14-19 September 1970.

13 Rudolf Moos, 'The Assessment of the Social Climates of Correctional Institutions', *J. Res. in Crime and Delinquency,* vol. 5, 1968, pp. 174-87.

14 I. e. T. and P. Morris (1963), op. cit.

Chapter 7   The social backgrounds of prison officers

1 Gordon Rose, *The Working Class,* London: Longmans, 1968. On this point see also D. V. Glass (ed.), *Social Mobility in Britain,* London: Routledge & Kegan Paul, 1954.

2 General Register Office, *Classification of Occupations 1966,* London: HMSO, 1966.

3 T. and P. Morris, *Pentonville: Sociological Study of an English Prison,* London: Routledge & Kegan Paul, 1963, p. 77.

4 Ibid., pp. 77-8.

5 Home Office, *Report of the Inquiry Into Prison Escapes and Security* (The Mountbatten Report), London: HMSO 1966.

Chapter 8   Prison officers at work

1 Carl Jesness, William De Risi, Paul McCormick and Robert Wedge, *The Youth Center Project,* vol. I and II, Sacramento: American Justice Institute, 1972. See also the three annual reports on this project up to 1970.

2 Tony Parker, *The Frying Pan: a Prison and its Prisoners,* London: Hutchinson, 1970.

3 Robert K. Merton, *Social Theory and Social Structure,* Chicago: Free Press, 1957 (esp. pp. 195-206).

4 Ibid., p. 198.

5 Ibid., p. 199.

6 Richard Sparks, *Local Prisons: the Crisis in the English Penal System,* London: Heinemann, 1971.

7 T. and P. Morris, *Pentonville: a Sociological Study of an English Prison,* London: Routledge & Kegan Paul, 1963, pp. 86-7.

Chapter 9 Policy implications

1 Borrowed from Robert Walpole for use in sociology by R. K. Merton, *Social Theory and Social Structure*, New York: Free Press, 1961, pp. 103 ff.
2 Classical studies are: D. Clemmer, *The Prison Community*, New York: Rinehart, 1958; and Peter G. Garabedian, 'Social Roles in Prison', in L. Radzinowicz and M. Wolfgang (eds), *The Criminal in Confinement*, New York: Basic Books, 1971, pp. 116-30.
3 Gresham M. Sykes, *Society of Captives*, New York: Atheneum, 1958.
4 Hugh F. Cline, 'The Determinants of Normative Patterns in Correctional Institutions', in Nils Christie (ed.), *Aspects of Control in Welfare States (Scandinavian Studies in Criminology*, Vol. 2); London: Tavistock, 1968, pp. 173-83.
5 Leslie T. Wilkins, *Social Deviance*, London: Tavistock, 1964, pp. 88-90.
6 Howard Jones, *Crime and the Penal System*, London: University Tutorial Press, 1968, pp. 242-3.
7 W. David Wills, *The Hawkspur Experiment*, London: Allen & Unwin, 1941. Howard Jones, *Reluctant Rebels: Re-education and Group Process in a Residential Community*, London: Tavistock, 1960. Hugh Kenyon, 'Concept of Shared Responsibility in Borstal', *Howard Journal*, vol. 8, 1952, pp. 189 ff.
8 Home Officer Prison Department, *Group Work in Prisons and Borstals, 1962-6*, London: Home Office, 1966. Norman Fenton, *Group Counselling in State Correctional Service*, Sacramento: State of California, 1962.
9 Robert N. Rapoport, *Community as Doctor*, London: Tavistock, 1967. S. Whitely, D. Briggs and M. Turner, *Dealing with Deviants*, London: Hogarth Press, 1972.
10 For example, H. Northen, *Social Work with Groups*, New York: Columbia, 1969, pp. 40-5.
11 Isabel Menzies, *The Functioning of Social Systems as a Defence against Anxiety*, London: Tavistock, 1961.
12 Jones, op. cit., chapter VII.
13 Sir Rupert Cross, *Punishment, Prison and the Public*, London: Stevens, 1971.
14 Howard Jones, *Prison Reform Now*, Fabian Research Series 203, London: Fabian Society, 1959, p. 7.

Appendix 5 A tentative evaluation of the Moos CIES

1 R. Moos, 'The Assessment of the Social Climates of Correctional Institutions', *J. Res. in Crime and Delinquency*, vol. 5, 1968, pp. 180-1.

Index